FOR THE WORK OF THE MINISTRY

FOR THE WORK OF THE MINISTRY

A Manual of
Homiletical and Pastoral Theology

WILLIAM G. BLAIKIE

SOLID GROUND CHRISTIAN BOOKS
BIRMINGHAM, ALABAMA USA

Solid Ground Christian Books
2090 Columbiana Rd, Suite 2000
Birmingham, Alabama 35216
(205) 443-0311
sgcb@charter.net
solid-ground-books.com

For the Work of the Ministry
A Manual of Homiletical and Pastoral Theology

By William Garden Blaikie (1820-1899)

Taken from sixth revised edition, J.S. Nisbet and Co., London, 1896

First Solid Ground Christian Book edition, June 2005

Cover done by Borgo Design, Tuscaloosa, Alabama
Contact them by e-mail at nelbrown@comcast.net

Special thanks to Ric Ergenbright for the photograph used for the cover. Ric's work can be viewed at ricergenbright.org

Additional thanks to Pastor Lenny Byerly of Grace Baptist Church of Salisbury Center, NY, and Andy Wortman of Greenville Theological Seminary for permitting us to use their copies of Blaikie for this project.

ISBN 1-932474-82-X

Introduction to New Edition

I don't remember where I first heard or read about *For the Work of the Ministry*, by William G. Blaikie, but I was sufficiently impressed by what I had learned of it that it was toward the top of my list of used books to try to secure during a trip to Grand Rapids, Michigan (the Mecca for used Reformed books!) some 20 years ago. I was not disappointed in my search, and I was not disappointed as I worked through the book with pencil in hand in the days ahead. I have recommended that young ministers secure reprints or photocopies of this rich volume, and I also recommend it in the pastoral theology classes that I teach for both Greenville Presbyterian Theological Seminary and the Ministerial Training Institute of the Orthodox Presbyterian Church. It is only because the book has been so difficult to acquire that I have refrained from making it required reading. Hence, I was delighted to hear that Solid Ground Christian Books would be reprinting it; and I am honored to be asked to write its Introduction. *To all of my future students:* Be forewarned that this will now be required reading! I assure you, though, that your duty will be a richly rewarding delight!

William Garden Blaikie (1820-1899) was one of the founding ministers of the Free Church of Scotland. Having studied at Edinburgh University (where he came under the commanding influence of Thomas Chalmers) he was ordained to the Christian ministry and served as a pastor for a quarter of a century before accepting a call (in 1868) to serve as Professor of Apologetics and Ecclesiastical and Pastoral Theology at New College, Edinburgh—the theological school of the Free Church of Scotland. Blaikie was seen at his best in teaching Pastoral Theology, drawing together "his wide experience, a comprehensive grasp of the facts, abounding sympathy, an extensive knowledge of man, and a great capacity for teaching." The marrow of all of this is found in the volume which follows this Introduction, *For the Work of the Ministry: A Manual of Homiletical and Pastoral Theology*. It is not the work of a seminary professor who has had little or no experience "in the trenches" of real pastoral work. Such volumes of "pastoral theology" by theoreticians and arm-chair theologians are generally worthless. This is the work of a true "pastor theologian."

Blaikie begins on exactly the right note: The Christian minister is always a minister of the word of God! For our day in which there is much muddled thinking about the character of a call to the Christian ministry, Blaikie gives a typically compact but thorough digest of the timeless counsel on this all-important subject. Following that, nearly half of the book considers various aspects of preaching, i.e. homiletics. This puts the emphasis where it should: Ministers must constantly remind themselves that the great engine of their pastoral work is the preaching of the inspired, inerrant, and infallible word of the living God.

Having recently completed the teaching of another class on homiletics, I was struck by the relevance of Blaikie's material. Men still must cultivate a "pulpit style" as a distinct species of public speaking. Blaikie addresses this in both a challenging and satisfying manner. Likewise, his treatments of sermon construction (including the necessary work on introductions, conclusions, and divisions of the sermon) and sermon delivery are a fine refresher for all preachers as well as a mini-homiletics course for those beginning to develop their skills. I especially commend to you his excellent treatment of tenderness and love in preaching. How I wish that I had read this and taken it to heart before I ever entered a pulpit to preach!

The "pastoral instruction" that follows touches every aspect of the varied work of the ministry in any age. The transition from preaching to pastoral work is, rightly, leadership in worship, and Blaikie gives a succinct digest of instruction for the minister as he leads God's people in the highest calling of the church, the worship of God. He even offers some helps to improve congregational singing. Given how well our Scottish brethren sing the Psalms, those of us who also sing hymns can learn some lessons, too!

One of the greatest strengths of the volume you are about to read is that an evangelistic zeal and a catholic spirit permeate the entire treatment of pastoral work and his thoughtful remarks on revivals. Blaikie welcomed Dwight L. Moody to Scotland on his first evangelistic campaign in that land, and

Moody housed with Blaikie for that trip. Without any compromise of the author's staunch Calvinistic and Presbyterian convictions, Blaikie welcomes what was good about the 19th century revival of zeal for evangelism and missions, and offers careful advice to help pastors wed earnest and practical zeal for the lost with the proclamation and inculcation of Reformed orthodoxy. How we need that blend today, as Blaikie did in his day. The author, also, had no sympathy for those who made the ministerial office virtually the only office for service in the church. His chapter on "Organization of the Work" is quite simply a primer on pastoral administration. It is a fine blend of the historic Protestant view of the church wed to the pastoral work of training and utilizing others to do what the minister alone neither can do, nor is meant to do.

Here, too, is invaluable counsel to the minister in his various public capacities (not least in the character he is to sustain in gatherings with other ministers!). Inexplicably, his chapter on the minister's character is at the end of the body of the book. Perhaps the author wanted that to be the final impression on those who read it. Whatever the reason, this magnificent section is full of weighty words and a multitude of necessary reminders for the one who must always remember that "the life of the minister is the life of his ministry."

I hope this is enough to whet your appetite for the feast that follows! *My fellow ministers:* Read this book to re-kindle your devotion to the highest calling that God gives to any male: the work of the ministry! *Ministerial students:* Read this book to get a huge picture window on what preaching and pastoral work are really meant to be! *Men aspiring to the ministry:* This book will help you "desire the work" with holy realism rather than with romantic unrealism. Thank you, Solid Ground Christian Books, for making the pastoral wisdom of William Blaikie available to another generation!

William Shishko, pastor
Orthodox Presbyterian Church
Franklin Square, NY

PREFACE.

THE object of this book is to present in short compass a comprehensive view of the leading subjects that bear on the work of the Christian Ministry.

It has been the aim of the writer of the volume to make it the completest work on homiletical and pastoral theology, and also the most practical. He is very grateful for the favourable reception which it has received in various churches and countries, and is especially pleased to hear of the aid which some foreign missionaries have derived from it, in the training of native preachers. It can never be expected that on such a subject all one's views shall be accepted ; the great matter is to bring the various points under the notice of young preachers, so that their own judgment may be exercised upon them, and their course in reference to them intelligently and deliberately settled.

The author has not deemed it necessary to remove a few things which have a somewhat local or denominational reference, believing that these will not essentially interfere with the catholic spirit and aim of the book.

CONTENTS.

CHAPTER I.

THE CHRISTIAN MINISTRY A MINISTRY OF THE WORD.

CHAPTER II.

THE CALL TO THE MINISTRY.

CHAPTER III.

PREACHING A CHIEF FUNCTION OF THE MINISTRY.

CHAPTER IV.

THE HISTORY OF THE CHRISTIAN PULPIT.

CHAPTER V.

QUALITIES OF EFFECTIVE PREACHING.—CHARACTER OF THE DISCOURSE.

CHAPTER VI.

QUALITIES OF EFFECTIVE PREACHING—SPIRIT OF THE PREACHER.

CHAPTER VII.

PREPARATION FOR PREACHING.

CHAPTER VIII.

PULPIT STYLE.

CHAPTER IX.

TEXT, PLAN, AND STRUCTURE OF SERMON.

CHAPTER X.

INTRODUCTION, DIVISION, AND CONCLUSION.

CHAPTER XI.

EXPOSITORY LECTURES.

CHAPTER XII.

MODES OF DELIVERY.

CHAPTER XIII.

PULPIT ELOCUTION AND MANNER

CHAPTER XVI.

PASTORAL CARE OF THE YOUNG.

CHAPTER XVII.

PASTORAL ENGAGEMENTS AND MEETINGS.

CHAPTER XVIII.

ORGANIZATION OF WORK.

CHAPTER XIX.

RELATIONS OF THE MINISTER TO PUBLIC INTERESTS.

CHAPTER XX.

THE INFLUENCE OF CHARACTER.

APPENDIX A.

SUPPLEMENTARY HINTS.

I.—On Style.

II.—On Visiting the Sick.

III.—On Conducting Bible-classes.

IV.—On Spiritual Counsel.

CHAPTER I.

THE CHRISTIAN MINISTRY A MINISTRY OF THE WORD.

THE great purposes for which the Christian ministry has been set up are familiar to us from such passages as these : " Go ye therefore, and teach all nations, baptizing them in the name of the Father, and of the Son, and of the Holy Ghost : teaching them to observe all things whatsoever I have commanded you" (Matt. xxviii. 19, 20). "I send thee to open their eyes, and to turn them from darkness to light, and from the power of Satan unto God, that they may receive forgiveness of sins, and inheritance among them which are sanctified by faith that is in me " (Acts xxvi. 18). " He gave some . . . pastors and teachers ; for the perfecting of the saints, for the work of the ministry, for the edifying of the body of Christ : till we all come in the unity of the faith, and of the knowledge of the Son of God, unto a perfect man, unto the measure of the stature of the fulness of Christ " (Eph. iv. 11, 12, 13. See also 2 Cor. v. 18—21 ; 2 Tim. ii. 24—26). It is impossible to conceive any change so great or so glorious as that which the Christian ministry is thus designed to effect. It aims at a radical change in the relation of men to God ; an entire change, too, of character and life ; it aims at bringing men habitually under the influence of the purest motives, and at making their life the best and noblest possible, and the fittest preparation for the life to come. The influence of the Christian minister does not terminate with his public services ; it is designed, under God's blessing, to be a silent power with his people during every hour of their lives ; in hours of work and in hours of rest, in the market-place and the counting-house, in the family and in the closet ; prevailing, through the power of the Spirit, above all contrary influences, counteracting some of the strongest natural inclinations, and bringing every thought into captivity to the obedience of Christ.

B

For accomplishing all these changes, the chief instrument furnished to the Christian minister is—the Word. He is to come into contact with men chiefly by means of spoken truth. What his Master has committed to him is "the *Word* of reconciliation" (2 Cor. v. 18). As a sower, "he soweth the *Word* (Mark iv. 14). As a preacher, he preaches the *word* (2 Tim. v. 2). That Word is "the word of salvation" (Acts xiii. 26). It is the forerunner of faith and all other vital graces—"faith cometh by hearing, and hearing by the word of God" (Rom. x. 17). We do not speak at present of the unseen power that makes the instrument efficient; we advert to what is outward and apparent —the means furnished to the minister for effecting the change. So far as he is concerned, that change must be effected by the delivery of a message from God—a message which, in the first instance, reveals the way to his favour, but which has bearings at the same time on the whole sphere of human life and duty.

The end of the Christian ministry is thus a marvel of sublimity; the instrument for accomplishing it is not less a marvel of simplicity. It is often hard to believe that so great results can be achieved by the simple weapon with which the soldier of the cross is sent forth to confront the Goliath that defies the army of the living God. As of old, the wisdom of the world is ever ready to despise the sling and the stone, and is for clothing the shepherd lad in more elaborate and imposing armour. Nothing could have been of less avail under the old pagan priesthood than words spoken to the worshipper; the pretended acts of magic and divination were needed to give power to the priest. In the Church of Rome, and in churches of similar spirit at the present day, the "word" sinks into insignificance before the other means employed to produce and deepen spiritual impression. The minister must become more than a servant, ἀδιάκονος, —he must be turned into a priest, a member of a sacred caste, possessing, among other mysterious faculties, the power of forgiving sin and dispensing grace, and a power more awful still—that of creating the Saviour out of a morsel of bread, and offering up his body and his blood as a sacrifice for the living and the dead. The services of religion must be turned into rites palpable to the senses and fitted to overawe the soul; the chief work of the minister must be the performing of these rites; and the more complete his ritual the greater is his success; so that a triumphant climax is reached when the faithful on their deathbeds receive from him one by one the last offices of the Church; their souls being, as it were, serenaded

into heaven, while their bodies, protected before burial from
infernal influences by lights and litanies, and carried forth amid
songs and prayers, are at last committed to that holy bed
which their ever mindful mother has prepared for them in the
consecrated earth of the cemetery.

But the true-hearted minister will reject all such substitutes
for his simple weapon as not only needless but pernicious. In
his work, influences that operate externally are to be used only
in the most sparing way. They are not to be altogether excluded, for baptism and the Lord's Supper appeal in the first
instance to the outward senses, and poetical rhythm and
musical sound—both outward things—are employed in the
simplest service of public worship. But these things are designed
for the purpose of elucidating the truth spoken, and making it
more impressive; they are not to supersede or to overlay it.
"The word," says Vinet, "does not become a rite; but the
rite becomes a word." The sacraments are designed to make
the message more expressive and its freight of blessing richer;
but not to substitute an impression on the senses or an *opus
operatum* for the intelligent and believing reception of the truth.
The Christian minister is not called a minister of rites and
ceremonies; he is emphatically a "minister of the Word"
(Luke i. 2). "Christ sent me," said St. Paul, "not to baptize,
but to preach the Gospel" (1 Cor. i. 17). The baptizing was
subordinate to the preaching, not the preaching to the baptizing.

If "the Word"—the spoken truth of God—be thus the great
instrument of the Christian ministry, it is clearly a matter of
overwhelming importance that all intrusted with this instrument become right skilful in its use. If the chosen men of
Benjamin have no weapon but the sling and stone, they must
be trained to sling stones at an hairbreadth, and not miss
(Judges xx. 16). Indeed, the great end of our theological
training in all its branches is to promote a thorough acquaintance, intellectual and experimental, with the Word of God.
Our theological studies would utterly fail if they did not bring
back the student to the Scriptures, illuminated and vivified,
filled with a clearer and richer meaning to himself, and more
capable of becoming in his hands, through the power of the
Holy Spirit, an instrument of spiritual influence over others.
Such a study of the Bible is a study for a lifetime; and when
it opens up in its true proportions, the longest liver has more
cause to fear that his life will be too short for the study than
that the study will be too meagre for his life.

However little the world may esteem the arrangement which makes the Christian ministry so emphatically a ministry of the Word, those who look deeper will readily discover in it elements of the greatest value, so that in this, as in other Divine arrangements, "wisdom is justified of her children." It may be enough for our present purpose to point out four such elements of value—to show how, from this arrangement, the instructions of the Christian ministry derive—1. Authority and power; 2. Originality; 3. Variety; and 4. Durability.

1. *Authority and power.*—The Christian pulpit has never been such a powerful engine as when it has kept most closely to the function of expounding and enforcing the Word of God. The English pulpit of the seventeenth century differed from that of the eighteenth in being alike more Scriptural and more powerful. Whatever else may be said of the Puritan preaching, it was certainly preaching of the Word. It kept in the foreground the great central truths—the fall, the doom of sin, the redemption of Christ, the work of the Holy Spirit, and the solemn consequences of the choice which every man is called to make between guilt and pardon, between sin and holiness, between hell and heaven. Whatever variations there might be in the successive bars of the music, the fundamental air was ever the same ; the communication came to men as a solemn message from heaven with which it was madness to trifle. That ministry, whatever its faults and defects in other ways, was certainly a ministry of power. But when the pulpit ceased to be a place for expounding and enforcing the Word ; when passionless essays and exhortations to the practice of virtue took the place of clear statements of Divine truth and earnest appeals to the conscience, the pulpit lost its efficacy. In the eighteenth century earnestness was deemed fanaticism, and a mild statement of some branch of the Christian evidence in answer to the charge that the Bible was a forgery, or a mild recommendation of some acknowledged virtue, was regarded as the most proper expression of Christian zeal. But, as Dr. Samuel Johnson remarked, men got tired of hearing the apostles tried once a week for the crime of forgery ; their souls longed for better food. In the hands of Wesley and Whitefield the pulpit again became an instrument of power, just because it returned to its great function of setting forth authoritatively the Word of God.

We are sometimes told at the present day that the scope of the pulpit is far too narrow. If by this is meant that preachers generally confine themselves to too narrow a circle of Divine truth, there is some ground for the criticism. But if it is meant that preachers ought to give up preaching " old Hebrew doctrines," and to turn the pulpit into a kind of popular platform, from which everything interesting in science, exciting in politics, beautiful in art, and even amusing in light literature, ought to be freely dispensed, we believe not only that such an institution would be a failure, but that the pulpit would then become in reality what a German Roman Catholic called it in ridicule—" the chatterbox." It is well that the pulpit should know wherein its great strength lies. There are Delilahs in the tent tempting Samson to part with his secret, and persuading him to allow a razor to come upon his head. And truly the Philistines would be upon us if we should ever forget our office as ministers of the Word, and be tempted to abandon those solemn truths which, uttered in God's name, fasten themselves to the conscience, and, even where they do not lead to conversion, leave an awful sense of their importance and of the madness of trampling them under foot. Far better no pulpit at all than a pulpit that did not, as its chief business, solemnly address men as lost sinners, summon them to repentance, faith, and humility, and entreat them, in Christ's stead, to be reconciled to God.

There are several incidental sources from which we may see what it is about the pulpit that lays hold on men and stirs their hearts. One of these is Christian art. The subject has a painful interest, art having been so often abused and perverted to unspiritual ends. Yet it is certain that whatever power belongs to the masterpieces of Christian art is due to the degree in which they represent the great supernatural truths of the Bible. Art is admitted to be powerful in proportion as it is biblical, and when mere tradition becomes its basis it sinks accordingly. The pictures that stir men most are those which somehow embody the great facts of sin and redemption. " It may at once be laid down," says Lady Eastlake,* " that the interests of Christian art and the integrity of Scripture are indissolubly connected. Where superstition mingles, the quality of Christian Art suffers ; where doubt enters, Christian Art has nothing to do. It may even be averred that if a person could be imagined deeply imbued with æsthetic tastes and sentiments, and utterly ignorant of Scripture, he would yet intuitively prefer, as Art,

* " Life of our Lord in Christian Art." By Mrs. Jameson and Lady Eastlake.

all those conceptions of our Lord's history which adhere to the simple text."

It is said that the music of Handel falls comparatively dead upon a French audience, where religious scepticism prevails, and demands for its appreciation some degree at least of sympathy with a scriptural creed. Its power lies in the expression it gives to great scriptural truths.

If from art we pass to literature, we arrive at the same conclusion. In Titanic strength and grandeur Dante stands without a rival; and is not the very soul of his poetry the Christian doctrine of retribution—" the soul that sinneth, it shall die " ? It is very plain that the mind of Shakespeare was deeply impressed with the nature and the doom of sin; it was as something much more than a weakness or imperfection that sin appeared to him; and his hell was very different from that coarse bugbear which it is often said to be. If we think of Milton, we think of one to whom the Bible was such a power, that without his faith in it he would not merely have been a different man, but he would hardly have been a poet at all. What a contrast in enduring power and interest between Milton and Pope ! The one the incarnation of the deep Puritanic faith of the seventeenth century (without the Puritanic bareness), the other the reflection of the deism of the eighteenth, or, as his Essay on Man has been called, " Bolingbroke in verse." Thus it appears that the very truths which the culture of the present day would explain away as mythical, or repudiate as barbarous, constitute in no small measure the enduring strength of the Christian pulpit.

2. *Originality.* No doubt our first impression is that Biblical preaching cannot be original. If the problem were stated thus : A certain book is furnished as the basis of instructions to be given age after age and century after century to the whole of Christendom, how long will it be ere its contents are exhausted, and every new or original view which it can supply brought forward ? the reply would probably be, that it was impossible that a single book, handled constantly by innumerable expounders, could furnish anything new after two or three generations at most. Every grain of wheat, it would be thought, must by that time have been separated from a mass subjected to such continual thrashing. But the case is quite different. To any thoughtful mind it must be a great marvel not that there are many commonplace preachers, but that there are still any original preachers at all. That out

of a book eighteen hundred years old, which preachers without number have been continually handling, men should still be able to gather anything fresh or vivid, should be able to construct discourses that command the attention of intelligent and well-read audiences, and to do this with apparently no more difficulty than their predecessors at the dawn of Christianity, is surely an intellectual phenomenon demanding some explanation at our hand.

Is there any other book in the wide world susceptible of such treatment? Plato, Aristotle, Bacon, Shakespeare—is it conceivable that any of them should be drained in like manner week after week, in all ages and in all countries, and yet should never run dry? Would the expositors never feel it a penance to be confined to a path beaten so hard by their predecessors, and the hearers to be for ever subjected to hearing the same names and being fed with the same food? The question, let it be observed, is not whether Scriptural preaching is never a weariness to any. No doubt it is. But to these persons all truth of the same kind would be a weariness. The phenomenon before us is, that in all ages and in all countries there are multitudes who listen to the lively exposition and enforcement of Scripture truth with the keenest interest, and that there are preachers who bring it out as freshly as if it had come but yesterday from heaven.* There must be something very special about the Bible to account for this. Our explanation is that the Bible is given by inspiration of God, and that it is as full of Divine forms and germs pertaining to the spiritual world as the book of nature is full of them pertaining to the physical. No age can exhaust the fertility of nature. There are combinations of her forms and colours to be detected ever and anon as fresh as anything seen by Adam; and neither painter nor poet can ever be constrained to weep, like Alexander, that he has exhausted the old world, and that no new world can be found to conquer. It is the same, too, with the Bible. Divine truth lies there in forms innumerable, and no single preacher, nor school nor age of preachers, can ever bring the whole to light. The more we penetrate into this treasury, the more shall we be enabled to bring out of it things new and old. If we content ourselves with an easy and superficial study of it, we shall

---

* "Novelty is a great means of interesting, and preaching can only maintain its ground in this respect by continually renewing itself. Men wish for novelty, and, all things considered, they are not wrong. . . . Every prudent preacher will bring forth from his treasury things new and old."—*Vinet.*

of course be able to produce nothing but what is familiar to all. But if we penetrate below the surface, if we dig in the Bible as for hidden treasure, we shall never cease to find what is fresh and interesting. The most original mind cannot create truth; it can only bring to light truth that already exists, or find out relations of truth which have not been formerly apprehended. God's Book of Revelation is no more exhausted in these respects than God's Book of Nature. It is to nature that the artist must look if he would freshen his mind—if he would get into some new line of representation that will fascinate and move the lovers of art.* It is to the Bible, in like manner, that the preacher must look if he would give fresh interest and power to truths that have begun to pall upon the general ear. But it must be the Bible worked by meditation and prayer into his own soul, producing a spiritual originality which will make his applications of it to actual life as vivid as if the book had been written for the present day.

3. *Variety.* In reference to this, too, as a product of biblical preaching, the first impressions of many are different. The notion is apt to prevail that a strictly biblical ministry must be a monotonous one. And in many cases, it must be owned, preachers getting into a round of leading truths, and repeating them again and again with little variety, do foster this impression. It is a fault into which some of our most spiritual preachers are apt to fall. They deem it unworthy of earnest men, yearning for souls, to preach on any topics but those which concern, in the most direct way, the relation of the sinner to the Saviour. But in leaving out, as they do, a great portion of the Word of God, they are apt to cultivate in their hearers a narrow type of piety, instead of embracing in their instructions in due proportion the whole scope of that Word which, in its fulness, is fitted to make the man of God perfect, thoroughly furnished unto all good works. It is quite remarkable, indeed, how very small is the number of texts usually made use of by the evangelist passing from place to place. But the pastor who has to feed the flock from week to week and from year to year, must study to combine the conditions of unity in variety, and variety in unity.

* Sir Walter Scott was once asked why he was so careful in examining and describing real scenes, when he could so easily have constructed his scenery from his own imagination. His answer was that his imagination would have been exhausted in a very few efforts; but that there was infinite freshness and variety in nature.

No better mode of doing this can be found than by trying to make the lessons of the pulpit co-extensive with the teaching of the Bible. Looked at even superficially, the Bible is a book of remarkable variety. Besides theology, in the stricter sense of the term, it presents history and biography, extending often to the minutest details; devotional writing, bringing out all the varied experiences of the human heart, especially in its search for God; the proverbial wisdom of men in whom a rare worldly shrewdness blended with the profoundest veneration; typical representations of God's kingdom, of great interest and variety, if only we could get the right key to their meaning; songs and poems equally remarkable for their appreciation of nature and for the depth of their spirituality. What shall we say of the Gospels, the Acts, and the Epistles? The person, the life, and the death of Christ—what a study is this, and how fitted to stir the heart to its depths! The kingdom of God set up on earth —what a wonderful conception! How solemnizing to think of this Divine creation being in the midst of us, and of our being citizens of it, with all its holy rules of living, and of the imme- diate relation of every member of it to the Divine King! Look across any part of the Bible, and passages of quite Divine beauty are sure to meet your eye. Take Genesis, the oldest book of all, with its first articulate utterance of the Divine voice, " Let there be light; " fit word to herald all the rest—morning star, as it were, of " the true light that lighteth every man that cometh into the world." The happy garden, the cursed temptation, the fall, the expulsion, the promise; the contrasted characters and dismal tragedy of Cain and Abel ; the gloom of a growing corruption relieved by the bright star of Enoch ; the flood, the destruction of all flesh, the salvation of the elect family, the bow in the cloud, the fall' and shame even of the chosen patriarch ; the rebellion of Babel and its memorable punishment ; the rise of the great empires on the banks of the Euphrates and the Nile ; the call of Abram, the chequered lives of the pilgrim-fathers, the prophetic blessing of the dying Jacob, the romantic fulfilment of Joseph's dreams, and the curtain falling on the embalmed remains that could rest nowhere but in the land of holy promise.

To master all the treasures of the Bible, to blend all its voices into à harmonious whole, is no easy attainment. Though one great line of doctrine runs through Scripture, it has its diversities, like the parts of a musical harmony. Superficial men are ever finding contradictions where the profounder student will find a remarkable balance and agreement. To preserve this balance we must follow the manifoldness of Scripture, and not confine ourselves to certain favourite lines. We must have breadth as well as intensity in our teaching, otherwise we may foster a feverish life which will be followed by a time of reaction and dreary lifelessness. The history of the Christian Church is too full of such cases. Eager to uphold some great truth which has been the object of assault, the teachers of the Church have sometimes suffered other truths, forming its true complement and balance, to drop out of view. Meanwhile a craving has arisen in some hearts for the nourishment to be derived from these neglected truths; exaggeration in one direction and disparagement in another have followed, till some most painful strife and lamentable schism have completed the process. There is something in the very nature of Divine truth, and its solemn bearing on eternal life and death, that renders good men liable to exaggerate, and to show excited and feverish energy in defending treasures of such inestimable value. The safeguard against such extremes would undoubtedly be if our pulpits were exponents of the whole counsel of God, and our pastors wise and faithful stewards, able to give to all their Master's household a portion of meat in due season.

4. *Durability.* We ascribe this property to biblical preaching as including both the endurance of the institution itself, and the permanence of the impression made by it on men's minds.

The Christian ministry has a singular vitality. Schools of philosophy, once full of life, have died away; bright popular enterprises, like that of chivalry, have come and gone; institutions for the advancement of art and science, guilds for the benefit of trade, mechanics' institutes, people's colleges, and what not, have tried to strike their roots into the deep soil of our social life without more than partial and transitory success. The Christian ministry has fared otherwise. We do not refer now to what calls itself the Christian priesthood, which depends for its endurance on quite another set of conditions. We speak of an institution which claims no magical powers, but stands out before the world simply as the pillar and ground of the truth. What chance of permanence would the Church have, if, severing herself from special connection with the revealed message of God, she were to become a mere agent of Christian civilisation and improvement?—if her churches were to become lecture-rooms and opera-houses, and, instead of showing to men

the way of salvation, she were to show them experiments
in chemistry and regale their ears with songs and jokes?
Clever men may no doubt draw audiences for a time on Sunday
evenings to hear expositions of the physical basis of life, illustrated by means of a black-board and a piece of chalk, and
interspersed with snatches of music; but what hold can such
things take of the masses, or what chance of endurance can
they have? Like those trees whose roots run along the surface
of the ground, such institutions can have but a short and fitful
existence; and never can you expect to see in connection with
them what you see so often under the Christian ministry—the
steady crowded congregation assembling from age to age, the
children taking the place of their fathers, their attachments
becoming stronger, their sympathies deeper with advancing
years. To give to the Christian ministry its vital attachments,
it must be plainly in connection with the saving truth of God,
affording ground for the conviction expressed by the poor
maiden of Philippi—"These men are the servants of the most
high God, which show unto us the way of salvation" (Acts
xvi. 17).

And as this connection is necessary for the permanence of
the institution, so it is also for the endurance of any impressions
that may be made by it. If the clergy aimed only at setting
forth such views of truth and duty as have commended themselves to their own minds, they no doubt might have a number
of attached and admiring hearers, but their words could not
sink very deep or turn the current of many lives. The echoes
would not live as do the echoes of many a scriptural sermon,
slumbering, perhaps, while life flows smoothly, but awaking in
the day of trial, and comforting the soul in the hour of death.
If we would preach sermons of such a kind as to arrest the
conscience and turn the will, we must fill them with the Word
of God. It is the enduring effect of such teaching, in contrast
with the transitory impression of what is merely of human
origin, that St. Peter thus describes: "Being born again, not
of corruptible seed, but of incorruptible, by the Word of God,
which liveth and abideth for ever. For all flesh is as grass,
and all the glory of man as the flower of grass. The grass
withereth, and the flower thereof falleth away: but the Word
of the Lord endureth for ever. And this is the Word which by
the gospel is preached unto you."

These views of the efficacy of biblical preaching are the more
worthy of consideration because of the tendency of some

preachers at the present day to appeal for the authority of what they say not to the Word of God, but to the reason of their hearers—their sense of what is right and fit, their innate perception of truth and duty. If the authority of Scripture were recognised as supreme, and it were sought, in addition, to draw out for its truths the testimony of reason and of conscience, all would be right; and the fresh vigour of such preachers would be a valuable help to the efficacy of the pulpit. But the authority of Scripture is not represented as supreme. Men are constituted in a sense their own guides, their own lawgivers, and their own rulers; and the degree of their deference to such authority cannot rise much above the authority itself. The desirable thing would be to combine the old appeal to the Word of God with that frank recognition of man's actual thoughts and feelings which this class of preachers make so copiously. It is a great duty to commend ourselves to every man's conscience in the sight of God; but whatever support we seek to derive for our lessons from the conscience must be secondary to that which we draw from our great standard—the written Word of the Lord.

Some will no doubt complain that this is the way to produce intolerant preachers, and that no men are so offensive in their intolerance as those who claim that all their views are identical with the Word of God. But, where there is real ground for this offensiveness, it arises from this claim being made in reference to lesser matters on which the Bible gives no direct utterance. If the Bible really is a message from God on the great matters of sin and salvation, he must be a poor messenger who has no definite conception of the substance of the message, and allows men to accept or reject it according as they like it or no.

To preach with power and effect, it is plain that the Christian minister must be in deep sympathy with the Lord of the Bible, habitually thinking, as it were, his very thoughts and breathing his feelings. Divine truth digested into the substance of his spiritual being, and reproduced as if it were part of himself, goes to the heart of his hearers with all the power of a Divine message, and with all the freshness of a human experience. A church replenished with such a race of ministers stands in no danger of extinction; her path will be that of the shining light that shineth more and more unto the perfect day.

CHAPTER II.

OF the New Testament ministry it may be said as really as of the Old Testament priesthood—"No man taketh this honour unto himself, but he that is called of God, as was Aaron" (Heb. v. 4). But the manner of the call is widely and obviously different. The call to the priesthood came through hereditary descent—it ran in the blood; but in the New Testament we find no trace of any such arrangement for the Christian Church. The manner in which men are called to the New Testament ministry corresponds to the nature of the New Testament dispensation. The evidences of this call are internal rather than external; they are to be found in inward qualifications, not in outward marks. Our theory of the ministry is that the existence of the qualifications is the foundation of the title to the office; that it lies with the applicant and the Church jointly to determine whether he has this title; and that when the Church ordains a man to the ministry, she proceeds on the principle that as he appears from his qualifications to have been called to the office by the Lord, he ought to be invested with it by man. The Church, however, is often not able to come to a very clear judgment on the question whether a man has really received a call from the Lord to enter into his public service; all the more, therefore, it is incumbent on applicants to be very careful in this matter, faithfully applying the rule—"Let a man examine himself."

While this lecture shall be occupied chiefly with considerations for the settlement of the personal question, we desire emphatically to lay down the position, that, however clearly it may seem to an individual that he has the Master's call, the approval and ordination of the Church are ordinarily necessary to constitute the ministerial office. Great evil has arisen in the discussion of this subject from looking only at one side of a

question which undoubtedly has two sides. Some look exclusively at the *inward* qualifications, and hold that if a man
has these the approval and ordination of the Church are worth
less ; others hold that if a man has the approval and ordination
of the Church, he is a true and authorised minister, let his personal qualifications be what they may. The latter is no doubt
by far the more dangerous error ; but there is danger, too, in
the other. The latter would invest some men with the character
of Christ's ambassadors whom He never sent, and never could
have sent, because they are evidently destitute of his spirit ; and
" if any man have not the spirit of Christ, he is none of his."
The other would allow men to assume the ministerial office
without any check on their own judgment of their fitness, thus
encouraging the rough and forward, and discouraging the self-
distrustful and humble, and doing away with all that comely
order which the Head of the Church esteems so highly. The
true view is that which combines both, holding that the thing
of intrinsic value—that which constitutes the foundation of a
real call to the ministry—is personal qualification ; but that, in
ordinary circumstances at least, there must be a trying of the
spirits and a judgment on their qualifications by the Church, in
order to the constitution of the ministerial office. On this footing we proceed to investigate the subject.

It is of great importance to accustom our minds to the idea
of a personal relation between the Christian minister and the
Lord Jesus Christ. This, in fact, is implied (1.) in the very
name ; a minister, servant, διάκονος, must hold a personal relation to a master ; an ambassador must be appointed to his office
by the person whom he represents ; an under-shepherd must·
receive the portion of the flock for which he is to care from the
hands of the Chief Shepherd. (2.) It is implied, further, in
the nature of the *work* to be done ; the establishment of Christ's
kingdom proceeds on a connected scheme, in which each part
of the work bears on the rest ; the building of the spiritual
temple is carried on in conformity to a comprehensive plan ;
and though men may work who are not called, and their work
may be overruled for good, yet the true and authorised work-
men must be subject to the call and instructions of the Master
Builder. (3.) It is implied in the fact that efficient ministers
are represented as the *gifts* of the Lord to those portions of the
vineyard that enjoy their services. " I will *give* them pastors
according to mine heart, which shall feed them with knowledge
and understanding " (Jer. iii. 15). " When He ascended upon

high, He led captivity captive, and *gave gifts* unto men, . . . and He *gave* some, apostles ; and some, prophets ; and some, evangelists ; and some, pastors and teachers ; for the perfecting of the saints, for the work of the ministry, for the edifying of the body of Christ " (Eph. iv. 8, 11, 12). (4.) It is implied in the analogical case of the Old Testament prophets, who were called by God to their mission—" Before I formed thee in the belly I knew thee ; and before thou camest forth out of the womb I sanctified thee, and I ordained thee a prophet unto the nations " (Jer. i. 5) ; while of unauthorised prophets it is said, " I have not sent these prophets, yet they ran : I have not spoken unto them, yet they prophesied " (Jer. xxiii. 21). (5.) It is implied further in the analogy of the apostles, all of whom were called by Christ and sent by Christ—" As thou hast sent me into the world, even so have I also sent them into the world " (John xvii. 18). (6.) And finally, it is implied in the promises made to Christ's ministers. " The Comforter, which is the Holy Ghost, whom the Father will send in my name, He shall teach you all things " (John xiv. 26). " When the Chief Shepherd shall appear, ye shall receive a crown of glory that fadeth not away " (1 Pet. v. 4).

It is important that such views as these of the relation between Christ and his ministers and the appointment they hold from Him be attentively considered, as some are disposed to regard the idea of a Divine call to the ministry as a fanatical one, unworthy of the consideration of sober minds. But if the Head of the Church knows his sheep and calls them by name, it is obvious He must know his shepherds ; and if even the foremost of the apostles could not be intrusted with feeding the sheep and tending the lambs till he had three times answered a question relating to his personal state, it is not only not unworthy of the attention of candidates for the ministry, but eminently the reverse, to inquire whether this office of shepherd is designed by their Lord for them. It is an inquiry relating to a matter of fact, and on the answer to it must depend a great question of right or wrong. If a man who consciously is not called assume the office, no sanction that may be given to him by a fallible church can reverse the fact, and make him a true shepherd of Christ's sheep. His career must be unblessed, unhallowed—a profane handling of sacred things, the intrusion of a thief and a robber into the sheepfold, to whose voice the sheep will not listen. How soon to such a man, when the first feeling of novelty is past, will the ministry in its true functions be a burden and a weariness! How sorely will he be tempted to make it a mere platform for benevolence or a theatre for self-display, or to add to it some more sprightly occupation, instead of keeping to Christ's grand object—building up that kingdom which is not meat and drink, but righteousness and peace and joy in the Holy Ghost. And how distressing his influence on the flock, guiding them not to the green pastures and still waters, but to the dry places of the wilderness— mountains where there is no dew, neither the rain falleth upon them!

The common application of the words " calling " and " vocation " to men's ordinary occupations shows that even there, in virtue of certain considerations, some men are providentially designed for particular modes of life. These considerations have a certain resemblance to those which determine a call to the Christian ministry. A person is understood to have a vocation to a profession or pursuit when three elements are combined—*inclination, ability,* and *opportunity ;*—and the more decidedly that all these point to that particular pursuit the more clear is his vocation. A man with *ability* to be an artist, with a *passion* for art, with the *opportunity* of learning and prosecuting the profession, may be held to have a calling to it, subject, of course, to the risk of error under the head of ability, which must at first be doubtful, and to difficulties under the head of opportunity, which, however, may be designed only to call forth the energy and resoluteness of his character. If we give a full scriptural interpretation to the terms, it may be sufficient to say that these three elements, inclination, ability, and opportunity, constitute the call to the Christian ministry.

But we must not leave the matter in this vague form, since these terms may be understood in a variety of ways. For example, *inclination.* Ministerial life may be attractive to young persons of particular temperament in some of its secondary aspects ; they may have a liking for a life of quiet usefulness ; their literary tastes may be attracted by the clergyman's little study and theological library ; they may have a personal attachment to some who are engaged in the pursuit ; or they may feel that, more than any other, it fulfils their ideal of a desirable life. Their *ability* may have been tested by the usual methods in their preparatory classes, and by the crowning evidence of their having passed the final examinations with éclat. Their *opportunity* may have been determined so far by the absence of any other pursuit which it would have been natural for them to

follow, by the encouragement and approval of their friends, and
by the probability of their obtaining a suitable sphere of labour.
Now there are no doubt instances not a few of young men
entering on preparation for the ministry with views as indefinite
as these, who, either in the course of their studies or in their
first grappling with the difficulties of the ministry, have been
led to a far more profound sense of its responsibilities, and have
proved themselves to be able and successful ministers of Jesus
Christ. Not seldom a man, while sitting in his place in divinity
class-rooms, has for the first time heard the voice of the Master
asking "Whom shall I send?" and for the first time been
moved in spirit to reply, "Here am I, send me." A man may
receive his real call to the ministry even after he has been
formally in the office. But let it be understood, that whatever
the grace of God may afterwards effect, a mere *leaning towards*
the ministry, based on such secondary grounds as we have now
adverted to, cannot be regarded as a call to it. It may be that
Christ destines some such for high usefulness in that office
ultimately, but with their present views and feelings they are
not entitled to regard Him as calling them to feed his sheep and
his lambs. The reason is plain. In the ministry of the gospel
there is need for a man's *soul* to help the work, while in the
cases that have been supposed the soul has received no adaptation for it. The work of Christ demands a glow upon the spirit,
a devotion, a fervour, arising from a deep experience of sin and
grace, and the power of the world to come—demands an active
desire for the salvation of souls, not always to be found in those
who favour the ministry as a quiet useful life. There are
various forms of Christian philanthropy or benevolence, to
which, according to their opportunity, all Christian men are
called ; but the philanthropy which is peculiar to the Christian
ministry is the love of souls. It is in many ways important and
desirable that the ministers of the gospel should encourage,
and, so far as other duties permit, personally promote, these
various forms of philanthropy ; but it must be clearly understood that these do not constitute their primary work, and that
an interest in them is not the specific qualification which indicates, on the part of Christ, a call to his ministry. The minister
is the servant to whom Christ intrusts the carrying out of the
grand purpose for which he came into the world. "This is a
faithful saying, and worthy of all acceptation, that Christ Jesus
came into the world *to save sinners ;* of whom I am chief"
(1 Tim. i. 15). In all whom Christ calls to be his servants in

this work, there must be found some fitness for it in this its highest aspect—a special interest in the salvation of souls, and a deliberate purpose to make this the great business of their lives.

1. Plainly, then, in the first place, a call to the ministry presupposes the existence of the great mark of a servant of Christ—conversion of heart and life.

It is not to be supposed that Christ would call men to his ministry, or the work of saving souls, whose own souls are not saved, and who are not partakers of that life which comes from the indwelling of the Holy Ghost. The order of his kingdom is, "Let the dead bury their dead." It is true, at the same time, that unconverted men have sometimes been the instruments of saving good to others, and instances could be given of persons who have been led to the Saviour, and have continued to adorn his doctrine, while he who first led them had come to wallow in the lowest depths of sensuality. This fact may well make students of divinity careful in examining the foundations of their Christian profession. No one is entitled to assume that all must be right with him in this respect, since otherwise he would not be an aspirant to the ministry. There is no such thing as an *official* road to heaven. Whatever may be the way in which he was led, he must have given himself to Christ before he can be his minister. There must be found in him that sense of unworthiness and emptiness which leads him day by day to the blood that cleanseth from all sin, which draws him to God, makes him hang upon the promise of the Spirit, encourages him to read and pray, and makes him earnest and unceasing in the conflict with sin and temptation. Carelessness in the keeping of his own vineyard can be no recommendation in the keeper of other vineyards ; and of all men the servant of the Lord should be the last to lie open to the reproach—"What meanest thou, O sleeper ? arise, call upon thy God" (Jonah i. 6).

2. More than this, a call to the ministry supposes a peculiar sympathy with Christ in his great enterprise as Saviour, and a strong desire to be of service to Him in that enterprise.

A deep sense of the guilt and misery of sinners, far from their father's house, and often fain to fill their belly with the husks ; much distress of soul at the thought of lives perverted by sin from their great end, and prostituted to objects shallow and unsatisfying at the best ; a yearning desire to gather the wanderers to the Saviour ; a sense of mental refreshment ; a seeing of the travail of one's soul and being satisfied in the accomplishment of this desire; a feeling that to help thus would be to apply one's life to the noblest purposes, and to reap a reward that leaves nothing to be desired; a fervent wish to be sent out by the Master on such errands, an eagerness to hear from his lips the command, " Go, work to-day in my vineyard ; "—some such experience as this is one of the spiritual conditions that mark off some out of the mass of young Christians as specially qualified to take part in Christ's ministry. We would not exclude those who, feeling deeply that this is the true spirit of his service, but lamenting their own poverty and emptiness in regard to it, are lifting up their souls to God, beseeching Him to pour it out upon them. We should indeed be most hopeful of such, knowing that as the air rushes most rapidly into an exhausted receiver, so the grace of God fills most readily the soul that is consciously empty. The Church has no such ministers as those in whose breasts the Word of the Lord so presses for utterance, that even if like Jeremiah they should say, "I will not make mention of him, nor speak any more in his name " (Jer. xx. 9), his word would be in their heart as a burning fire shut up in their bones, so that they could not keep it from bursting forth. Natural temperament—that part of a man which it is least easy to alter—may have something to do with this ; but be our temperament what it may, we have little cause to believe that we are called to Christ's public service unless it be at least our aim and prayer to have his word so dwelling in us that " we cannot but speak the things which we have seen and heard " (Acts iv. 20).

3. It follows that where there is a real call to the ministry, along with this sympathy with Christ in his great enterprise of salvation, there will be a readiness for those habits of life and modes of service that tend to its accomplishment.

A genuine aspirant to the ministry must have the power of contemplating what has now been described as the main part of his life-work, and of setting himself to accomplish it accordingly. Of course, young men at the beginning of a race cannot know experimentally all its difficulties and temptations, and cannot therefore have before them all the circumstances that would enable them to say intelligently that they never would tire of it. But this is not necessary. It is enough that, so far as they know themselves, and know the work, and know the promises and helps that are available for it, their hearts go with it, and that, recognising this state of mind as the gift of God, they feel the necessity of continually asking Him to renew and deepen it, so that as time rolls on they may like the work better, and live for it more. It ought not to be concealed that the experience of life that will come to you by-and-by will bring with it temptations which you may feel but feebly now. To renounce the world, with its aims and prizes, is often an easier thing for a young man in the free independence of youth, than for one whose position is complicated by domestic relations, and who is sometimes tempted to desire for the sake of others what he could quite freely renounce for himself. But, under any circumstances, an aspirant to the ministry must see to it that he is content, with God's help, to lead a life which cannot well fail to be one of much labour and self-denial ; that he possesses those habits of self-command which shall preserve him from the snares of indolence and fitfulness ; that, like Moses, he can turn aside from the allurem nts of wealth and pleasure, feeling that the humble path he has chosen has rewards of its own far higher than those of Egypt ; that he has faith enough in his Master to keep his mind at ease as to temporal things, in the belief that God will supply all his need, according to his riches in glory, by Christ Jesus ; that he has a special abhorrence of all those vices, such as sensuality, deceit, or dishonesty, a single act of which, openly committed or disclosed, might be enough to discredit if not ruin his character and usefulness for ever ; and, above all, that he is so alive to the necessity of maintaining this spirit and these habits of life by daily fellowship with the Fountain of Life, that they form the subject of his most earnest supplications at the throne of grace.

The maintenance and culture of this spirit is indeed one of the most important elements, if it be not the most important element, of preparation for the work of the ministry. Unfortunately, it cannot be said that literary and philosophical studies have a direct tendency to foster it. Rather, perhaps, the other way. Breadth and expansion of intellect they do give, and, what is extremely valuable in education (for it is education itself), they enable you to use your mental powers, to work and control that wondrous machinery of the brain which would otherwise lie idle like an unmanageable ship, or rush about wildly like a flooded stream. But the spirit of consecration cannot be said to arise from either classics, or physics, or philosophy. Sometimes, indeed, we see students entering on their literary studies with more of Christian fervour and devotedness than they show at the close. It is of vast importance, therefore, that pains be taken, not only to ascertain the existence of a spirit of consecration, but to foster and deepen it. The student's own private exercises of devotion, in which he must never allow the pressure of other work to lead him to become slack; his Sabbath-day communion with the upper world ; his home-mission work, so useful at this period of his career ; his private reading, embracing, as he will strive to make it embrace, the memoirs of earnest ministers, and all else that stimulates the spirit of consecration—will serve, by God's blessing, to nourish this habit, and thereby make it the more apparent that it is in obedience to Christ's own summons that he is entering on the work of the ministry.

It must not, however, be supposed that an intense sympathy with Christ in the great enterprise of salvation, and the preva-lence of all those feelings and habits of life which we have noticed in connection with it, constitute, in all cases, a call to the ministry. That they constitute a call to some form of service is undoubted ; in the case of women, for example, where such feelings are often peculiarly strong, the call to serve Christ in some shape is unquestionable ; but few females, how-ever enthusiastic, fancy that their vocation is to preach the Gospel. To complete the elements that go to constitute a call to the ministry, we must consider what is peculiar to that mode of service, and therefore indispensable to the successful per-formance of its duties.

4. We remark, then, further, that a certain amount and form of *intellectual* ability must be regarded as a requisite for the ministry of the Word. There must evidently be a certain capacity of *intellectual acquirement.* No man is qualified for the office of the ministry (except in cases of great rarity, where other qualifications are extraordinary) who is incapable of furnishing himself with the ordinary branches of theological knowledge, to whom Greek and Latin are but unknown tongues, philosophy a region of mist and cloud, theological discussion a battle-field of hard words, and the history of the Church a mere labyrinth of facts and conflicts, schisms and heresies, that no memory can carry and no brain digest. There must be some capacity to feel at home in such walks, because in these times especially, when speculation is so much in vogue, when educated laymen are often so much in need of guidance, when the library of every Mechanics' Institute has its comple-ment of sceptical works, when young tradesmen and ploughmen are becoming familiar with the infidel arguments of the day, it were presumption in any one to aspire to the office of a

spiritual guide who did not know more about these subjects than his people, and who was not better qualified to discuss them. We say that it is only in cases of great rarity, where other qualifications are extraordinary, that the want of such a capacity can be excused. We can conceive men of such spiritual force, such power of making the truth appear as its own witness, such skill in attacking the conscience, moving the will and touching the feelings, and in such obvious alliance with the Spirit of God, that the absence of human learning would hardly be felt to be a defect, and at the feet of such teachers the greatest scholars might be content to sit. But men of this calibre are rarely to be met with, and when they do occur, they will either, by their extraordinary spiritual momentum, assert their right to be regarded as exceptions, or they will find a special sphere of usefulness of another kind. Let it be observed, however, in regard to such men, that it would be a great mistake to regard them as uneducated, even if they have but little of human acquirement. They possess one thing which it is the great aim of education to impart—the power of using their powers—a command over their own faculties—a capacity of launching their weapons with an instinctive certainty of aim, and with a force which is all the greater that the operation is so natural and so sure. Where a natural gift of this kind is consecrated by the Holy Ghost the impression is marvellous; but so far from proving that human culture is of little consequence in ordinary cases, it proves just the reverse. For that marvellous development and command of one's mental faculties which such men seem to have as a natural gift, the great mass of men have to acquire by education and by practice. The enlargement of our mental powers, the capacity of using them at will, the ability to have them in orderly array, so that they shall not jostle nor impede one another, but shall multiply the force which is exerted by each, is a more important and valuable result of education than any amount of undigested acquirement.

Some measure of this intellectual ability is doubtless to be regarded as a qualification for the ministerial office. Some measure of intellectual grasp, some readiness of intellectual movement, some skill in intellectual concentration. And let it not be said that in thus dwelling on the importance of intellect in the ministry we dishonour the Spirit of God. The fact is, that from the Apostle Paul downwards it is men of great learning and high intellectual culture who have been the mightiest instruments of spiritual results. Augustine, Calvin, Owen, Baxter, Jonathan Edwards were all men of full acquirement and well-developed intellectual power. But their reliance on the great source of spiritual strength was not impaired either by the fulness of their learning or the force of their intellect. They laid all their attainments at the foot of the Cross, and would have entered very cordially into the remark of Archbishop Leighton to a friend who admired his books, and congratulated him on having produced them : " Ah," said Leighton, " one devout thought outweighs them all."

5. There are also certain *physical* qualifications which are not to be overlooked in judging of a call to the ministry.

Extreme bodily feebleness, especially feebleness of the throat or the chest, on which the faculty of utterance is so dependent, is certainly a disqualification, and can be disregarded only on the strength of an unusual measure of other qualifications.   So also is a nervousness so extreme that it will never allow one to forget one's-self, while it produces a kind of mental paralysis in presence of an audience that makes a public appearance a kind of martyrdom, and renders one most helpless when one ought to be strongest.   It is scarcely possible to draw a hard and fast line between that measure of natural shyness which may be overcome by practice, by courageous efforts to do one's duty, and by earnest prayer for the help of God, and that extreme nervous feebleness which unfits one for ever being a good public speaker.   But it is certain that nothing appears to the lay mind more out of place than the appearance in the pulpit of one whose feeble accents and general helplessness make him more an object of compassion than of respect.   And on no occasions are people more disposed to pass hard judgments on theological institutions and those who conduct them than when such men appear as their instructors.   The public are but little in the way of accepting the lesson which an eminent man used to say that he could always draw even from the poorest sermon he ever heard—a lesson of patience.

6. And perhaps we ought to advert to certain *social* elements not to be overlooked.   The ministry is a social office, and men of unsocial temper, who shrink from the company of their fellows, and instead of being disposed to let out their hearts to others ever keep them defended as by a coat of mail, are *pro tanto* disqualified.   This tendency, too, is one which, unless overcome in youth, will grow with years, creating at last a positive repulsion between the minister and at least the younger

members of his flock. To encourage his people to speak on religious topics, and to enter freely into his plans of work, a measure of frankness is indispensable ; for it is frankness that draws frankness, it is cordiality that begets cordiality, that breaks down the barriers of reserve, and knits the bonds of brotherhood. Considering, too, how much it is his duty to " beseech " and " persuade " men, it is evident that a genial, kindly, persuasive spirit must be of eminent service.

Yet, on the other hand, seeing that the minister of Christ is called to deal in the pulpit and elsewhere with very awful realities, it is essential that he be free from all levity of character, from everything that would lower in men's eyes the dignity of his office, or connect paltry or ludicrous associations with the grand truths he is called to proclaim. Called too, as he is, to aid in the work of the great Peacemaker, and often finding it his duty to endeavour to adjust the differences that arise in families and in communities, he has need of a calm and peaceable temper, and of that prudence which enables one to steer one's course calmly, without stirring elements of strife which lie around one on this side and on that. A morose, reserved, and surly temper, or an irascible and violent one, are therefore serious disqualifications for the ministry. For " the servant of the Lord must not strive ; but be gentle unto all men, apt to teach, patient, in meekness instructing those that oppose themselves ; if God peradventure will give them repentan e to the acknowledging of the truth ; and that they may recover themselves out of the snare of the devil, who are taken captive by him at his will " (2 Tim. ii. 24—26).

It is quite true that some of the qualifications for the ministry that have now been adverted to are of secondary importance, and that the partial absence of them does not conclusively show that the person has no call from Christ to this office. On the other hand it is also certain that several men of true excellence have not only done no good service, but much mischief in the ministry, by the want of talent for public speaking and public instruction, by a feeble, nervous, awkward manner, by an ungenial, mule-like temper, or by a pugnacious, exasperating spirit. We are constantly hearing expostulations from persons outside against some of those whom we send forth to preach, but who are utterly unfit for the charge of a congregation. If young men only knew themselves, and knew their natural infirmities, they might do a great deal at the present stage in checking and overcoming them ; they might learn a lesson of humility and watchfulness from the very knowledge of them ; they might be thrown into that relation of conscious dependence on God into which Paul was thrown by his thorn in the flesh, and taught to prize, as he was, the ever-glorious promise, " My grace is sufficient for thee : for my strength is made perfect in weakness " (2 Cor. xii. 9).

It would be matter of deep regret if these observations had only the effect of making any conscientious young man uncomfortable, of stirring doubts in his mind as to his Divine vocation to an office which hitherto he may have been contemplating with unclouded satisfaction. If, however, any doubts have been raised, let them not be suffered to remain. In the first place, let him bear in mind that though he is responsible for presenting himself as a candidate, and though that does imply that he thinks this is according to the mind of Christ, it is the Church that is responsible for ordaining him. The ministerial office will not be formed till a congregation calls and the Church ordains him. But if doubts have arisen as to whether he should even offer himself as a candidate for the ministry, then let him frankly and honestly lay his case before the Master whom he desires to serve, and pray that in his light he may see light on the question, whether or not He calls him to his ministry. Let it be frankly owned that on such a subject as this, we who teach teach through our own errors, and become experienced through our infirmities. We serve a kind and most considerate Master, who, if we but have humility and docility, will bear with innumerable defects, will bless our poor endeavours, and kindly lead us on, through failures and blunders innumerable, to a respectable measure of success. The years glide on with pleasure when we are doing his work, and contributing our mite to the grand result—the establishment of the kingdom of God in the world. Our disappointments and sorrows are comparatively bearable when we remember that they are shared by Him who has power to place them among the all things that work together for good. And when the joys of harvest are accorded to us, when souls are blessed through our word and living stones are added to the spiritual temple, the satisfaction is increased by the thought that He too rejoices, and looks down on this product of the new creation with even livelier satisfaction than He felt at the close of his creative week, when He saw all that He had made, and behold, it was very good.

CHAPTER III.

PREACHING, or the public proclamation of the truth by the living voice of preachers or heralds, is pre-eminently an ordinance of the New Testament. Occasionally it was practised in Old Testament times; but as a permanent and universal ordinance it was the institution of our Lord. Enoch and Noah were in some sense preachers. The author of Ecclesiastes is called expressly "the Preacher," but it is a question whether the original term (קֹהֶלֶת) would not be rendered more fitly "the Compiler." Jonah, when sent against Nineveh, was instructed to preach the preaching that God gave him—that is, to utter the proclamation, "Yet forty days and Nineveh shall be overthrown." On the return from the captivity, Ezra, from his wooden pulpit reading the book of the law to the assembled people, giving the sense and causing them to understand the reading (Neh. viii. 4), presented probably the nearest approach to modern preaching in Old Testament times. In the synagogues the practice seems to have been common; and our Lord at Nazareth, first reading a portion of Scripture, and then giving an address on it, seems to have followed the usual practice. John the Baptist was expressly and conspicuously a preacher; but, perhaps, it was as the forerunner of Christ that he brought forward so prominently the mode of influence which Christ himself was to establish and perpetuate.

Preaching was not resorted to by the philosophers or founders of ancient schools. Even after they had instructed their disciples, they did not send them out to public and populous places to speak in light what they had been told in darkness, or preach upon the housetops what they had heard in the ear. Methods more select, and apparently careful, were taken to preserve and perpetuate opinions which it would have been counted sacrilege to fling abroad on the rude ears of the *profanum vulgus.* Nevertheless, the method instituted by Christ has proved itself far more effectual than any.

" The systems of the wisest philosophers," says Dr. Kidder " have passed away, but the preaching of the Gospel has continued, and so multiplied itself, that it more nearly fills the world than any system of teaching or influencing mankind has ever known." There is probably no order of educated men in the world more numerous than that of Christian preachers. In spite of the rivalry of the printing-press, the superior attractions of other professions, and the fears that sometimes arise lest the supply should fail, it is renewed from age to age ; and the prophetic announcement of the Psalmist still finds its fulfilment in every Protestant country—" The Lord gave the word ; great was the company of them that published it."

In the New Testament no fewer than five expressions are employed to denote the employment of the preacher.

1. Εὐαγγελίζω, in the middle voice εὐαγγελίζομαι, to bring glad tidings, to declare the good news—with special reference to the salvation of Christ ; as the angel said to the shepherds, εὐαγγελίζομαι ὑμῖν χαρὰν μεγάλην (Luke ii. 10). It is well to mark the prominence of the element of good news in this leading word, corresponding to which a tone of gladness ought habitually to mark the delivery of the preacher, as if he were bringing a piece of good news to persons in trouble. In very many cases the word is used simply for proclaiming, but without excluding the notion of good tidings. The corresponding noun, εὐαγγέλιον, is the Gospel, the good news, what old writers used to call the Evangel.

2. Καταγγέλλω, usually translated to preach, but sometimes to show, to teach, to declare. The use of the intensive κατὰ denotes emphasis and urgency—" Whom ye ignorantly worship, him I καταγγέλλω ὑμῖν—emphatically make known to you " (Acts xvii. 23). " Be it known unto you, therefore, men and brethren, through this man is preached (καταγγέλλεται) unto you the forgiveness of sins " (Acts xiii. 38).

3. Κηρύσσω, to make proclamation like a herald ; spoken, for example, of John the Baptist—" He came into all the country round about Jordan, κηρύσσων βάπτισμα μετανοίας εἰς ἄφεσιν ἁμαρτιῶν " (Luke iii. 3). Κηρύσσειν Χριστόν, to preach Christ—" Philip went down to a city of Samaria and preached Christ unto them " (Acts viii. 5).

4. Διαλέγομαι, to speak to and fro, to discuss, to reason— " He reasoned in the synagogue every Sabbath, and persuaded

Jews and Greeks" (Acts xviii. 4; xix. 8, 9; xxiv. 25), &c.   It
is emphatically used of the preaching of St. Paul, as when at
Troas he preached (διελέγετο) to the disciples, and Eutychus
fell down, διαλεγομένου τοῦ Παύλου ἐπὶ πλεῖον (Acts xx. 9).

5. The word λαλέω is also rendered to preach, as in Mark
ii. 2—" He preached (ἐλάλει) the word unto them;" but also
sometimes simply to speak—" they so spake that a great
multitude both of Jews, and also of Greeks, believed." It is
instructive to find the plain word for speaking interchanged
with the other terms, because this shows that preaching is in
fact just speaking; it is not essentially different from our
ordinary way of communicating our thoughts to one another by
the faculty of speech, the chief difference being only that which
is demanded by the nature of the truths uttered and the size
of the audience addressed.   Our Lord's own preaching was
emphatically *speaking* (διατί ἐν παραβολαῖς λαλεῖς αὐτοῖς); it
derived much of its force from its being so, from its being the
natural expression of his thoughts ; nor, because He spoke
naturally, did he seem to find difficulty in giving to his voice
a tone suitable to the subject, or in moving all up and down
the scale of emotion, from the gentlest expression of sympathy
to the most impassioned utterances of indignation, or the most
solemn denunciations of doom.

The ordinance of Christian preaching, to which all these
expressions point, is nowhere very formally defined ; nor are
the functions of New Testament preachers anywhere set forth
with the exactness which marks the regulations prescribed for
the priesthood.   The truth is, as Vinet has well remarked, that
"Jesus Christ instituted little, but inspired much."   Instead
of forming exact patterns, like the moulds in an iron-foundry
which the melted metal is to fill precisely, he gave a formative
quality to the views with which he inspired his followers, by
which, rather than by express instructions, the shape of his
institutions was to be determined.   In regard to preaching, it
was left to assume whatever form should be found to be most
in accordance with its two great purposes—CHRISTIAN INSTRUC-
TION and CHRISTIAN PERSUASION.

1. Instruction, the announcement of the message, the communication to men of the truths with which the ambassador
has been intrusted, must obviously be the first object of the
preacher.   In the earliest times the wonderful facts of Christ's
history formed the chief topics of instruction, and the gospel
preached was little more than a transcript of the gospel after-

wards written—an account of the marvellous life and death of the Son of God. With the progress of the Church and of Christian knowledge, it was less necessary to be constantly preaching these elementary facts ; indeed they came to be assumed as known, and the element of instruction in preaching then consisted in explanations of the relations and bearings of the great fundamental truths, both as to what man ought to believe concerning God, and the duty which God requires of man. Some are inclined to say that there is now no longer occasion for the element of instruction in preaching, sufficient provision for that being made previously in the school-room and the Bible-class. But even if it were certain that the fundamental facts of the Christian faith had been taught there with sufficient clearness and fulness, a vast field for instruction would remain in the elucidation and application of these facts. The truths of Revelation are so vast and manifold in their reach and bearing, that as no teacher can ever grasp the whole, so no congregation can be beyond the reach, and therefore beyond the need, of further instruction in regard to them.

2. But while instruction is certainly to be regarded as one of the great purposes of the pulpit, it is certainly not the *terminus ad quem ;* it must be subordinate to its other great purpose, that of *persuasion.* Under this term we include the *moving of the soul* by means of the truths which are handled by the preacher. His duty is not exhausted when he has laid down his message, like a cargo of coal, at his hearer's door, leaving him to accept or reject it as he may please ; he must prevail on him if possible to open his door, admit his goods, and place them in safe custody under lock and key. Knowing the terror of the Lord, he is to persuade men (2 Cor. v. 11) ; to beseech men in Christ's stead to be reconciled to God (2 Cor. v. 20) ; to warn every man, and teach every man in all wisdom, that he may present every man perfect in Christ Jesus (Col. i. 28). It is this business of persuasion—this moving of the springs of human hearts, and bending them Godwards, that constitutes the great difficulty of the preacher's office, and leads him most to feel the insufficiency of human strength, and the need of the special grace of the Holy Ghost. But the more a preacher recognises this as the great end of his labour, the more successful, with God's help, will his preaching be. And the greater the number of such preachers in a church, the more remarkable and the more prevailing will be the influence of its pulpit.

It is chiefly in the fact of its being designed for persuasion, that the vindication of the pulpit as a permanent institution of the Christian Church is to be found. If instruction were the only or even the chief purpose of sermons, that end could be secured better through books, or through the recorded discourses of the best preachers, presenting the truth with a fulness, a clearness, and an exactness to which the greater part of preachers can make no claim. It is of the utmost importance to keep prominently in view that it is the living element in the pulpit that not only gives it its chief value but justifies its very existence. It is the presence in it of a man of God who has not only received Divine truth into his own soul, but who regards it as his great business to get it into the souls of his hearers. It is not the wires and posts that constitute the value of our telegraph system ; without the living fluid that runs along the wires all that is seen by our eyes would be worthless. It is not to present men with any mere body of divinity, however clearly stated and skilfully articulated, that the Christian pulpit has its being ; but that the truth may be mingled with the warmest feelings of the preacher's soul ; that he may use all his tact to recommend it to his actual congregation ; that prejudices may be removed, existing motives stimulated, objections answered, and indecision rebuked ; and that this living element in the preacher may be blended with a life-giving element from above—the living power of the Spirit of God. If this were constantly borne in mind, and if the actual pulpit corresponded to this ideal, we should have far fewer of those diatribes against it with which we have been made so familiar in our day.

Within the present generation the pulpit of this country has been exposed to rougher handling than usual. Something like a crusade has been preached against it, and when it is not believed by those who run it down to possess any self-reforming power, it is confidently consigned to the *limbus patrum*, as a fossil of a bygone age.

The objections to the pulpit come from various quarters, and possess a greater or less degree of virulence. While some would utterly demolish it, others would curb it or push it into a corner—making it endurable by making it insignificant.

1. The first blast of the trumpet against the pulpit in recent times appears to have come from the Tractarian school. The objection of that school to the pulpit was that it tended to depreciate the sacraments. One of the later Tracts for the Times (No. 87) described the sermon-loving spirit as the off-

spring of a " worldly system," as " not conducing to a healthful and reverential tone toward the blessed sacraments," and as " the undue exaltation of an instrument which the Scripture, to say the least, has never much recommended." We can easily understand this objection. It is the voice of the sacerdotal school, exalting the sacraments above the Word, regarding the sacraments as channels of grace *ex opere operato*, and substituting a spirit of blind dreamy wonder in reference to the sacraments, for that intelligent appreciation of the mind and will of God as revealed in the gospel, which the Protestant pulpit fosters. It is just what we might expect that when men take to sacerdotalism they should disparage the preaching of the Word. But in those who consider the character and tendencies of the sacerdotal theory, the depreciating remarks on the pulpit that have issued from that quarter cannot but produce an impression the opposite of that designed. Nor is it any contradiction to these remarks that in some instances, and for some purposes, the sacerdotal party have had recourse to earnest preaching. In some of their mission services daily preaching has had a leading place. But it is preaching as subordinate to the sacraments and the Church. It is not like the preaching of the Reformers, nor the preaching of which the sum and substance is " Believe on the Lord Jesus Christ, and thou shalt be saved." It is rather designed to lead to the Church and the sacraments as depositories of the grace which alone fills and satisfies the sinner's heart. It does not say, Come to Christ, in simple faith, that you may be saved, and then join the fellowship of the Church, that your new life may be sustained and helped on ; but, Come to the Church which has Christ to give you, and which will give you Christ and salvation when you show your desire to receive them at her hand. It does not say, Look to Christ, and your faith will receive the grace of salvation ; then resort to the sacraments that you may enjoy that grace more largely and luxuriantly ; but, Come to the sacraments both for the beginning and the continuance of grace. The essential difference between Popery and Protestantism is here ; nor is it surprising that under such a system the preaching should be depreciated which points every hearer at once to a Saviour in whom all fulness dwells.

2. Again, it is objected to the pulpit, and especially to the more Protestant section of it, that it overlays *worship*, casts into the shade the devotional parts of Divine service, and deprives men of what is the real, the truly precious blessing

of public worship—conscious nearness to God.   Men go to
church, it is maintained, not to worship God, but to listen to
man.   The devotional services are "the preliminaries," hurried
through as quickly as possible that the main part of the time
may be left for the chief part of the business—the sermon.   We
freely but sorrowfully allow that there is some ground for this
objection ; but it evidently bears not against the institution
of preaching, but against the abuse of it.   For neither in point
of length nor of anything else is it desirable or necessary that
the sermon should be such as to monopolize attention, or
supersede the deliberate and earnest worship of God.   It ought
beyond doubt to be subservient to such worship.   It should go
to form and foster those feelings toward God which find their
suitable expression in acts of worship.

Other objections to the pulpit may be stated separately, and,
being somewhat kindred, answered together.

3. It is alleged by some that the pulpit is unnecessary in the
present age.   It is an age of books and intelligence, and it is
easy for men to get from books whatever religious instruction
they desire, much more conveniently and completely than from
the cursory and miscellaneous essays that are doled out to them
from the pulpit.   The state of matters was quite different when
the clergy were the only educated men in a community, and
alone in possession of the key of knowledge.   The pulpit might
be a necessity in such an age, but it is no necessity in ours.

4. More than this, the pulpit is an impertinence.   It is quite
opposed to the spirit of the age.   The present is an age of
independent thought and critical inquiry, while the pulpit
represents an age of authority on the one side and blind submission on the other.   Opinions now are not given forth *ex
cathedrâ*.   Everything has to run the gauntlet of criticism.
The head of the State cannot read a speech to Parliament but
next morning it is pounced upon, if not torn to pieces, by a
thousand newspapers.   The pulpit, with its one-sidedness, its
dogmatism, and its freedom from public challenge and criticism,
remains the only protected article in an age where every other
statement of views or opinions lies open to the four winds
of heaven.

5. It is alleged that the pulpit is actually unworthy of the
age.   It is below the level of its intelligence and vivacity.   It
is dull, clumsy, unsuitable ; meeting no wants, satisfying no
cravings, either of high or low.   Ever and anon we have in
our leading English newspapers, as well as in other journals,

a run of letters and articles uttering and echoing these views. The dulness of sermons is proverbial ; but from time to time the proverb is renewed, with an additional adjective or two to give it force. " Modern preaching," it is said, " is poor." " The great majority of our religious teachers are feeble, incompetent." There has been of late comparative " failure, alike in the quality and quantity of pulpit power." " Preachers as a class have been degenerating ; or rather, to speak more correctly, they have failed to keep pace with the general advancement around them ; the strength of English character goes forth in other directions ; the bone and sinew and muscle of the country's manhood are elsewhere and otherwise employed than in the pulpit, and this has been the case for some time past." " By friend and foe a common conclusion seems to have been reached on this question. It is said that the pulpit has reached the period of its decadence ; that it has ceased to be a great formative power amongst us, and that the influence it once yielded over the intellect and life of the nation is gone."

Such words are held to express the views of the more educated class in England. But it is not from this class only that we hear of the dislike to the pulpit. In an anonymous writer we find the following representation of the bearing and spirit of a great portion of the working classes of England towards religion and religious ordinances. We say of *a great portion* of these classes, because we believe that it would be a great error to regard it as true of the whole.

" The people *en masse* have come to smile both at religious teachers and at the system they represent. . . . There is so wide a gulf between the clergy and the great body of our working classes in our large towns, the former possess so little knowledge of what the latter are reading and thinking about and discussing, that evil often results from attempts to approach our irreligious classes. . . . The tendency here is to settle down into a dry, hard, unimaginative secularism, pushing aside, with an impatient gesture, every claim that may be urged in the name of religion. This tendency does not show itself now, as formerly, in a menacing attitude ; but for this very reason its progress and ultimate results are all the more to be dreaded. The comparative silence that reigns just now among our industrial orders is full of grave admonition. I wonder how many ministers of religion could answer the question, What are the working classes doing ? What is the tone and colour of their

D

thoughts just now? Those who know could answer in a word—*material*. I believe that times of agitation, such as those of the days of socialism or chartism, are, in some respects, preferable to the present treacherous stillness. Men at least talked and discussed then about something higher and more spiritual than strikes and co-operation schemes. Now, on the contrary, materialism in some form is that to which every thought is given and every energy applied. Thus we have atheism in fact without the odium of the name ; and just here lies the danger in the present temper of the public mind. Formal, positive, organized infidelity is not the danger of the hour, though there is a startling amount of this in our large towns and cities; but it is a sullen, apathetic indifference, combined with an eager devotion to schemes which practically ignore all religion, that is just now to be dreaded." *

Such statements are made of the working classes of England, but the pulpit of Scotland is not exempt from unfavourable criticism of the like kind. In a volume entitled " Strictures on Scottish Theology and Preaching," by a Modern Calvinist, the writer finds fault with the tone of *stern severity* which in matter and manner alike characterizes the Presbyterian pulpit ; the *abstract nature* of its lessons, dealing so much with theology, and so little with the actual realities of life ; the ascetic view which it commonly takes of the world and all that pertains to it ; its morbid dread of encouraging self-righteousness, by insisting on moral duties; its unreal and exaggerated pictures of humanity ; its suspiciousness of the professions of men, and slowness to recognise what is good in them ; and pleads for " a more consistent, large, and liberal explanation of the gospel, and an advance in all those simple and natural conceptions of it that may relieve God's message of the crotchets and incumbrances which have rendered it, to popular apprehension, in no small measure nugatory and contradictory."

In trying to assign their just value to such objections as have now been specified, we may dismiss at once the notions of those who think that the pulpit is a mere fossil of the past, doomed to oblivion, except in so far as antiquarian museums may preserve it, along with flint arrows and copper-headed spears. Christian preaching is a Divine ordinance, and it will share the permanence which belongs to everything Divine. We do not need to say of it, with trembling hearts, " *Esto perpetua ;* " a voice not to be gainsaid has settled that.

* " Preachers and Preaching." By a Dear Hearer.

As to the relative quality of the preaching of the present day, the state of the question is often put unfairly. It is not whether there are but few great preachers ; it is not whether there are very many extremely poor preachers ; it is not whether the vast body of preachers are very mediocre ; but it is whether in these respects the pulpit of our age contrasts so unfavourably with that of other ages as to exhibit the evidence of organic decay. That the pulpit has epochs of unusual brilliancy, and that the present is not one of those epochs, we may quite freely admit, without allowing that its vitality is essentially abated, or that the time of its decadence has come.

The answer to the objection that the pulpit is unnecessary in an age of widely diffused literature and intelligence has been given by anticipation. If the pulpit were a mere vehicle of instruction, this might be relevant, but not when the living and breathing soul of the preacher forms an essential element in its very *raison d'être.* So also we may dismiss the objection that the pulpit is an impertinence, as continuing an authoritative style of dealing with people in an age which discards such authority. If the preacher's function be to deliver God's message, not his own, and if he speak accordingly, he cannot but speak with authority ; but while doing so he should take care to show, by his humble and loving tone, that the authority is all his Master's, and that for himself he is but the voice of one crying in the wilderness.

With the other objections to the pulpit it is not possible to deal in so summary a way. It is true that certain preachers are to be found at the present day whose style of ministrations justifies many if not all of the criticisms that have been adverted to. But it is just as true that there has hardly ever been an age in which the same thing might not have been said. When an institution is served by so vast a number of officers, it is easy to find samples enough apparently to justify any kind or class of accusations. But it does not follow that the whole institution partakes of the faults that are undoubtedly in some parts of it. How far the pulpit of the present day is liable to the charges we have referred to is a question which we cannot settle here, but for settling which materials may be supplied as we proceed with our subject. One remark, however, in the way of caution it may be well to offer. There is a vast difference between criticisms offered on the pulpit when its origin as a Divine institution is recognised, and also its great purpose for persuading men to believe on Christ and do his will, and criticisms that regard it as but an instrument of human culture, designed to help men onward in the path of civilisation. Criticisms of the latter order have little claim on our consideration; criticisms of the former kind, however sharp and serious, should be received with respect and examined with candour.

But apart from the question whether or not modern strictures on the pulpit are just, there is an obvious lesson to be drawn from the fact that they are so remarkably abundant. You, students of divinity, are about to take up this Divine weapon at a time when it has fallen widely into discredit. You are about to use it for the highest purposes, while many are declaring that it is fit for no purpose. The credit of a Divine ordinance is to be intrusted to you, and it will rest practically with you to show whether preaching be that contemptible device of human priest-craft which some allege, or the product of the wisdom and skill of the Church's Head. Surely, in such circumstances, you must be satisfied with no common pains to acquit yourselves well. And the obligation to do your best in this matter is all the stronger if the number of " born preachers " among us is small. If we have few orators in our ranks, who by touching some hidden spring can open the heart and move it at will (within the spheres to which human powers are equal), all the more need is there for the mass of young preachers to make the most diligent improvement of the powers they have, and to seek with the utmost earnestness to become able ministers of the New Testament. To be an efficient preacher does not demand the gifts of genius; but it does demand a most careful discipline of the mental and moral powers, a thorough knowledge of the Word of God, familiarity with the collateral fields from which the preacher's illustrations must come, familiarity with some of the best models of pulpit eloquence, personal fellowship with Christ, and much tender sympathy for men. It implies a careful watch over your own hearts, lest the breath of temptation or the chill of worldliness should unfit them for your work; and, finally, it implies that not only as a general habit, but especially when you are preparing for the pulpit, you shall plead the promise of the Father—that your tongue may be a tongue of fire, and your words, words of the Spirit, and thereby words of life.

CHAPTER IV.

THE HISTORY OF THE CHRISTIAN PULPIT.

IF it were necessary to vindicate the wisdom of Christ in making preaching the chief means of the establishment and extension of his kingdom, a sufficient defence would be found in the remarkable power which the Christian pulpit has wielded, especially at certain periods in the history of the Church. The pulpit has a history of its own ; and the style of eloquence that has characterized it in its better periods is as well marked, as distinctively *sui generis*, as that of any other kind of eloquence. While no other religion than Christianity has produced an oratory dealing with the unseen and eternal, the Christian preacher, at many epochs, and in not a few tongues, has risen to heights which no secular orator has approached, and has stirred men's hearts with truths that have gone to the very depths of their being.

Hardly had Christ left the world, when the power of his institution, replenished with the might of the Holy Spirit, was remarkably displayed. Never before, except under the preaching of John and of Jesus himself, had such appeals fallen from human lips as those of Peter and his companions, and, a little further on, of Stephen, Paul, and Apollos. What was said of the winning manners of David might almost have been said of the addresses of these preachers—they " bowed the hearts of all the men of Judah, even as the heart of one man " (1 Sam. xix. 14).

The apostolic preaching was not the less powerful that it was so artless ; it was the preaching of men who, for the most part, had studied in no school of rhetoric or philosophy, and who had no skill to shape their message in words that man's wisdom taught ; but who, apprehending that message with unexampled clearness, feeling it with overwhelming force, and trusting to an Unseen Arm to send it home, poured it out in the might of the Spirit, making the people fall under them, not by the power

of man, but by the power of God. As to any school or form of
eloquence, it cannot be said that they founded any ; nor can
we find more for our imitation in the apostolic model than its
directness, its simplicity, and spiritual earnestness. Even at
this day a preacher marked by these qualities—an " apostolic "
preacher, as we call him—exercises a great influence in a
community ; and if such men were only given to us in sufficient
numbers there would be little need for cultivating preaching as an art. But while such men are occasionally raised up,
as at the beginning of great eras, or after a long slumber in the
Church, or at the commencement of great enterprises in heathen
lands, they are not common in ordinary times ; and it becomes
necessary to combine all the means by which the power of
efficient utterance may be increased, and possession taken of all
the avenues to the heart of man.

During the second and third centuries there were few great
preachers. The work of Christian edification was carried on
quietly and unostentatiously, the discourses consisting of simple
expositions of Scripture, or exhortations to steadfastness, or
admonitions regarding current duties, dangers, and trials. The
era of persecution was not favourable to bold, aggressive
preaching ; the " Apologists " bent their energies on vindicating
themselves and repelling the misrepresentations of their foes ;
while some able minds were drawn into the region of philosophical speculation, and tried to reconcile the revelations of
the gospel with the theories of the philosophers. In homiletical
literature the second century is almost wholly barren ; though
some works remain, like the Pedagogus of Clement of Alexandria, that were probably materials for sermons. About the
end of the third century we find more traces of pulpit power.
Origen, who, with all his errors, gave the greatest impulse to
the exegetical study of the Scriptures, appears to have done a
great work likewise in elevating the pulpit. Not only by his
own great powers as a preacher, but as the head of the catechetical school of Alexandria, he did much to give shape and
form to the Christian sermon, and to establish that mode of
address which has become so closely connected with Christian
worship. The sermon came to have a wider scope and a more
careful structure, and was directed more systematically towards
the establishment of the faith, the explanation of Scripture, and
the moulding of the hearts and lives of men.

But if the second and third centuries were somewhat wanting
in homiletical products, the case was wholly different in the

fourth and fifth. The period embraced in the latter half of the fourth century and the earlier part of the fifth was one of unusual brilliancy, unequalled by any period in the history of the Church previous to the Reformation. The union of culture and piety, of great oratorical gifts and great earnestness in preaching, was the feature of this period. Such names as those of Ambrose, Augustine, and Jerome in the Latin Church, and of Basil, the two Gregorys (of Nazianzus and Nyssa), Cyril, and Chrysostom in the Greek, shed a singular glory over this age. The causes that conspired to produce this result were numerous. Christianity had ceased to be a despised and persecuted religion, and had won many devoted adherents in the highest circles of society, both social and intellectual. Christian congregations were no longer meeting in upper rooms, or hiding from observation in catacombs and caves, but assembling in spacious churches, to fill the pulpits of which demanded oratorical qualifications of a higher order. The revolting excesses of heathen luxury and self-indulgence had caused a strong recoil in the bosom of many a noble Christian; and while such men did not as yet adopt all the extremes of asceticism, they made a vigorous protest in their own practice against all forms of worldly indulgence, and boldly summoned their fellows to follow their example. The age, too, was blessed with many Christian women of intense devotion, who bent their whole energies to induce their husbands and their sons to consecrate themselves to Christ. There was hardly one of the distinguished men whom we have named unconnected with a warm-hearted female relative, who as mother, sister, or grandmother, had besought him, with prayers and tears, to give himself to the Lord. The instances were numerous of men of high gifts and culture, who had been educated for the profession of lawyers or rhetoricians, abandoning their secular pursuits and devoting themselves to the Christian ministry. Sometimes they hovered for a time between the monastic and the active life; and even when they abandoned the former they remained unmarried, and practised no small measure of austerity in the regulation of their lives. No doubt they were on the very edge of that morbid view of the world which afterwards developed so disastrously into the monastic system; but as yet the morbid element had not advanced much beyond the point at which it gives a very powerful impulse to self-denying zeal. When men of high birth and lofty character renounce the world, and, as the result of deep conviction, give themselves to the service of Christ, they are commonly distinguished by a spiritual intensity and earnestness beyond the common; and when, as in the case of the great preachers of this era, they possess high talents, assiduously cultivated, the result is unique, and a spiritual force of remarkable efficacy is enlisted on the side of Christianity.

Remarkable though the preachers of this period were for ability and earnestness, we shall be greatly disappointed if we expect to find their homilies characterized uniformly by clear expositions of doctrine, or by solid and satisfactory explanations of Scripture. In both these respects they were, as a whole, far below the standard of the present day. We miss greatly in them clear statements of the way of salvation for sinners. But in showing the significancy and the practical bearing of the great facts of Christianity; in rebuking the spirit that regards the interests of this world with more anxious concern than those of the world to come; in urging men to earnestness and self-denial in the great duties of religion—many of the preachers of this period show a remarkable power. There is no mis-taking, too, the reality and sincerity of their appeals to their hearers. Their tone is intensely real; they are doing business with those whom they address; they are as far as possible from merely delivering essays or dissertations in their hearing. In this respect, and as a corrective to the tendency to heaviness with which our preachers are so much affected, the homilies of this period deserve the careful study of divinity students. And if you have not time to become acquainted with many of them, it is easy to make a selection. Augustine will naturally be selected from among the chiefs of the Latin Church. Among those of the Greek Church, Basil and Chrysostom have long maintained the reputation of the most eloquent and earnest. The great preacher of Antioch and Constantinople, as is well known, derived his name, Chrysostom, or the Golden-mouthed, from the marvellous quality of his eloquence. Many of the best preachers of modern times have owned their obligations to Chrysostom; nor can any preacher be familiar with his eloquent and powerful appeals without imbibing something of his spirit and adopting something of his manner.

Between the fifth century and the sixteenth the Christian pulpit had but little to boast of. On the one hand, however, there were not wanting men who preached a mystic devotion, or who urged the renouncing of the world, like St. Bernard, or the imitation of Christ, after the manner of Thomas à Kempis;

and, on the other hand, there were missionary preachers, especially in the earlier period, like the Culdees of the school of
St. Columba, who did much for spreading Divine truth among
the ignorant and careless, but of whose sermons we have hardly
any remains. Then there were the preachers of the mendicant
orders, some of them very powerful in their time, sent out to
counteract the preaching of the Waldenses and like-minded men,
in pre-Reformation times. As a rule, however, the pulpit was
feeble, and for a long time previous to the Reformation it had
in many instances been wholly neglected, or, if used at all, used
not to proclaim the way of life, but to communicate to the
people legends of the saints. Nor is this to be wondered at.
It was now that a system reached its full dimensions which
aims at instructing and impressing men by a different instrumentality from the preaching of the Word. Ritualism, *as a
method*, is essentially antagonistic to preaching. In its *object* it
may not always be so; in certain cases, no doubt, Ritualists
honestly seek to bring men's souls under the influence of spiritual truth. But it is characteristic of Ritualism, as a method,
that it aims at instructing, or at least impressing, men through
services that appeal to their senses, and in this respect it is
antagonistic to preaching, which seeks by means of the truth to
work directly on the soul. The method of Ritualism is very
tempting, where the men to be dealt with are ignorant, and
their mental faculties have never been roused into activity. It
seems unreasonable to suppose that spiritual truth should be
apprehended by such men directly, and the wiser method is
thought to be to treat them as children, and make their senses
the chief medium of impression. It is forgot that there is
nothing better fitted to exercise the mind and rouse its dormant
faculties than the great saving truths of Christianity; that there
has never been any community too degraded to be beyond the
reach of these truths when the Spirit of God has accompanied
their proclamation; and that the employment of the Word as
the chief means of spiritual impression is the appointment of
God, and is not therefore within the discretion of men. In
point of fact, wherever external ordinances have been chiefly
relied on as the means of impression, the mind has usually
become stunted, and spiritual stagnation has followed. The
dark ages were marked by the prevalence of Ritualism, but
along with Ritualism there was the prevalence of death.

It was inevitable, therefore, that as a general rule the pulpit
should stagnate while Ritualism prevailed. It is natural to find

the authorities of the Church of Rome resorting from time to time to new sensational devices, in order to stimulate the appetite which is so ready to tire of sensational food ; introducing miracle plays and passion plays, in addition to all the sensuous accompaniments with which they had already overlaid the worship ; ready to welcome every device which could throw fresh interest into the services of religion. But though here and there a voice was raised in favour of preaching the Word of God, such a proposal was systematically discouraged. The pioneers of the Reformation instinctively resorted to the method of preaching, and utterly distrusted and disliked the whole system of Ritualism. Men like Savonarola and Wycliffe were powerful preachers of the Word, and they believed that that Word was capable, through the power of the Holy Spirit, of effecting all that was needed to bring men to God and guide them in his ways. The Reformation itself was the result of a revived Christian pulpit. It was the preaching of the Word of God that made the Reformers popular, and that roused the souls of the people. Wherever the pulpit was set up, the Reformation spread, and wherever the Reformation spread, the pulpit was set up. Where the pulpit was most free, and was used most vigorously, the Reformation was most thorough. By-and-by the Church of Rome came to see the power of this weapon, and from time to time she has used it, as a means both of producing a diversion from Protestantism and of extolling the authority of the Church and the value of her ceremonies. But her use of the pulpit has always been somewhat restricted— generally in the centres of intellectual life, among educated men who were becoming tired of her ceremonies and sceptical of her whole claims and authority. It is contrary to the genius of her system that she should place much reliance on preaching, or represent it as other than subordinate to the elaborate ritual in which she puts her trust.

The Reformation era was one of great triumph for the pulpit. Never was its power more conspicuously or more conclusively shown. The greatest revolution of modern times was in the main the fruit of this weapon. And if the preaching of the Word had not been forcibly suppressed, if fire and sword had not stopped its action in France, Spain, Italy, and Austria, its triumph would have been still greater, and Europe, with but trifling exceptions, would have owned its power.

The preaching of the Reformation was a decided advance, in doctrinal clearness and solidity, on that of the fourth century, and even on the best specimens of the mediæval period. Compared with the former, it was more clear, full-volumed, and definite—dwelling on man's fallen state, and on the way of salvation through the sacrifice of Christ, as well as on the scriptural means of maintaining the life of faith and holiness, amid the trials and temptations of the world. Compared with the preachers of the mediæval period, the Reformers were more hearty, hopeful, and rejoicing. Living secluded from the world, as even the best of the mediæval preachers did—Bernard, Anselm, and the like—and subjected as they were personally to a rigid discipline, they were little fitted to proclaim heartily the glad tidings of free forgiveness ; they rather gave themselves to probe hearts, to awaken pensive feelings, to wean from the world, and to urge the carrying of the cross. The preachers of the Reformation mounted to a higher platform, and unfurled the true banner, the real Evangel, the glorious news of the kingdom of God. In their lips the grace of God that bringeth salvation was no mere speculative dogma, it was the pearl of great price, it was the treasure hid in the field, it was the unspeakable gift of God to men. To press on them this grand discovery, to urge them to lay hold of this treasure and thus secure their eternal peace and happiness, afforded scope for the highest eloquence, and was fitted, indeed, to create an eloquence where it did not exist. There was thus a rejoicing element in the Reformation pulpit, such as had not been since the apostolic age. The ring of Luther's joyous nature was in it, and the melody of his triumphant hymns, in opposition to the minor key of many preceding centuries. It was genuine, hearty, earnest. It filled the world with its sound. Everywhere men were brought up out of a horrible pit, out of the miry clay ; their feet were set on a rock, and a new song was put in their mouths, even praise to their God.

The German pulpit, which became so great a power under Luther and Melancthon, has not sustained the fame of its early days. We all know how it was deadened and all but destroyed by the withering blight of Rationalism. Towards the end of last century many of the sermons preached were on such topics as the care of health, the necessity of industry, the advantages of scientific agriculture, the duty of gaining a competence, the ill effects of law-suits and the folly of superstitious opinions—topics of which some might well enough form part of a parochial minister's instructions, but which it is fearful to think of as a substitute for the great and saving doctrines of

sin, grace, and redemption.* Since the revival of the evangelical spirit among some of her theologians, Germany has been
more conspicuous for her important contributions to literature
than for eminent service in the pulpit. Yet there are not a few
names of great preachers, scattered along her history, which are
worthy the attention of the German scholar. Spener, the
founder of the Pietists, who was preacher to the Court at
Dresden, occupied in the pulpit the first rank in his day, and
was in the highest repute for his sweet devoted spirit and his
pure eloquence, in respect to both of which he has been
compared to Fénélon. Zollikofer, who died at Leipsic in 1788,
was compared to Cicero. John Godfrey von Herder, famed in
German literature, and court preacher at Weimar, who died in
1803, was an earnest and holy man, and his sermons are
" characterized by solid thought, a chaste and lofty eloquence,
and a deep religious spirit." Reinhard, court preacher at
Dresden (died 1812), was one of the princes of German
preachers ; his sermons fill thirty-five volumes, and are full of
most interesting expositions of the secondary aspects of Christianity, but defective in the great fundamental truths. Schleiermacher, Harms, Theremin, and Krummacher may be mentioned
among those who have attained eminence in more recent times.

It can hardly be said, however, that the German pulpit has
yet attained a position corresponding to the extraordinary
vigour and attainments of the German mind. We doubt
whether German theologians have a high enough conception of
preaching as the great method of advancing the kingdom of
God. Should they attain to such a conception, and should
something of the old earnestness of Luther's days come again
into the German pulpit, the most glorious effects might be expected ; the German Church might become the reviver of the
gospel throughout Europe.

From Germany we pass to France. The phenomenon that
presents itself here is very remarkable. In some respects
France was the theatre of the greatest triumphs of the pulpit.
The Protestant Church in some degree shared the glory ; in
solid thought and evangelical light and warmth no French
preacher equals Saurin. Of Daniel de Superville, who, after
the revocation of the Edict of Nantes, had to fly to Rotterdam,
Dr. Doddridge used to say that he never met with any French
sermons to be compared with his, especially for beauty of

* " Hagenbach's German Rationalism," pp. 104, 105. Clark's translation.

imagery and tenderness of expostulation. But many of the
lights of the French pulpit were in the Church of Rome, and,
what is rather startling, some of them were Jesuits, though but
little affected with the spirit of their order. They approached as
near to Protestantism as was possible for members of the Church
of Rome, and, though the enlightened Protestant will miss in
their sermons elements of great value, he cannot fail to be
charmed by their eloquence, and often warmed and stimulated
by their fervour.

What the French pulpit achieved in the age of Louis XIV.
was due in chief measure to the example and influence of
Bourdaloue. A man of high culture, yet earnest Christian
character, breathing the æsthetic spirit of an Augustan age, yet
weeping over its unbelief, profligacy, and hollowness, and feeling deeply the utter effeteness of the Church's ceremonial, he
sought from the pulpit to appeal to something higher than the
senses—to rouse the soul and conscience of his audience. Dis-
daining the empty rhetoric of his predecessors, he sought to
express real and rousing thoughts in the most perfect forms of
language, to make the most exquisite and finished diction his
vehicle for conveying to the highest circles the unwelcome
truths which they were so shamefully neglecting. Bourdaloue
was followed by Bossuet, Fénélon, Massillon, La Rue, Fléchier,
and others hardly less eminent. The pulpit became the great
centre of attraction. It was an age of singular brilliance, the
age of Condé and Turenne, of Corneille and Molière and Racine,
of Pascal and La Fontaine and Montesquieu, of Malebranche
and Boileau and Fontenelle ; and yet the pulpit held its own in
the midst of all this splendid rivalry. But it was not like the
pulpit of the Reformation. Highly elaborate and artificial, it
did not address itself to the masses, but rather to an *élite* circle
of cultivated men and women, to whom nothing is acceptable
unless it be presented in the most faultless style. It did not
deal so directly with the doctrines of salvation, nor had it the
same joyous ring, as the utterance of men who, having found
the pearl of great price, were calling on their brothers to share
the treasure. While it called men to tremble and be in awe
before Him who is of purer eyes than to behold iniquity, it did
not so clearly proclaim the grace that hath appeared bringing
salvation. It was not free from that gloomy tone that always
characterizes the devotion of the Church of Rome ; it did not
quite bring the worshipper away from the mount that might
be touched, and that burned with fire, to the new Jerusalem

with its songs of jubilee, or to the glorious liberty of the sons of God.

Yet we should err much if we concluded that this wonderful era of the French pulpit was not worthy of our careful study. Mr. Jay, of Bath, who was so distinguished as a plain, earnest, evangelical preacher, but who at the same time felt profoundly that no legitimate means ought to be neglected by which preaching might be made more interesting and impressive, learnt French in his old age, simply that he might be able to read and study the sermons of the great French preachers. To make them models would be out of the question, yet from the study of them we may gain many collateral benefits. The emotion that burns in them may stir our spirit; the boldness and force with which they address the conscience may rouse our courage; the brilliance of their diction may enrich our style; their innumerable felicities of thought and expression may give us useful hints in the handling of topics which are never out of date, however different the circumstances of the time. But while we profit in these respects, we must go far beyond the French preachers in spiritual power; for they failed to arrest the growing corruption of the times, or to produce any such spiritual revival as that which followed the preaching of Wesley and Whitefield, and other plain but spiritual men.

The English pulpit has never presented anything so systematic or so finished as the French. It has exhibited a much more varied style of pulpit eloquence, sometimes excelling in the form, sometimes in the substance, sometimes in the spirit of preaching, and sometimes in all. The sermons of the Reformers were not finished compositions, but they were the gushings of full and earnest hearts. In the seventeenth century we have two types of preaching, one more characteristic of Churchmen, and the other of Nonconformists. In general, the Nonconformists excelled in fulness of doctrinal statement, while the Churchmen addressed themselves to the practical ethics of daily life. In the sermons of Howe, Baxter, or Flavel, man is dealt with as a lost sinner, to whom the Saviour is stretching forth his hands, and he is urged to fly to him for deliverance from the wrath to come. In Tillotson, Barrow, South, and Atterbury, there is what we may call an underground recognition of redemption, but man is dealt with rather as a denizen of this world, where he has duties, trials, and temptations numberless, in which he needs help and guidance. What was once said of South, that his sermons were not Sabbath-day but every-day sermons, is more or less applicable to the whole school. Jeremy Taylor, indeed, rises to a higher level. But the tone of most of the classical preachers is somewhat cold and dry, and this dryness becoming more and more characteristic of the English Church pulpit of the eighteenth century, reduced it ultimately to dust and ashes.

Yet there are some notable qualities in the great Church preachers of the seventeenth century. They had a great faculty of planning and arranging, often a remarkable breadth of view, embracing all the aspects of a subject, and a great power of clear, correct, and forcible expression. The evangelical intensity which they lacked found its place in the Nonconformist pulpit, which seldom failed to proclaim the high doctrines of grace and salvation. But this severance of the evangelical from the ethical element—the restriction of the evangelical preachers to the one, and of the Church preachers to the other—was unfortunate, and helped, perhaps, in conjunction with other causes, to produce the miserable state of things in the eighteenth century. When at last the Nonconformist interest was in a great measure stamped out, the evangelical and earnest element nearly disappeared.

But the extinguished torch was rekindled by Wesley and Whitefield, and the pulpit resumed its former power. The one element which they flung into it, and by which it became so effectual, was gospel life. Then followed the great evangelical revival of the present century, in which Churchmen shared so largely. Like the Nonconformist pulpit of the seventeenth century, the evangelical pulpit of the nineteenth has confined itself almost wholly to the doctrine of salvation—the soteriology, as theologians call it, of Scripture—and has bestowed only the most sparing attention on ethical and social questions, and on the numberless problems, speculative and practical, which the inquiring spirit of the age is ever starting. It is another class of preachers than the evangelical that are commonly discussing these questions in the pulpit.

But while the old types of English preaching are still to be recognised, there is much more variety, both in style and matter, than in any former age. And the question of how the pulpit is to be made most efficient is as important and difficult as ever. If only it can be made to combine the old evangelical message with the guidance which men need in the special circumstances of the time, there is no reason why it should not have before it a time of as great power and as rich blessing as ever.

The pulpit of Scotland has had a history of its own. In the early days of the Reformed Church of Scotland, and in the Covenanting period too, the pulpit was a great power. But the literary remains of the period do not convey a just impression of the force which they represent. Knox, Bruce, Rollock, Rutherford, William Guthrie, Livingston, and others, were doubtless powerful preachers. The samples that we have of their pulpit work, however, are somewhat uncouth, rough, and hard to read. Hardly any man in Scotland of the seventeenth century—Archbishop Leighton excepted—was a master of the English tongue. The truth is, their style was formed out of three languages, their native Scotch, English, and Latin. Latin was the language of theology, Scotch of the people, and English of the press. It was not till towards the end of the eighteenth century that the English of Scotch writers and preachers came to approach in ease and finish what is to be looked for in educated men speaking and writing their native tongue.

The great features of the Scotch pulpit have been its close adherence to Scripture and its love of dogmatic theology. With these features its greatest masters have combined a closeness in the application of scriptural doctrine to the heart and conscience from which it is difficult to escape. But, as in England, two very opposite types of preaching have developed themselves—that which deals earnestly with souls on their relation to God, and that of calm, sensible, ethical instruction. The former style may be said to have culminated in such men as Boston of the *Fourfold State*, and the Erskines of the Secession ; the latter in Dr. Hugh Blair and his contemporaries. Seldom has gospel truth been preached with the fulness of view, the rich flavour, the fervour and the earnestness of Ralph and Ebenezer Erskine. Often wild and unpruned, their preachings were evangelical festivals, and the feast was " a feast of fat things full of marrow." But, as in England, the ethical or practical element was but little attended to. Dr. Blair and his contemporaries found a neglected vein, which, however little fitted to supply to souls the bread of life, was at least left unworked by preachers of the other school. It is the vein which is always resorted to by men who wish to preach usefully without committing themselves, or their people to the distinctive doctrines of the gospel. It is much to be regretted that evangelical preachers in the present day seldom give it the place which it holds in the Bible ; in its place in the evangelical system, ethical preaching would have its proper force ; and there would be no ground for the common accusation that the evangelical system is not much concerned for moral interests.

The weak point in Scottish preaching has commonly been heaviness; and this has arisen from a tendency to an excess of dogmatic and expository teaching, and a want of familiar fellowship with the hearers in the ordinary moods and workings of their minds. The preacher has too often stood on a pedestal, delivering his dissertations before the people, or expounding to them from the Scriptures God's dealings with men in former days; he has not so readily come down to their level, nor touched their actual feelings, difficulties, and aspirations, nor sought to deal with them as he found them, nor, taking them kindly by the hand, endeavoured to help them on the way to heaven. In his expositions of Scripture he has taken extraordinary and often wearisome pains to explain the feelings and the actings of the men and women introduced to us there ; but he has only in the vaguest way spoken to his people of their own feelings, or exercised direct influence upon them. It was one of the great benefits conferred on the Scottish pulpit by Chalmers, that while he maintained its foundation of sound dogmatic and Scriptural teaching, he dealt with his audience as a reality and not an abstraction, and in all his teaching seemed to have in view their actual wants and tendencies. We have a school of preaching rising up in our day, not always the most orthodox, which purposely avoids abstract dogma, and strives to deal only with what is living and stirring in the minds of the people. The true policy is to combine the two—to keep ever in the foreground the great message which God sends to men, but to give this message not in a heavy, abstract, uninteresting form, but so as to take living hold of the people who are gathered before us.

It is an interesting fact that the most characteristic contributions of America to our pulpit literature have been marked by this feature of adaptation. To hit the human heart through some joint of the armour ; to touch its actual feelings; deftly, sharply, palpably to transfix it with the arrow of conviction, so as to leave it in no doubt as to its being struck ; then bring gospel truth in its more comfortable aspects to bear on it, in a way equally pat and pertinent—is what an American can do as it is done by no other. Popular religious literature in America abounds in papers of close, pithy application, compelling the exclamation, " Thou art the man." Preachers like Dr. Cuyler and Dr. Talmage get to close quarters with their

E

hearers, and having pinned them to the ground to show them their helplessness, encourage them to look earnestly to the great source of help and blessing. Or, taking up the human side of life, they point out to them errors and failings that are apt to escape their notice, and ply their consciences with the obligation to conform more closely to the high standard of the Divine will.

It is a common observation that in the present age the pulpit is not what it was. And in one respect there may be ground for the remark. It has not the brilliancy of other times. There are not many born orators in its ranks. But the general average of pulpit power is probably greater than at any former time. In any case, the lesson for us is obvious. When less is given of the extraordinary, more must be made of the ordinary. When the soil is poorer, the husbandry must be better. When there are fewer men of genius, there must be more men of persevering industry and holy application. When fewer men are sent, able, by a holy instinct, to command the attention of their fellows, there must be more men who are resolved, by God's grace, so to improve every faculty that the message with which they are put in trust shall not suffer in its treatment at their hands.

CHAPTER V.

1. IT is too obvious to require proof, that the most essential requisite for effective preaching is that it be scriptural. The substance of the preaching must be the substance of the message which the minister has been called and commissioned to proclaim. The word spoken must be a transcript of the word revealed ; the preacher must at once receive of the Lord that which he delivers, and deliver to his hearers that which he receives. For the preacher of the gospel merely to retail the truths or enforce the duties of natural religion, with a slight colouring of Christianity, would be far more preposterous than for the player to act the play of *Hamlet* without the part of Hamlet. Obviously the backbone of the Christian revelation must be also the backbone of Christian preaching. Man must be dealt with as a sinner, and told, as he was told by Christ himself, that the Son of Man came into the world to seek and to save that which is lost. There must be no concealment either of the nature, the desert, or the doom of sin. And here, perhaps, is the point where the temptation to unfaithfulness is strongest ; partly because it puts a strain on your faculties to take in the Bible doctrine of sin, partly because it demands much courage to proclaim it as something which you believe, and partly because such teaching interferes with a certain amiable feeling that likes to make things pleasant, and that shrinks from inflicting humiliation and pain.

Faithful preaching must further set forth the character of God in its twofold aspect of righteousness and mercy ; " the Lord merciful and gracious, long-suffering and abundant in goodness and truth, forgiving iniquity, transgression, and sin, and that will by no means clear the guilty." It must draw the line between salvation by works and salvation by grace ;

turning the sinner's eyes away from himself, turning them
wholly to the Cross. It will dwell largely on the person of the
Saviour, and the redemption achieved by the shedding of his
blood. The great work of the life-giving Spirit, quickening the
soul from spiritual death, and maintaining in it the life of holiness, will have a prominent place. The inseparable alliance
between privilege and duty will be brought out clearly—the
connection between God working in the believer, and the obligation on him to work out his salvation with fear and trembling.
Men will be called to lives in all respects well-pleasing to God,
and required to maintain an inviolate purity of conscience, and
in every relation of life to cultivate a self-denying spirit of
love and goodness. This great body of truth will be pressed
home by the solemn prospect of the great white throne, and
the awful alternatives of everlasting bliss or misery that hang
on their decision.

Keeping such truths in the centre, the preacher may sweep
round them in a circle wider or narrower, according as he
deems his hearers sufficiently or imperfectly grounded in the
great central truths. Taking the whole Bible into account, the
circumference of its teaching is remarkably wide. There can
hardly be a greater contrast than that between the wide sweep
of the Bible orbit and the narrow circle of ordinary evangelical
preaching. The majority of preachers adhere to a somewhat
limited range of topics. Either it is that they are afraid to
leave "the principles of the doctrine of Christ," though this is
urged in the Epistle to the Hebrews, or that they fail to make
themselves so familiar with other topics as to be able to preach
upon them. It cannot be denied that there is great meagreness
of ethical teaching, for example, in most evangelical pulpits.
Undoubtedly, too, there are many forms of temptation in the
actual world, as well as antidotes to the spirit of unbelief; many
quiet resting-places for the weary soul, many subtle incitements
to the higher life, and many refinements and beauties of Christian character, which are almost wholly passed over by the
evangelical pulpit. There are moods of the soul, sin-worn and
world-worn, with which some of our imaginative writers sympathize, but which are hardly ever approached by the evangelical preacher. And when these topics are touched, as they
sometimes are with remarkable freshness, by preachers who are
not evangelical, inquiring spirits are drawn away from the great
central truths. No man ought, in any case, to meddle with
experiences which he does not understand, or to try to open

doors of which he has not the key. But while he makes the cardinal truths of revelation his centre, he should try to make his circumference wide enough to embrace all that is embraced in the Bible. There is nothing to which we are more prone than a narrow traditional notion of what is comprehended in the whole counsel of God. Little can be said for the preacher who fancies he knows it all, or who does not find on his right hand and on his left glimpses of unexplored territory which are continually inviting his research. Only let him see that what he does teach from the pulpit is truly the message of God, and not the mere fancies of his own mind. It is of immense service for him to be constantly recalling the fact that his is a message of life and death, to be spoken to men, " whether they will hear, or whether they will forbear " (Ezek. ii. 5); and if in the delivery of ordinary messages between man and man, such as are now sent by the telegraph, fidelity is the first requisite, how much more when the message comes from God, and when heaven or hell hangs on the reception!

2. Next, we notice *clearness* as another great quality of effective preaching. It is plain that no vivid impression of a truth can be conveyed to others by one who sees it mistily and expresses it vaguely. " Fire low," says Dr. Guthrie, " the order which generals have often given to their men before fighting began, suits the pulpit not less than the battle-field. The mistake common to both soldiers and speakers is to shoot too high, over people's heads, missing by a want of plainness and directness both the persons they preach to and the purposes they preach for." *

It sometimes happens that plainness in the pulpit is hindered through an erroneous idea of what is due to its dignity. This leads some preachers not only to speak in an artificial tone of

---

* In Tennyson's " Northern Farmer " the effects of this mistake are hit off with remarkable cleverness, though doubtless with a dash of exaggeration. The farmer is dying, and is turning over his past life in a half-accusing, half-excusing spirit. Naturally he thinks of his relations to the parson, and here is his statement of how he improved the ministrations of his spiritual guide :—

" And I hallus com'd t's church afoor my Sally wur deäd
An' eerd un a bummin' awaay, like a buzzard clock ower my yead,
An' I niver know'd what a mean'd, but I thowt a 'ad summut to saäy,
An' I thowt a said whet a owt to a said, an' I comed awaay."

The farmer would never have been content with this view of his duty if the parson had started like the great Preacher—" Behold, a sower went forth to sow."

voice, but to make use of circumlocutions for the very purpose
of avoiding plain terms. Probably this habit arises from unconscious unwillingness on the part of the preacher to come into
near mental contact with the people—a grievous error, since
such closeness of mental contact is one of the chief aids to
spiritual impression. In other instances the use of unusual
words is a wretched piece of pedantry, a device of the preacher's
for showing off the superiority of his training.

But a fault of this kind is trivial compared to that of preaching on a subject that has not been clearly thought out. There
is a snare in natural fluency, the fluent man being often tempted
to neglect clearness and directness of statement and simplicity
of method. He is tempted to dispense with that most useful,
though often intensely irksome, process—getting hold of his
own thoughts, ascertaining precisely what they are, and sepa-
rating them from every particle of obscurity. Perhaps he thinks
it enough in his preparation to get hold vaguely of a thought,
and trust to its clearing itself, as it were, and coming out with
sufficient plainness, under the excitement of delivery. Far more
may be expected *ultimately* of the man who, though at first he
sees his subject enveloped in mist—sees a fragment of an idea
here, and the shadow of one there, and knows that there must
be a connection between them, but is baffled, bewildered, and
almost maddened as he attempts to define and express them—
perseveres, nevertheless, with the persistency of a martyr, jots
down with his pencil everything as it occurs to him, concen-
trates his attention more earnestly, keeps his temper, walks
about his room, is frequently on his knees, or with his hand
over his eyes ; possibly finds it necessary to take a quiet walk
in a retired place, or to wait till a night's sleep shall have
freshened his brain, or given him a better point of view ; but at
last, when his work is finished, finds an abundant recompense
for these pangs of parturition in the clear consecutive form in
which his thoughts come out. If we admire the marvellous
precision, clearness, and force of the thinking of John Foster, it
will be well for us to remember what labour composition cost
him, how very far the pen which *he* wielded was from that of
the ready writer. Nothing can be more valuable than the
mental discipline of clearing the obscure and marshalling the
tangled in our own minds ; nor does it follow that the same
toil and trouble will always be required. A habit of clearness
will be attained, which will by-and-by supersede the necessity
of the efforts through which it was acquired.

3. A third quality of effective preaching is *adaptation* to the capacity and circumstances of the hearers. Of all public speakers, the preacher has most need to cultivate this quality. An ordinary congregation presents more *variety of capacity* than almost any other audience. Persons may be found in it of almost all varieties of education, from the most crass Bœotian to the most cultivated sage. The child of eight will be found side by side with the grandfather of eighty, and the babe in Christ with the mother in Israel, who, taught for half a century by the Holy Ghost, has been gaining wonderful insight into the things of God. One hearer may be ignorant of the very elements of Bible history and theological knowledge ; another may possess an acquaintance with both, wonderful for his years and opportunities. The ability to feed the sheep and the lambs together, to write like the apostle in the same letter to little children, and to young men, and to fathers in Christ, is a marvellous achievement of Christian tact and wisdom.

In general, we may say that the more biblical any discourse is, the more will it be found to suit the several varieties of capacity. Our Lord's own discourses are full of instruction here. And many of them—his parables for example—have this remarkable feature, that while fitted to interest all classes, even the humblest, they are adapted at the same time to give exercise to minds of the highest calibre, suggesting views of truth which such minds may find it most useful to ponder. And generally, the Bible, from first to last, will be found to be quite a model of adaptation to all the diversities with which the Christian minister has to deal, both in its general adaptation to the average capacity, and in the portions which are specially fitted for those above that level and for those below.

Let it be observed, however, that while a preacher must aim at hitting the existing capacity of his audience, he ought at the same time to try to *enlarge* it, to accustom them to the *higher levels* of truth and experience. Some ministers have been wonderfully successful in this way, not merely conferring benefit on individuals in their flocks, but educating the flock itself—expanding its intellectual and spiritual capacity, and enabling it to find enjoyment and profit in regions that would at one time have seemed dark as a mine or inaccessible as an Alpine peak. In such cases, the effect has been largely due to the silent impression which an able and well-instructed, and at the same time modest, man produces, of the reality of these higher levels, and of the precious deposits which they afford, by creating a strong sympathy with himself. He lifts them up, or excites in them the desire to rise, whereas an instructor who is himself content to dwell in the more common levels creates no conception of anything higher, and inspires no upward desire. It is between two extremes that the true preacher must steer : between preaching so high that the people cannot rise with him, and preaching so low that they have no wish to rise. The golden mean is to strike their average capacity, but carry them gradually up.

4. In all effective preaching there is an *arresting* element. It must seize on actual thoughts and feelings in the breasts of hearers, and use them as auxiliaries for spiritual impression.

It is of great importance, in this point of view, to get a common starting-point with one's hearers. This is often furnished by special occurrences—remarkable providences that every one is struck by, or by human feelings, common to most men, but that commonly lie, as it were, in deep rock-pools, seldom stirred by other hands. Very often the preacher will excite a wonderful interest by quietly using his own experience of sin and infirmity, hope and fear, joy and sorrow, effort and disappointment, as the basis of his instructions. Few that have done so have failed to meet with illustrations almost ludicrous of the remarkable degree to which their lessons have struck home. A hearer will sometimes ask a friend with the most ingenuous solicitude, " Who could have told the preacher all about me ? I felt that he was describing me to the very life." Most likely the preacher did nothing but delineate some common human experience : *e.g.* the disgust one has in certain moods of mind at some besetting sin ; the vivid conviction at these times that one will never again fall into it ; the gradual disappearance of that conviction, and one's horror at discovering by-and-by that one has fallen into it as badly as ever.*

This mode of rousing feeling in the heart of a hearer has an effect on the mind corresponding to that of a touch on the body. Abstract discussion may leave a hearer utterly unmoved, as much so as if he were asleep. But touch such a person, even though his face be turned in the opposite direction ; the effect is

---

* " A man," says Cecil, " who talks to himself will find out what suits the heart of man ; some things respond, they ring again. Nothing of this sort is lost upon mankind ; it is worth its weight in gold for the service of the minister. He must remark too what it is that puzzles and distracts the mind ; all that is to be avoided. It may wear the garb of deep research, great acumen, and extensive learning ; but it is nothing to the mass of mankind."

first a surprise, then a concentration of his attention upon you. So if you come into contact with a hearer's mind by rousing some living thought or feeling, the effect is first a surprise, and then a concentration of his attention. And for a time at least he is at your command, and will hear anything you may say. The metaphorical meaning of the word " touch " illustrates our position. A touching appeal is an appeal that rouses a living feeling—a chord vibrating in your soul comes into contact with a corresponding chord in another's, and sets it vibrating too ; and when the power is wielded by a man of much emotional sensibility the effect is overwhelming.

But whether by a touch or otherwise, it is of the greatest consequence to a preacher to get his lessons associated with something that has life and motion in the heart of his hearers. A dry preacher is one that pays no regard to this law of interesting discourse, but is content to let the stream of his thoughts, if there be a stream, flow on, without an attempt to bring them into contact with any thought or feeling that is active in his hearers. A commonplace preacher, in like manner, is content to utter statements, not because they are fitted to lay hold of anything living, or give life to anything dead, but simply because they are the things that it is most proper to say on the subject. No amount of fluency can atone for this defect. A flow of words without one arresting thought can never stir heart and soul. On the other hand, there are low clap-trap arts which some preachers resort to for the purpose of creating a surprise. There are men who utter *outré* things from the pulpit, on a principle not much higher than that on which the clown in a pantomime throws his body into grotesque attitudes or wears a dress of motley. If educated men know so little of what is stirring in the minds and hearts of their fellows, and have so few resources for attaching the great lessons of Christianity to these, as to be obliged to resort to the *outré* and the sensational, it is surely an indication that they are unequal to their task.

5. A fifth quality of effective preaching arises from its making use of a *variety of faculty* in order to obtain access to the souls of the audience. It is not content to gain or to hold possession by a single avenue, such as the reasoning faculty ; it aims to bring into play the whole round of faculties by which the mind can be approached or influenced. In other words, it seeks to make the mode of appeal as varied as it is in the Bible.

All of us have probably known instances of very admirable discourses failing to produce much impression, because from first to last they were addressed to the logical faculty, and when that faculty became tired, as it does very quickly in uneducated hearers, no other was called in to relieve it. Men who are trained to follow the movements of the logical faculty may indeed find much pleasure in discourses where it is used almost alone, but used to excellent purpose; few intellectual treats are greater than a piece of powerful reasoning, where, either by clear statements that commend themselves to our intuitions, or by more formal modes of reasoning, light is thrown on the obscure, and truths that lay in shadowy corners are brought out into the clear sunshine. But in preaching, even the most logical minds are intolerable if their logic is not steeped, so to speak, in emotion; great masters of the art, like Jonathan Edwards or Canon Liddon, would be utter failures if the fervour of a burning heart did not glow in their discourses. Cold logic, like that of Butler's "Analogy," is unsuitable for public preaching. In common minds, and indeed it may be said in all minds, the imagination is the indispensable handmaid to logic. It is easily excited, even in the uneducated; it works for a considerable time not only without fatigue, but with an intense sense of enjoyment. Appeals to the feelings are also very effective, when managed with skill and moderation; but it must be remembered that if the feelings do not at once respond to such appeals they are liable to become hardened, and if they do respond, being tender and excitable, they are easily overpowered. The same remark may be made of the conscience. Obviously the part of a skilful preacher is to appeal in due proportion to all the faculties, as he finds them appealed to in the Word of God.

Take, for example, the Epistle to the Romans. For the logical faculty there is noble exercise there, especially in the earlier chapters; but that unrivalled epistle would have been a very different production had no other faculty been appealed to. How skilfully, all through, are the other faculties called into operation! What a striking summons, for example, is given to conscience in the beginning of the second chapter : "And thinkest thou this, O man, that judgest them that do such things, and doest the same, that thou shalt escape the righteous judgment of God?" Nothing, by the way, can be more effective than to wake up conscience by a sudden and unexpected appeal like this; as is done also in some of our

Lord's parables, or in Nathan's parable of the ewe lamb. It is like the sudden uncovering of a masked battery in war. In another part of the epistle we find the moral instincts or intuitions brought skilfully into play : " If our unrighteousness commend the righteousness of God, what shall we say ? Is God unrighteous who taketh vengeance ? (I speak as a man.) God forbid ; for then how shall God judge the world ? " A little further on we are borne on the outspread wings of imagination to hear the creation groaning and travailing in pain, and waiting for the adoption, to wit, the redemption of the body. And in other places our feelings are laid siege to and carried captive : " O the depth of the riches both of the wisdom and knowledge of God ! how unsearchable are his judgments, and his ways past finding out ! " It is this variety of appeal that makes the Bible such a lively book, and such a contrast to the productions of those who by addressing themselves for ever to a single faculty wear out their hearers. The best preachers in this respect are doubtless those who with as little effort as is apparent in the case of our Lord, or in that of St. Paul, are able to appeal to the several faculties in due proportion, and to get the best work out of each. In no case, of course, must the reasoning faculty be denied its own place. It is less shy, and at the same time more honest, than the feelings, which, if pressed too hard, will hide themselves altogether, or give, at best, but a one-sided decision. Direct appeals to the feelings are effective in proportion as they are rare. It is better to aim as a habit at moving them by sympathy ; if the heart of the preacher be moved intensely by what he utters, that will serve to move the feelings of his audience. Indeed, it is only when the feelings of an audience have been brought up to a certain pitch by this process that the direct appeal carries the day.

6. From the preceding remarks it follows that in effective preaching copious *illustration* is indispensable.

The capacity of the human mind to appreciate resemblances and contrasts is one of its most invariable characteristics, and it may readily be turned by the preacher to valuable account. It enables him to lay stepping-stones along paths where otherwise he could not hope to conduct the larger portion of his hearers. It lends bright hues to subjects which would otherwise be too sombre, and catches the attention that in cases innumerable would be sure to be lost. It is in this light that we speak of it now. When ordained to the charge of his first congregation, the late Dr. Guthrie determined that whatever he

might fail in, he would compel his hearers to attend. Watching,
in the course of his first efforts, to discover what part of his
discourses seemed to be most attended to, he saw that it was
the illustrations. He accordingly resolved to cultivate that
department with peculiar care. Cultivate it he did, and to the
greatest purpose, for a greater master of illustration has never
appeared in the pulpit, nor one who by means of it could more
closely rivet the attention of his audience. But the copious use
of illustration has higher sanction. Our Lord's discourses
abound in it. His parables are illustrations all through. The
Sermon on the Mount has hardly started before we find the salt
of the earth, the light of the world, the city set on an hill, the
candle under a bushel, and the candle on the candlestick. In
their most solemn and impressive periods, too, Christ's discourses are pointed with illustrations. The Sermon on the
Mount fills us with an overwhelming sense of the retributions
of the day of doom, by the illustration of the house on the rock
and the house on the sand. The parable of the last judgment
makes a similar impression, by the illustration of the shepherd
dividing his sheep from the goats. Nothing could repress the
outflow of illustration from the mind of Jesus. In the deepest
agony of the garden his sufferings were spoken of as a cup.
The farewell discourse begins with the house of many man-
sions, has for its central subject the vine and its branches, and
near its end introduces the woman in travail having sorrow
when her hour is come, but after the child is born forgetting
her anguish for joy that a man is born into the world. Probably
it is not less instructive in another connection, that there are
no figures, and hardly any illustrations, in the *intercessory prayer.*
When the address was to God, they were not needed. But on
the way to Calvary the ever busy faculty again asserts itself
in the address to the daughters of Jerusalem : " If they do
these things in the *green tree,* what shall be done in the dry ? "

There is this further to be said in favour of illustration, that
it is adapted to take hold of all classes and ages of hearers. An
apt illustration is fitted to interest the most cultivated philosopher and the youngest child. Illustration, in fact, is one of the
chief instruments for enabling a preacher to fuse his audience
together, and treat it as a unity. Some parts of a discourse
may be adapted to one class, and some to another ; but the
illustrations are for all. They are the pictures of spoken
instruction. Pictorial illustrations of Scripture, provided they
be true, even if slight and almost rude, are not beneath the

notice nor the interest of the most intellectual reader. And it is one of the signs of the times that illustrated works are far the most popular. Illustrated sermons are popular too. And where the illustrations are wanting, the sermon is like a tree in winter, or a skeleton, or the bare ribs of a ship on the stocks; skilfully constructed it may be, but incomplete, and very soon tiresome.

Illustrations, however, even when good, and in good taste, may be overdone. They may be so superabundant as to overlay instruction, and make the discourse illustration *et praeterea nihil*. Care must be taken that a body of solid instruction underlies the more illustrative part. How wonderfully this was verified in the discourses of our Lord a single instance will suffice to show. In a sense, the parable of the sower was all illustration, but it was not illustration only. There lay underneath every one of its figures an amazing amount of solid truth—a nucleus, so to speak, capable of being expanded to an all but unlimited extent. Our Lord's habit is equally adapted to correct the error of those who despise all illustration and of those who present it in a style of gorgeous and tawdry embellishment.

We have said that illustrations are especially useful for the young. Indeed, if one desires to train one's self to the habitual use of suitable illustration, one cannot do better than teach a class of children. In breaking down scriptural truth to them, and getting them to understand it, one will constantly find the benefit of illustration. Men are but children of a larger growth, and the habit which one learns in dealing with the young will be of eminent service with the old. In dealing with children you are not likely to introduce illustrations merely for their own sake. You are not likely to get them up elaborately, as if your object were to show how beautiful a picture you can draw. Mr. Ruskin maintains, elaborately and truly, that whenever Art sets up on its own account, when it becomes the end of its own existence, instead of the handmaid of truth and the spur to duty, it loses its legitimate function, it becomes a bastard. The same is true of the art of illustration. Illustration ought always to make what is on the other side *more clear*, never to obscure it. In the case of a Christian sermon it should make the Saviour, his person and his work, more conspicuous and more commanding. Dr. Kidder* gives this anecdote of a Spanish painter of the Lord's Supper: "It was his object to

* "Homiletics," p. 185.

throw all the sublimity of his art into the figure and countenance of the Saviour ; but on the table in the foreground of the picture he painted some cups with such extraordinary beauty and skill that the attention of all who came to see the picture was at once attracted to the cups, and every one was loud in their praise. The painter observing this, saw that he had failed in his design of directing attention to the principal object in the picture, and exclaiming, ' I have made a mistake, for these cups divert the eyes of the spectator from the Master,' he immediately seized his brush and dashed them from the canvas."

So should we dash from our sermons everything that obscures truth rather than brightens it, and throws its shadow on Him whom every power should be employed to delineate " fairer than the children of men."

CHAPTER VI.

WHEN deep impression has been made on a hearer, and it is
attempted to trace it to its source, the remark is sometimes made that it was not so much what the preacher said as
his way of saying it that left its mark behind. The truths
uttered may have been long familiar ; but as spoken by the
preacher they had an edge and power that made them tell on
the hearer as they had never told before.

This is in thorough harmony with the great scriptural doctrine
that the power which quickens and changes the heart, through
the word preached, is in all cases the Spirit of God. That
power may go with the same truth as spoken by one man, and
not as spoken by another. It may go with it as spoken by him
at one time, and not at another. The reason may be that the
human instrument is adapted for the Spirit's use in the one
case and not in the other. It must be of great importance,
then, to know under what conditions the instrument becomes
adapted to the Spirit's use, and it will be the desire of every
loyal preacher that in his case the instrument may ever be
found in the state of highest meetness for such Divine employment.

This leads us to consider the spirit of the effective preacher—
first, in relation to God ; and second, in relation to the people
before him.

I. When is the spirit of the preacher in such a relation to
God that the Holy Spirit may be expected to work by him, and
give Divine efficacy to his words ?

The answer is short and simple : when he feels that his place
is that of a mere instrument in the Spirit's hands ; when he
desires and prays that the Spirit may work by him for the great
ends of the ministry ; and when he goes to work in the belief

that the Spirit will give the blessing promised, and in the
expectation of witnessing the fruits of His work.

The deepest humility is thus immediately connected with the
highest power. All confidence in our natural ability to impress
our fellows has to give way to a supreme trust in the Divine
power working through us; and when fruits of that Divine
working appear, we are filled with awe at God's nearness to us,
and at his condescension in making use of us for so glorious
a work.

The case admits of no compromise. We dare not divide the
work with God, as if we were partners on somewhat equal
terms. Far less can we take the chief place as ours, and merely
ask God to help us, thinking, perhaps, how well we do when
we recognise Him thus. In our regard God's place must be
high above all other. The part that we sustain is that of mere
servants or instruments, placing ourselves at his disposal. We
seek to deliver God's message in the best form in which it can
be delivered, but we look to God alone for the power to make it
effectual, and when it is made effectual we give all the glory to
Him.

It is this spirit that makes a human ministry a ministry of
power. God honours those that honour Him. The Wesleys and
the Whitefields, the Nettletons and the Moodys, and all the other
preachers whose words have proved words of life and of
marvellous power, have all habitually stood in this relation to
God, owning Him as the only source of efficacy, and ever giving
Him all the praise.

II. Next, we have to consider the spirit of the preacher in
relation to the people to whom he speaks. We have to remember, too, that the preacher is not merely an evangelist, but a
pastor who from week to week seeks that his people may be
built up in knowledge and in grace. The work is so important
and so difficult that no element can safely be neglected that may
be used by the Spirit for this end. The utmost attention needs
to be given to fit the instrument for its work, which implicit
reliance should at the same time be placed on the power that
makes it effectual.

It may be well now to enter somewhat into detail on the state
of the preacher's spirit in reference to his audience.

1. The preacher must himself be *interested* in what he preaches
to others. Interested, we say; but that is a feeble term, not
expressing by any means all that needs to be aimed at, but only
the first element in the process. The opposite state is, when

the preacher is so lifeless as to go through his discourse as a
mere matter of form, much as he might go through a sermon
written in an unknown tongue. It is not likely that in any
living church this extreme will often be found. But without
approaching it, a preacher from various causes may deliver a
discourse on an important topic without being himself interested
in it, or without being interested in it at the time. Suppose
that he hastily preaches a discourse prepared years before,
without taking any pains to get it fresh into his own mind and
soul, the probability is that it will be to his audience like
ditch-water rather than a draught from a limpid stream. To
be really effective it must be a rill of living water ; it must be
the expression of thoughts and feelings that are alive within
him, not dropping out helplessly, like water from a leak, but
streaming forth with the freshness and energy of a fountain.
And this condition is by no means inconsistent with the great
requisite that what he preaches be essentially the thoughts and
word of God. For as the water that issues from a fountain
comes originally from the clouds, but in its passage through the
earth acquires the sharpness and sparkle of spring-water ; so
Divine truth, coming first from above, but passing through
the soul of the preacher, acquires that element of freshness on
which, under God, its efficacy depends. " Whosoever drinketh
of the water that I shall give him," said our Lord, " shall never
thirst ; but the water that I shall give him shall be in him a
well of water springing up into everlasting life " (John iv. 14).

Great preachers have commonly felt many such springs of
heaven-born thought and feeling stirring in their hearts, and
have been eager to pour them out. But the freshness which
one feels in first preaching on a subject may disappear or may
be lessened after a time. The fountains of interest and feeling
are sometimes intermittent, or, like some famous spas, they may
dry up at one time to burst out at another. The repetition of
an old discourse, with which one has been unfamiliar for some
time, is always a somewhat perilous experiment, and is not
likely to be resorted to by the conscientious preacher *unless he
still feels a fresh interest in the subject*, or takes some pains, by
additions or otherwise, to connect it with processes that are
active in his own mind.

2. The next quality we mention is, in one sense, only the
superlative degree of that which has just been illustrated—
earnestness. The earnest preacher has vividly before him the
circumstances of the audience ; he feels the awfully solemn

F

nature of the truths proclaimed to them, and his very soul flows out in the longing desires he cherishes and the appeals he makes for their everlasting welfare. If the main function of the preacher were to reiterate the truths of natural religion, and to urge men to be more conscientious and consistent in their lives, there might be less occasion for the quality we now speak of. But it is otherwise when the preacher has to address immortal beings ruined through sin, to tell them of the blessed propitia-tion, and to urge them to commit their souls at once to the Saviour, under fear of a doom more aggravated than ever, if their other sins be crowned by their rejection of Him. If all carelessness in regard to important interests be offensive, care-lessness in the handling of such themes must be surpassingly so. No man can estimate the deadening effect of handling such topics in an indifferent tone.* It is of all things most incumbent on the minister of Christ to treat them as realities. And in order to do this it is equally indispensable that he feel them as realities himself. For there is an earnestness which is not real but assumed, and which can never accomplish the end of that which is real. There is a got-up manner, an artificial vehemence of tone, a violent gesticulation in the pulpit, which, however it may please the ignorant, has only the effect of sham and clap-trap on the genuine heart. To speak earnestly one must feel earnestly on subjects of such awful solemnity. And that earnest feeling is something not to be sought merely before preaching, or in the process of preaching, but to be habitually cherished, and often renewed and intensified, during the whole course of our lives.

There are some aspects of human life which are fitted to create a certain feeling of earnestness in the heart of any man of ordinary sensibility and benevolence, whether he be a Chris-tian or not. But this feeling by no means comes up either to the pitch or the quality of evangelical earnestness. At the brightest, human society is a chequered scene. To most men life's little span is crowded with sorrows and disappointments, often bitter beyond expression, and protracted beyond the hope of remedy. Philanthropy is moved by the spectacle, and labours to mitigate these sufferings. But this philanthropy is not tan-

* Garrick, it is well known, was once asked by a clergyman how it was that he, the actor, dealing in fictions, made so powerful an impression, while the clergyman, dealing in realities, sent the people to sleep. " Because you treat realities as if they were fictions, and I treat fictions as if they were realities."

tamount to evangelical love, although often, directly or indirectly, set in motion by it. The Howards and Wilberforces, the Chalmerses and Shaftesburys, that have shown most anxiety for the relief of human suffering, have in point of fact been men of earnest evangelical views. But the spirit that animates the right-hearted minister of the gospel is far deeper than that of common benevolence, and the sorrow that compassionates men's miseries in this world is in him but the lighter play of that deep and awful emotion which is roused by the thought of their state before God, and their hopeless condition for the life that is to come.

So solemn and awful are the views of life and eternity presented in the Word of God as applicable to a large proportion of the men around us, that were it not that our nature, by its very structure, is incapable of perpetually realising the awful, or of living in the future, the evangelical minister would be overshadowed by a continual horror. As it is, if his heart be true, as often as he thinks vividly of the state and prospects of a world that lieth in wickedness, he must feel a new impulse to earnestness in inviting sinners to lay hold on the Saviour. His soul will be stirred to its depths as he pleads with God to open their hearts and draw them to himself. And even after this great object has been gained, there are ulterior objects that must continue to exercise the most earnest feelings of his heart. There are old habits which the new convert must be induced to abandon ; there are holy graces which he must be trained to covet ; there are enterprises of Christian love in which he must be enlisted. The spirit of evangelical earnestness implies a heart panting for such results, and incapable of finding rest until the objects of its solicitude are in full training for the inheritance of the saints in light.

In the pursuit of these objects, the earnest preacher combines the coolness of a man of business with the fire of a warrior. Professor Blackie has given a striking definition of the earnest preacher—"a man of business on fire." A man of business, having a special business to transact, a definite object to accomplish, requiring the use of means adapted to the end ; arguments, illustrations, and appeals that must be thought over, put in proper form, and arranged in due order, as carefully as an engineer plans a bridge or a general arranges his army. But once the materials are chosen and made ready, the process itself needs to be carried on at a red heat. Unless it is besieged with urgency and fervour, the citadel of Mansoul had better be let alone. The neglect either of the business element or of the propelling element in the process is disastrous. Artillery without powder and powder without artillery are equally in vain. If you neglect the business part, if you are not provided with solid reasons in orderly array, your harangue will become rant—soft, pulpy declamation, with little power to move. If you have an ample stock of strong considerations but no fervour to propel them, your arrows will fall at your feet, instead of sticking fast in the hearts of the people. The great preachers of all times and countries have been marked by both qualities. The resources of well-trained and well-furnished intellects and the fervour of deeply exercised hearts have been yoked together for their pulpit work. They have tried to open their hearts to the full influence of the solemn truths of revelation—placed them, as it were, at the very roots of their being, and sought to have their hearts saturated by them ; and they have diligently trained their faculties of thought and speech to give expression to their convictions in a suitable way.*

3. Kindred to the qualities of efficient preaching now considered is a third—*affectionateness.* The command to "speak the truth in love" (Eph. iv. 15) is of course not equivalent to a command to speak it in softness, or to serve it up in what has been called the "goody-goody" style. It is not a command to intersperse discourses with many epithets of endearment—a thing which our blessed Lord dealt in very sparingly, and which even the most warm-hearted of his apostles, John and Paul, did not employ much. Such endearing words, when they do occur in the Epistles, are generally near the close, after the writer's heart has warmed with his subject, or with some very pathetic thought which has presented itself to him. Christian affectionateness does not imply the opposite of manliness, but is rather the true quality of manliness. It is a quality in the handling of Divine truth which, among hearers, the manly

---

* It is recorded of William Burns, so eminent as an earnest preacher, that, in his youth, his mother on one occasion observed him walking in deep reverie in a side-street in Glasgow. Though she went up straight to him he was quite unconscious of her presence, and started, when addressed, as from a dream. "Oh, mother!" he said, with deep emotion, "I did not see you; for when walking along Argyle Street just now, I was so overcome with the sight of the countless crowds of immortal beings eagerly hasting hither and thither, and all posting onwards towards the eternal world, that I could bear it no longer, and turned in here to seek relief in quiet thought."—*Memoir,* p. 53.

heart desiderates, and which, among preachers, the manly heart tries to supply. It does not imply anything that would prevent the outburst of holy indignation on occasions suitable to the expression of such a feeling; for neither our Lord, nor John, nor Paul had any difficulty, on suitable occasions, in giving expression to indignation in the most unqualified terms. Indeed, there is something almost startling in the thunder-like roll of denunciation which both our Lord and his apostles poured out, and with which, on the very eve of his martyrdom, the meek heart of Stephen met the wickedness which was directed against him. Observe, however, that indignation is properly a burst, and is therefore entirely different from a settled harshness or hardness of temper. Observe, too, that the wickedness with which the prophets as well as our Lord and his apostles had to contend was of the most undisguised and outrageous character; and observe, further, that if you have singleness of eye, and if you hold pride, selfishness, and irritability in check, there is hardly any risk of your mistaking the occasions on which indignant denunciation is the proper mode of dealing with wickedness.

These exceptional cases, however, do not invalidate the position that ordinarily a tone of affectionateness is both the right tone for the preacher, and that it is especially to be cultivated when disagreeable truth has to be spoken, or when a spirit of opposition has to be overcome. For the preacher is one who has to win souls, and there is no way of winning without love. The preacher is the representative of the great Father, whose great power for winning men back to himself is love: "I drew them with cords of a man, with bands of love" (Hosea xi. 4). The gospel of which he has charge is the gospel of infinite love. "God so loved the world, that He gave his only begotten Son, that whosoever believeth in Him should not perish, but have everlasting life" (John iii. 16). To preach such a gospel, to represent such a God, without the habitual spirit of love, would be as outrageous as for the bearer of a flag of truce to aim at his object by scattering oaths and curses among those whom he approached.*

We have said that there is a special call on the Christian preacher to stir up the spirit of love when disagreeable truth

---

* "I have never felt," Mr. Moody has said, "that I could get hold of an audience unless I had previously filled my heart with thoughts of their eternal condition, and felt compassion and a yearning for their welfare working in my soul."

has to be spoken, and when a spirit of opposition has to be overcome—disagreeable truth, such as the doom of the sinner, the Divine retribution on sin, the awfulness of the wrath to come. To handle such topics in ordinary circumstances in a tone of stern severity is utterly revolting, and one cannot but admire the question of M'Cheyne, when, in answer to his inquiry, a brother minister told him that his sermon on the previous day had been on the punishment of the wicked. "And were you able," asked he, "to preach it *tenderly?*" There are not a few subjects in our theology that are capable of becoming frightfully repulsive in the hands of hard and heartless preachers, and in such a case the more able the sermon the more terrible is the perversion it is likely to cause.

But if it be incumbent on preachers to stir up the spirit of love when painful truth has to be spoken, it is still more so when opposition has to be overcome. Guardians of Divine truth are very liable to excited feeling. It is an unpleasant thing when your hearers will not attend to you. It is still more so when they actively oppose you. It is deeply unpleasant when truths that you prize as the very foundation of eternal life are assailed by others, when the cause which you admire and support is held up to scorn and ridicule, and when all manner of unfairness is made use of to damage truth and prop up error. It is in such circumstances that the spirit of love needs to be specially sought. One needs to take great heed lest one give way to that impatience of opposition which is common more or less to all, and which, in some temperaments, rises to the height of a fever. Such impatience is but a carnal feeling, and can never be sanctified by any connection with religion. It is not zeal for truth but impatience of opposition that commonly tempts theologians to aim those hard hits, which no doubt enliven controversy, but make it extremely dangerous. Looking back along the history of the Reformed Churches, there is much cause to regret the tremendous bitterness that has characterized these periods of religious controversy. This fact, which can hardly be questioned, shows the tendency of the earnest religious mind to fall under carnal influences, and to forget that in Christianity the greatest of all the graces is—Charity.

4. Still kindred to the qualities of efficient preaching that have been illustrated, is a *fourth*—the spirit of *sympathy.*

This is St. Paul's spirit—"all things to all men" (1 Cor. ix.

22) ; trying to understand men's feelings, as the springs of their actions ; considering from what causes their temptations arise, and dealing with them accordingly; thinking how we should feel and act under similar circumstances and influences ; adapting our instructions to their circumstances and even prejudices, as far as we can do so honestly ; coming down to their level, as our blessed Lord did, in order that we may carry them upwards to his.

Such a spirit is especially valuable in addres-ing persons whose mode of life or habits of thought are quite different from our own. Let it be supposed that we, being strangers to all shade of doubt, are dealing with persons of speculative habit, with a morbid distrust of traditional judgments, and a strong determination to prove all things ; persons who halt at every step, and question positions on which we feel that our very salvation rests. Obviously such a case, instead of being scornfully denounced, as it often is, demands a very unusual degree of consideration and forbearance. Or suppose that we, leading a leisurely life, aided by all the appliances of civilisation, going to church and meeting at the regular hours without effort or difficulty, have a number of hearers struggling for very life under the heaviest burdens, toiling without rest from morn to dewy eve, and depressed by sorrows and anxieties that gnaw them like a grinding toothache by day and by night. Nothing can be more unsuitable than to address them as if they were in comfortable circumstances like ourselves.

The most persuasive preacher, other things being equal, is the preacher who has the most correct apprehension of the circumstances of his hearers, and the largest consideration for them. Let it not be said that this spirit leads to a good-natured apology for all vice and all error. On the contrary, it is when true sympathy is in operation that you are most free to denounce sin and condemn error—to deliver God's testimony against them most uncompromisingly. Consideration is not indulgence, but the opposite. You tell the people that you know what has tempted them into sin, but you warn them to think what sin is—how fiercely, how horribly God hates it, how it robs Him of all his due, how it poisons and ruins their whole nature, and yet what a frightful hold it has got of them. If only we have, in union with sympathy, such zeal and intensity as that of men like St. Paul or Chalmers, we shall not be liable to apologize for sin. Chalmers presented a marvellous instance of the union of sympathy and enthusiasm, great breadth and

great force, ample consideration for the circumstances of different classes, and yet extraordinary power of urging them
upwards. But the most memorable of all instances of the
union of sympathy and intensity is in the case of our Lord.
He who shielded the miserable adulteress from the harsh violence
of her accusers ; He who looked with such love on the young
man who, though he failed, was not far from the kingdom of
God ; He who burst into tears at the grave of Lazarus, when
He saw the distress of Mary ; He who prayed on the cross,
" Father, forgive them, for they know not what they do "—
became to us all a wonderful example of sympathy. Need we
speak of *his* loyalty to truth and duty ? or of the impulse He
gave in the direction of what is pure and noble, and in opposition to all falsehood and wrong ?

But while cultivating sympathy with man, we must never
forget the necessity of a predominant sympathy or fellow-
feeling with God. If, on the one hand, we would avoid the
hardness of tone that looks at truth and duty only in the
abstract, and enforces their claims by sheer pressure on soul
and conscience ; on the other hand, we must beware of treating
men as if they were simply unfortunate, the victims of unfavourable circumstances. We need to keep in the forefront of our
teaching the fact that sin dishonours God, and would fain
dethrone Him. God has claims on us as Creator, Jesus Christ
has claims as Redeemer, the Holy Ghost has claims as Teacher
and Sanctifier. To enforce these claims is not a secondary but
a primary part of our duty. Due weight and due order must
be given to every part of the angel's proclamation :—First,
glory to God in the highest ; then peace on earth, good-will
to men.

There is something yet to be mentioned as a quality of
effective preaching—not, however, as a separate quality, but
rather as an atmosphere or aroma gendered by the rest. It is
the indescribable something that is called *unction;* what all
understand, but what no one can define. It is, indeed, amusing
to observe how variously unction has been attempted to be
defined. According to one, it is the joint product of the Holy
Spirit's influence on the heart of the speaker and of his
sanctified efforts on the hearts of the hearers. According to
Blair, it is the union of gravity and warmth ; or, more fully,
that affecting, penetrating, interesting manner, flowing from a
strong sensibility of heart in the preacher to the importance of

those truths which he delivers, and an earnest desire that they may make a due impression on the hearts of his hearers. To Vinet, unction appears to be the total characteristic of the gospel, recognisable, doubtless, in each of its parts, but especially observable in it as a whole ; it is the general savour of Christianity ; it is a gravity accompanied with tenderness, a severity tempered with mildness, a majesty united with intimacy ; it is the true temper of the Christian dispensation, in which, according to the Psalmist, "mercy and truth are met together, righteousness and peace have kissed each other." Dutoit-Membrini, as quoted by Vinet, represents it as "a gentle warmth which makes itself felt in the powers of the soul. It produces in the spiritual world the same effects as the sun in the physical. It enlightens and it warms. It gives light to the soul and warmth to the heart. It makes us know and love, it interests. . . . Its only source is the spirit of regeneration and of grace. It is a gift which is spent and lost, unless we renew this sacred fire which must always be kept burning ; and that which preserves it is the cross within the soul, self-denial, prayer, and penitence. . . . Unction is felt, is known by experience ; it cannot be analyzed. It produces its impression secretly, and without the aid of reflection."

Our purpose in quoting so many definitions where nothing is defined, is simply to bring out the fact that in preaching of the true order there are qualities which have no separate genesis, but are the results of the purer forms of Christian feeling and experience. "There are no artificial means," says Vinet, "of acquiring unction ; oil flows of itself from the olive ; the most violent pressure cannot produce a drop from the earth or the flint." Unctuousness you may produce by something like the apothecary's art ; but genuine unction defies your chemistry. The artificial product differs from the genuine as the scents extracted from coal-tar differ from the fragrance of myrrh and aloes and cassia. True unction belongs only to true grace, and to humble gracious feeling ; it refuses to associate itself with the coarse arts of the pretender.

CHAPTER VII.

PREPARATION for preaching is of two kinds : the habitual training of all the faculties to be engaged, so as to bring them up to the highest state of fitness and efficiency ; and the study of particular passages or subjects, with a view to the delivery of discourses upon them.

It is with the former of these that we are to be occupied in this chapter. To young and inexperienced preachers it is hardly possible to convey a deep enough sense of the importance of this species of preparation. Usually it is by experience that a sense of the difficulty of good preaching comes. A sermon that seemed splendid to a young man at twenty-five, will possibly appear pitiful when he looks over it at fifty. "If I were sure of living ten years," an able preacher once remarked, "I should spend nine of them in preparing to preach during the tenth." Experience shows us how much is lost in our ordinary preaching ; how few hearers we move even feebly, how many we fail to move at all ; what need therefore there is for asking more strength from above, and taking more pains to be plain, pointed, interesting, and impressive. "Preaching," said the distinguished Jansenist, St. Cyran, "is a mystery not less terrible than that of the Eucharist. By preaching, souls are begotten and raised to life for God ; in the Eucharist, they are only nourished, or rather healed. In order to render ourselves worthy of this office we must labour to obtain a great mastery over self, and after we have brought the heart to desire nothing in this world we must bring the tongue to silence—which is, as I understand it, the last perfection attained by the man who labours to attain unto virtue. Only thus can we become worthy of presenting the Word of God before the world, and of publishing its truths, without thinking in the least of ourselves or others, as we are required to do in *prayer*, from which exhortation and preaching can never be separated, if they are performed according to the will of God. . . . In the pulpit, we should be more apprehensive of offending God than in any other place, and only enter it after having laboured diligently to mortify our own spirit, as well as to mortify that itching curiosity to learn many and fine things which all men have, and which is the greatest temptation which remains to us from Adam's transgression."

For the most part it is highly desirable that the young preacher should habitually place before his mind a very high idea of what a sermon ought to be. As far as opportunity serves, let him listen to the ablest preachers, and select for reading and study the productions of some of the great masters of the art, of whom, as we have seen, both ancient and modern times furnish so large a number. It is probably the circumstance of a low standard being in view that accounts for much inferior preaching. Preachers are apt to fall into the notion that it is enough to produce what will *decently serve the turn*, instead of cherishing the deep conviction that on every occasion they ought *to do their very best.* The remark has been made, even in regard to secular matters, that no great success attends the labours of those who, instead of aiming at the best, are content to do things merely in a passable way. The constant endeavour to find out the very best way of doing things, and the doing of them accordingly, is what has given to the greater part of our countrymen so high a position in industry, in engineering, and in the arts and manufactures generally. But how much more incumbent is it on those who have had committed to them the interests of immortal souls, to fling from them the indolence that is content with decent mediocrity, and strive, God helping them, to do their work in the best possible way!

But let us come more to particulars, glancing first at the intellectual, next the spiritual, and lastly the physical preparation.

I. And, first, preparation for preaching implies a thoroughly disciplined state of the *intellectual* powers. It implies that the young preacher has been trained, and has trained himself, to bend his powers to the investigation and exposition of truth, has acquired the mental habits favourable to that exercise, and a measure of freedom and familiarity in the pursuit. It implies that while engaged in mental labour he is not at the mercy of every impulse or freak of fancy that may rise within him; not

tempted, like a child at play, to run after every butterfly that
may flit across his path, but able to keep his attention bent on
the proper object before him, and to regulate his habits accordingly. It implies, further, that his mental powers have acquired
some measure of *robustness* and *skill* in the investigation and
exposition of truth; that he has attained a measure of self-
reliance, in the proper sense of that term, and is not at the
mercy of any strong-minded or strong-willed person, who,
however confidently, may come pressing contrary views upon
him. The degree or amount of this intellectual preparation
which a student brings to the work of preaching, must obviously
depend on the diligence and perseverance with which he has
prosecuted the various branches of a literary and theological
education. But he who enters on the ministry with a fair
measure of self-discipline and command of his mental powers
and habits, will find the benefit all through life. The struggles
which it cost him at first to subdue himself will have their
reward. He will find, as years roll on, that with comparatively
little effort his powers can be brought to bear on his work, and
can achieve results quite wonderful in the eyes of those who do
not consider the long preparatory process that has been silently
but steadily gone through.* A well-disciplined preacher, after
years of exercise, may be able to prepare a discourse in comparatively little time, showing a marvellous combination of
faculties, and marvellous perfection of each. He may even be
able to preach extempore, and thoughtless men may ask, What
is the use of young men spending hours on the preparation of
discourses, when this preacher does so much better by an extempore effort? But in truth that extempore effort may be the
result of a lifetime of discipline. The self-possession, the power
of orderly thinking and expression, the lines of thought that
have been opened, the stores of illustration that have been made
available, represent the discipline and the industry of a lifetime.
There may be a few cases in which genius springs, almost at a
bound, to these heights, but in ninety-nine cases out of a
hundred they are reached only by the slow process of elaborate
self-discipline.

* It is said that Sir Joshua Reynolds was once asked how he could
charge a hundred and fifty guineas for some picture when it had taken
him but three days to paint it. "Three days!" said the indignant painter;
"it has taken me five-and-thirty years." The capacity to paint it in three
days represented a course of discipline extending over his whole professional life.

There is no little consolation in this view for able ministers when they happen to occupy small and obscure positions. For the most part it is the tempter's voice that tells them that in these humble spheres they are wasting their energies. Wasting them they certainly are, if they are tempted to think that they may take their ease, allow their minds to run wild, as it were, and content themselves with the most careless performance of duty. But they are doing the very opposite of wasting them if they are binding on their consciences the obligation to do their very best—if, in that humble sphere, they are resolutely strangling every temptation to indolence and self-indulgence, and are resolved to hear no voice but that of Him who has given them their talents saying, " Occupy till I come." It is this, and not an impatient contempt of an insignificant sphere, that forms the true road to promotion. But even should their conscientious endeavours pass without acknowledgment and reward in this life, they must not suppose that they have laboured in vain. The training acquired in this life, we may be sure, is not lost in the life to come ; and even though the Master's voice of encouragement should not be heard till the day of judgment, it will not be too late to hear the glorious announcement, " Well done, good and faithful servant ; thou hast been faithful in a few things ; I will make thee ruler over many things ; enter thou into the joy of thy Lord."

In passing from the subject of intellectual *discipline*, to advert to the intellectual *stores* that ought to be laid in as a preparation for efficient preaching, we should have, first of all, to speak of the whole course of study carried on in our divinity halls. Obviously it is unnecessary to say much of this now, but on one branch a few words must be said, namely, biblical study. The systematic study of the Holy Scriptures manifestly holds the first rank in the category of preparation for preaching.

It may be doubted whether any man, not even excepting the celebrated preachers in the Church of Rome, ever became great in the pulpit without drinking in copiously of the Word of God. What Lamartine has said of the famous Bishop of Meaux illustrates in one aspect the value of biblical study to preachers, though there are higher aspects of the subject to which the poet does not advert : " The Bible, and, above all, the poetical portions of Holy Writ, struck as if with lightning and dazzled the eyes of the child : he fancied he saw the living fire of Sinai, and heard the voice of omnipotence re-echoed by the rocks of Horeb. His God was Jehovah ; his lawgiver, Moses ; his high priest,

Aaron; his poet, Isaiah; his country, Judea. The vivacity of his imagination, the poetical bent of his genius, the analogy of his disposition to that of the Orientals, the fervid nature of the people and ages described, the sublimity of the language, the everlasting novelty of the history, the grandeur of the laws, the piercing eloquence of the hymns, and, finally, the ancient, consecrated, and traditionally reverential character of the Book, transformed Bossuet at once into a biblical enthusiast. The metal was malleable; the impression was received, and remained indelibly stamped. This child became a prophet: such he was born, such he was as he grew to manhood, lived and died: *the Bible transfused into a man.*"*

The study of Scripture proper to a theological student or to a preacher may be said to be threefold—critical, personal, homiletical. His critical study is directed to the ascertaining of its true meaning; his personal study to the edification of his own soul; his homiletical study to the instruction and edification of his people. It were a happy state of mind if he could at one and the same time study the Scriptures critically, practically, and homiletically. And no doubt it is an attainable state of things. A man like John Albert Bengel in his mature years could not have separated the three. But in most cases it seems desirable that the student should begin with separate readings, at least for personal or devotional purposes.

1. No student of divinity ought to want his sacred season of daily personal fellowship with God, or to stand in need of being urged to the solemn perusal of the Scriptures during that season, in order that he may hear God's message to his own soul. The very life of the soul depends on this and kindred exercises; they supply the oil that keeps the lamp burning; they are parts of the breathing process that give oxygen to the blood.† The Romish priest is bound to read daily a considerable portion of his breviary; but it is otherwise in most branches of the Protestant Church; and there is a risk when no formal rule is prescribed, and the matter is left to conscience alone, that the devout reading of the Bible for personal edification may either be omitted or carelessly performed.

---

* See Potter's " Sacred Eloquence," p. 51.

† "An hour of solitude, as has been well remarked, passed in sincere and earnest prayer, or the conflict with, and struggle over, a single passion, or subtle bosom sin, will teach us more of thought, will more effectually awaken the faculty and form the habit of reflection, than a year's study in the schools without them."—SHEDD, p. 132.

2. As little ought it to be necessary to stimulate students of divinity to a full critical and exegetical acquaintance with Scripture. To be able to grasp the great purposes of Divine revelation as a whole ; to see at the same time the drift and bearing of its several parts ; to apprehend the great lessons of the various histories, biographies, and epistles, the parables, the sermons, the doctrinal statements, the allegories, the lyrical effusions, that make up holy Scripture ; to know where to find the most striking statements on any subject which Scripture embraces, to make one part throw light on another, and bring out the chief lessons of the whole—are attainments of inestimable value to the future preacher of the Word.

3. But beyond this, though not much beyond it, there is a homiletical object to be kept in view in the study of Scripture. The mind of the student ought to acquire a homiletical habit, and to get into the way of thinking, as he goes along, what use for preaching purposes can be made of this and of that part of Scripture ; while a record will be kept of what strikes him as available, and of the line of thought which it has opened up to him. No farmer can be acting wisely who does not look well to his seed-corn, and make sure of enough to sow all the acres that are to be under crop the following season ; and no preacher can be acting wisely who does not take care to provide himself with a sufficiency of germs or homiletical seed-corn for future use. This homiletical habit, while connecting itself mainly with the reading of the Scriptures, will operate also upon any other material that may be made available for the purpose. We are told of a Grecian general who, when he travelled and viewed the country around him, revolved in his mind how an army could be there drawn up to greatest advantage ; how he could best defend himself if attacked from such a quarter; how advance with greatest security, how retreat with least danger. "Something similar to this," says Dr. Shedd, " should be the practice and study of a public speaker. It is as fitting that the preacher should be characterized by a homiletical tendency as that the poet should be characterized by a poetical tendency. If it is proper that the poet should transmute everything he touches into poetry, it is proper that the preacher should transmute everything he touches into sermons. This homiletic habit will appear in a disposition to skeletonise, to construct plans, to examine and criticise discourses with respect to their logical structure. The preacher's mind becomes habitually *organific*. It is inclined to build. Whenever leading thoughts are brought

into the mind, they are straightway arranged and disposed into
the unity of a plan, instead of being allowed to lie here and
there, like scattered boulders on a field of drift. This homiletic habit will appear again in a disposition to render all the
argumentative and illustrative materials, which pour in upon
the educated man from the various fields of science, literature,
and art, subservient to the purposes of preaching. The sermoniser is, or should be, a student, and an industrious one, a
reader, and a thoughtful one. He will, consequently, in the
course of his studies, meet with a great variety of information
which may be advantageously employed in sermonising, either
as proof or illustration, provided he possesses the proper power
to elaborate it and work it up."*

The variety and richness of the stores that may be rendered
thus available are very great, provided you have the eye that
detects them, and the hand that diligently lays them up in
storehouses, in the shape of note-books or literary indexes.
Mr. Spurgeon once remarked that he would think little of the
man who, from a daily newspaper, could not find material in
large quantity that would be of service in the construction or
illustration of a sermon. Passing facts are often of great value
to a preacher, if wisely used. Any one may notice how the
drooping attention of a congregation is often caught up by a
reference to a fact of the day. The preacher had been losing
himself in the cloud-land of abstractions, but when he came
down to the sphere of actual fact, his hearers, almost without
exception, rallied round him. It was like blowing a trumpet to
collect scattered troops. To a certain extent this explains the
influence of anecdotes. Be they good, bad, or indifferent, they
seldom fail to command attention. In the way of illustrations,
one's daily reading and daily observation are fitted to yield a
constant supply of useful material. The preacher that reads—
be it travels, history, biography, philosophy, speeches in parliament, poetry, fiction, reviews, or ballads—with an eye all the
time to the pulpit, will be gathering a store of illustrations
which he will never be likely to meet with if he merely begins
to search for them when he needs them. " Go to the ant "
may be addressed to the preacher in more senses than one ; be
always storing, so that on an emergency you have only to step
into the storehouse and take out what you need. But be the
store what it may, it is indispensable that it be passed though
the mill of the preacher's own mind, so as to come out with his

* Shedd's " Homiletics and Pastoral Theology," pp. 108, 109.

image and superscription. A sermon ought not to be a piece of conglomerate, nor a coat of many colours, but an organized structure with a pervading unity.

II. The next branch of habitual preparation for effective preaching is what we have called the *spiritual.* If preaching be a thing of the heart as much as of the head, the heart as well as the head must be brought into a state of preparation. And this can only be achieved through the maintenance of high spirituality of mind. That is to say, by keeping the soul much in contact with unseen and eternal realities, and by having one's impressions of these renewed and intensified from time to time. In the history of certain preachers it may be remarked that at certain times their ministry has been marked by a manifest increase of Divine power. Such times have been seasons of remarkable visitation, of deep personal affliction, of overwhelming public calamity, or of powerful spiritual awakening. It is said of M'Cheyne that one Saturday afternoon being met by a brother on his way to visit a dying person, and asked how he could spare such a time for that purpose, his answer was, " I always like before preaching to look over the brink." And the more a preacher's mind is filled with the views of life which the deathbed gives, and the tremendous significance which the doctrine of the cross thus derives, the more powerfully and impressively will he be likely to preach. To this qualification there is no royal road. No brilliancy of mental gifts, no success in study, no natural fervour, can enable a preacher to dispense with the habit of spiritual contemplation, the fellowship with the unseen which is required to give the true tone to his sermons. If only, by God's great mercy, we could attain just impressions of the state of man, the love of God, the grace of the Saviour, the malignant energy of the devil, the doom of sin, the fearful conflict raging around us between the prince of this world and the Lord of Heaven, and the awful issue of the strife in which we are engaged, how much more powerfully should we preach ! If we could only realise vividly the actual life of some one to whom we may be called to preach—the blinding power of lust by which he is wont to be assailed, the frightful craving he experiences, the loathsome ruin of which he is on the brink, the troubled life, the dark death-bed, the horrible resurrection, the eternity of despair ; on the other hand, the glorious results of a saving change, of a vision of the Saviour to his soul, and new life in Him ; if, moreover, we could see the difference of the effect or impression *on others* in the two

G

cases—in the one, the corrupted heart a propaganda of pollu-
tion, misery, and death   in the other, the regenerate heart a
fountain of strength, joy, and beauty, on every side—would not
our hearts fill with the noble dignity of our office, and the
prayer go up like a lightning-flash to heaven for Divine strength
to fulfil this ministry !

In order to maintain this spirituality of mind, it is useful,
among other instrumentalities, for preachers to include some
earnest spiritual treatise in the list of what they habitually
read. It is desirable that they should be in daily contact with
earnest thoughts and feelings, and especially when preparing
an address for the pulpit. To many of the old writers, Augustine, Bernard, à Kempis, and others far remote, or Baxter,
Bunyan, Leighton, or Rutherford among those more recent,
there was granted a singular clearness of spiritual vision, and a
marvellous fervour in writing what they knew. A kind of
magnetic influence goes forth even from their writings, and
tends to inspire in kindred hearts a corresponding feeling. It
must be a cold nature indeed that is not warmed into a higher
fervour than usual by the perusal of the appeals in which
Baxter, for example, remonstrates with ministers on the habitual coldness of their feelings, and humbly rebukes his own
indifference : " For myself, as I am ashamed of my dull and
careless heart, and of my slow and unprofitable course of life,
so the Lord knows that I am ashamed of every sermon that I
preach ; when I think what I am, and who sent me, and how
much salvation and damnation of men is concerned in it, I am
ready to tremble, lest God should judge me a slighter of his
truth and of the souls of men, and lest I should in my best
sermon be guilty of their blood."

Time will not allow us to follow out the lines of thought
which these views open up. If the preacher would have his
heart as well as his head in a due state of preparation, let him
frequently cultivate solitude, or rather the solitude in which he
has the company of his Master. Let him recall the ends for
which He came into the world and gave himself up to be the
Redeemer ; try to enter afresh into sympathy with Him in
these ends ; take encouragement from the fact that the work is
Christ's, and all power in heaven and earth is given to Him ;
let him meditate on the abundant promises of the gift of the
Holy Spirit to as many as wait for his grace ; let him ask the
strength that is made perfect in weakness ; and let him remember that solemn day of reckoning, when all that he has

done shall be brought to the touchstone of *faithful service*— Was it done to please himself, or was it done to serve the Master ?

III. It now remains to say a few words on *physical* preparation for preaching.

The present generation is much more disposed than some of its predecessors to believe in a certain connection between good health and good preaching, although to many persons it may seem that there is no such connection, while a smaller number may think that a preacher's delicate health actually aids a right impression. And no doubt there is a certain class of truths which are taught more impressively by a man who bears the seal of death on his wasted face ; but, on the other hand, such a man's influence in other respects is feeble, if not injurious. " It is impossible," says Mr. Beecher, " for an invalid to sustain a cheerful and hopeful ministry among his people. An invalid looks with a sad eye on human life. He may be sympathetic, but it is almost always with the shadows that are in the world. He will give out moaning and drowsy hymns. He will make prayers that are almost all piteous. It may not be a minister's fault if he be afflicted and ill, and administers his duties in mourning and sadness, but it is a vast misfortune for his people." *

The sad, sombre, melancholy look of the invalid preacher, and, indeed, a heavy, dull, dreary look in any preacher, has a specially repulsive effect on the young. It insensibly leads them to associate with church services the very opposite of those happy feelings which they so readily associate with their sports. Under any circumstances, the solemnity of Divine worship constitutes something of a trial for the buoyant, playful tendencies of youth, but infinitely the more on that account is it matter of regret if the trial is aggravated by the repulsiveness of a countenance on which nothing bright and radiant ever appears to settle.

But even where there is no positive disease, there may be a physical languor that reflects itself in feebleness of voice, dulness of tone, stiffness of manner, and a general want of lively and attractive power. It may be difficult to persuade some preachers that physical causes have to do with this, but the connection is beyond all reasonable doubt. And the fact that such symptoms are the effect of some transgression of the laws

* " Lectures on Preaching," i. 189.

of health makes it incumbent on the student to attend to the
condition of his outer man.   Not—as he values the temper of
his friends and his congregation—that he is to bore them by
constantly obtruding the state of his health on their attention.
One should be able to look after one's health quietly, without
plaguing the world either with the process or the reasons for
it.   Sometimes, indeed, it is impossible for the student to care
for it as he might, and as he would if he were driven less by
the *res angusta*, or if he could content himself with a lower
standard of qualification ; and sometimes without knowing it he
exhausts that reserve fund of strength which ought to be hus-
banded in youth, so that the spring of his constitution is broken,
and the seeds of early decay are sown.   Everything points to
the duty of caring for the health and vigour of the body, and
especially of the three organs on which the preacher is specially
dependent—the stomach, the nerves, and the lungs.

Of the *stomach*, we say, because from any disorder there
spring those nameless morbid feelings which gender depressing
views of life and duty, sour thoughts of one's position, and
bitter onslaughts on one's rivals or opponents.   Of the *nerves*,
because nervous feebleness and nervous irritation, besides
destroying one's own spring and motive power, bring one into
ominous neighbourhood with dark temptations and terrible
diseases.   Of the *lungs* and other organs of speech, because a
clear metallic voice is so indispensable to efficient utterance,
and feeble lungs cannot but be accompanied by a sense of difficulty, and by feebleness in other forms.

It is very certain that due attention to physical exercise is
an essential condition of sustained vigorous preaching.   The
command to be " strong in the Lord " includes strength of body
as well as strength of soul.   A whole Saturday spent in the
study, and particularly a whole Saturday night, is not favourable to that physical vigour which usually underlies good
preaching.   " The speakers that move the crowd," says
Beecher, " men after the pattern of Whitefield, are usually men
of very large physical development, men of very strong digestive
powers, and whose lungs have great aërating capacity.   They
are men of great vitality and recuperative force. . . . They are
catapults, and men go down before them."

Some men may affect to despise these things, but it is a
foolish affectation.   Subordinate though their place may be, it
is a real place notwithstanding ; at least in every case where
" the bow *abides* in strength, and the *arms of the hands* are

made strong by the hands of the mighty God of Jacob " (Gen. xlix. 24).*

* Very probably some will dispute our position as to the connection of good health and good preaching. And not without some plausibility. Of the three classes of powers of which our nature is made up—bodily, mental, and emotional—it has been remarked that the development of any one class *to its utmost capacity* is seldom effected without damage to the rest. In the prize-fighter and the acrobat both mind and soul are stunted. In the senior wrangler, the development of intellect is commonly far beyond that of the body and the soul. In the spiritual enthusiast, the intensity of the soul dwarfs mind and body. We may therefore find more spiritual intensity in one whose body is enfeebled—say by fastings and vigils—than in another. But even allowing for such exceptions, the general rule in ordinary life will remain but little modified.

CHAPTER VIII.

PULPIT STYLE.

THE subject of style, in connection with the delivery of God's message, is one which some persons may think it were better to pass over entirely. Their fancy is that no good can come of instructions or rules fitted to make preachers nice as to the language in which they express themselves. If we should send a man through the town to announce that a house was on fire, should we lecture him on the style in which he should make the announcement ? If we should despatch a life-boat to the rescue of a shipwrecked crew, should we instruct the captain how to throw a figure of speech or two into his invitation ? Only let preachers be in earnest, it is said, and they will have no difficulty in finding appropriate words. Of course, when a man has only to shout " fire," or when a life-boatsman has only to invite shipwrecked sailors to jump on board, there is no need for instructions on style ; but it is absurd to represent these acts as parallel to those to which the preacher is called from week to week, or to speak as if the simple monosyllable suitable to the one were a fair representation of the mode of address essential to the other.*

Style has often been defined " the dress of thought; " but it is a mistake to suppose that language and thought may be separated from each other as completely as dress may be separated from the body which it covers ; it is nearer the truth to say with Wordsworth, that style is the incarnation of thought. In common parlance, style denotes the more conspicuous quali-

---

* " Let us not forget that to preach is to instruct. If we had only to drive the sinner to the foot of the Cross the gospel might be soon unfolded. But the good news is found in many subjects. . . . To terrify is not everything ; it is not even a very small matter. We must touch the heart, and in order to do that we must instruct. There is a great number of souls that can only be gained to Christ at this price."—*Vinet*.

ties, whether of thought or language, or of both combined, by which the writing or the speaking of any one is distinguished. Sometimes the two things are placed in antithesis, as when we say of some one that his thoughts are good but his style is bad ; in which case we mean that he has taken no pains to set forth his thoughts in a suitable and attractive form. But more frequently the term style is used to denote qualities that belong more or less both to the thought and the expression. If we say that one's style is clear, that is applicable to both. If we say that it is forcible, or figurative, or diffuse, or concise, both elements are comprehended. The idea of the language is probably more prominent ; but the language covers the thought, and the thought, to a large degree, determines the language. Style, therefore, is not a mere affair of words. It combines the properties both of the cuticle and the *cutis vera ;* with an outer surface apparently detached, or detachable, but a lower layer, from which the outer is formed, in immediate connection with the vital forces of the system.

Before proceeding to specific suggestions on pulpit style, it will be useful first to consider the question, Whether there be any fundamental difference between the style of conversation and the style of the pulpit ? And also, Whether there be any such difference between the style of the pulpit and other modes of public speaking—parliamentary, forensic, or platform ?

At first sight it might seem as if there were a fundamental difference between the style of the pulpit, especially in its higher flights, and the style of conversation. If men were to converse as they sometimes preach, the result would be bombastic ; if they were to preach as they usually speak, it would be bare, passionless, and tame. But this may be because their actual preaching is bombastic, and their actual conversation poor and tame. It is obvious that the conversational style has many advantages. It arrests attention ; it keeps the voice natural ; it obliges you to bear in mind your object, viz. to convince and persuade the person or persons addressed ; it compels you, by an instinctive process in your own mind, to adapt yourself to your audience, and to see that, as you advance step by step, you carry them along with you. These are very substantial advantages of the conversational style, not to be lightly sacrificed. Is it possible, then, on the basis of such a style, to rise to those heights which the public orator counts his peculiar domain—to become impassioned, flowing, poetical ? The question is nearly equivalent to this, Could such a style of speech become natural and appropriate in conversation ? Can it be conceived as natural that a friend, talking to another friend, should get so raised above the ordinary level as to pour his soul out in sentences resembling the most eloquent periods of the greatest pulpit orators ?

In theory we can see nothing to prevent this supposition from being realised ; but ordinarily there are insuperable hindrances *in practice.* Thus, it is very seldom that any one would think of *preparing* to give expression, in conversation with a single person, to his fullest, intensest thoughts and feelings on any subject, or of so arranging them that they should come out in the best possible order, and with the greatest possible force, each sentence and clause intensifying the rest. Further, the circumstances of an ordinary two-handed conversation, as we call it, prevent the rise of that excitement and enthusiasm which the presence of great numbers gives to a public speaker ; they fail to supply that uplifting power which makes him forgetful of common things, and enables him to carry up his audience to a more ethereal region. An ordinary conversation, in a word, has a down-tying or tethering effect on a speaker, and hence the bareness and tameness by which it is usually characterized. But fancy some man with a great conversational gift, like Coleridge, thoroughly interested and thoroughly roused ; the words of such a man will probably have as much of passion and poetry, of glowing warmth and flowing fulness, as the best periods of a sermon. May it not be, that the circumstances characteristic of the *pulpit* are designed to give to a speaker the benefit of that power that carries one upwards, and of that wider sweep and intenser feeling which belong to oratorical discourse ?

This seems to be the true theory of style. The style for the pulpit is essentially the conversational, but with the added wings of an eagle, and with a capacity of uttering things, grander, richer, and fuller than would be practicable in actual conversation.

This view of the matter receives strong confirmation, if not actual demonstration, from the range and capacity of feeling and expression which conversation commands in our great dramatical, poetical, and fictional writers. No one ever actually conversed as many of the characters of Shakspeare, Milton, or even of Sir Walter Scott converse. In point of fact, many of the most eloquent, imaginative, and impassioned passages in the English language occur in the form of dialogues. And yet no one, with common sense, accuses these brilliant authors of making their characters talk bombastically or unnaturally. The explanation is what has just been adverted to : they take advantage of the *theoretical* capacity of the conversational style to make it express what, by reason of practical drawbacks and difficulties, it hardly ever does express in actual life. They make men and women talk, not as they do talk in the work-a-day world, but as it would be suitable for them to talk under the influence of excited feelings, if they had easy command of the richest stores of language, and if this great faculty of speech were so common as not to excite the idea of a prodigious effort or of an affected display. Now it is just these conditions, so seldom realised in actual conversation, that preaching and other forms of oratorical speech admit of. And it is the fact of their admitting of these conditions that justifies the use of that full, ornamented, and impassioned language, which in other circumstances would be so unnatural.

This view of the proper foundation of the pulpit style receives further confirmation from the fact that all our Lord's discourses were framed on the conversational model. The Sermon on the Mount is conversational, and it is instructive to observe how, as He goes on, He seems to get nearer to the people ; how the plural *ye*—" Ye are the salt of the earth "—passes into the singular *thou*—" If *thy* right hand offend thee, cut it off and cast it from thee." But in not a few instances we see our Lord, in his discourses, rising up to what is more strictly the oratorical region, becoming impassioned, flowing, and poetical, holding his hearers in breathless attention, exercising all the fascinating influence of the highest eloquence.

If we inquire into the practice in other forms of public speaking, we shall find a similar state of things. In parliament, on the platform, or at the bar, great speakers start from the conversational level, securing thereby the attention and the sympathy of their audiences, and it is only as their feelings warm, or as the subject unfolds itself, or as the audience inspires them, that they rise to the oratorical heights. So also with great preachers. Their opening sentences are almost invariably sentences that might have been spoken in conversation, either with a single hearer or a party of half-a-dozen. Take at random any of the sermons of Whitefield, or Mr. Spurgeon, or Mr. Robertson of Brighton, and you will find this remark wonderfully verified. In your own case it will be of inestimable service to fashion your preaching style on the conversational basis, understood as we have explained it. Start conversationally, and never for one moment forget that you are to preach *to* the people, and not merely to deliver a discourse before them. You are certain by this means to secure an attentive audience. You may or may not feel that you can spread your wings very wide, or carry them up to the higher realms of oratory. If you are not sure of yourselves in the upper regions, you will be content with the lower. You will feel it far better to establish the character of useful and instructive preachers than that of orators. Oratory is doubtless a most kingly gift, but for that very reason its counterfeit is a contemptible abortion.

Proceeding now to the details of pulpit style, we shall confine our attention to what seem to be the four leading qualities, namely, Clearness, Force, Fulness, and Beauty. This may be taken also as the order of importance : clearness being undoubtedly the first requisite, and beauty almost as certainly coming in after the rest.

1. *Clearness,* being the quality of plain and accurate representation, obviously demands clear and accurate thinking. According to Cicero, the first requisite of an orator is to know what he has to say. It would be flattering many speakers beyond their merits to suppose that they possessed this requisite. The criticism once passed upon a preacher that " he aimed at nothing in particular—and he hit it," might be extended to not a few. Vague in their thinking, they are equally vague in their writing. A foggy atmosphere does not admit of photographing, nor does a foggy mind admit of clearness. " Reading," as Bacon has told us, " makes a full man, writing a correct man, and speaking a ready man." One of the chief uses of writing is that it puts a great pressure on a man to understand himself. Hurried extemporaneous writing has no such effect, and is worse than useless ; nor can a conscientious preacher ever write a single page without asking himself as he goes over it what precisely he has been trying to say, and whether he has succeeded in saying it with the greatest possible clearness.

The object of *words* being to convey *ideas*, it is obvious that clearness is the most indispensable of all the qualities of style, just as transparency, or at least translucency, is the most indispensable of all the properties of glass. The first object of the public speaker is to find words that will most clearly express to his audience the ideas that he wishes to convey. Now it may be that the words that are absolutely most correct are not the words that are best adapted to this purpose. A botanist, *e.g.*, wishes to describe a plant to a non-botanist. The scientific terms are, of course, those which are absolutely the most correct, but to the non-botanist they are an unknown tongue, they convey no idea whatever. Consequently the botanist must try to find words intelligible to his hearer that will convey to his mind the most accurate notion of the plant. So also it is with the preacher. He, too, has to bear in mind that in preaching his object is not merely to express or record his ideas, but to *convey* them. If he were making out a scientifically constructed record of truth, he would be warranted in using technical words, and other words, which, however, he must not use when his object is to convey truth to a miscellaneous audience. He must consider what terms his audience are likely to understand. He must think what illustrations will be likely to aid them. If he go beyond this mark, it must be exceptionally and cautiously, remembering that he runs the risk of failing in the first object of the public speaker—failing to convey anything to his hearer's mind.

There are some forms of writing, and also of speaking, that are designed only for thoroughly educated audiences, and that admit, therefore, of the widest range of language. But preaching in almost all instances being addressed to a general audience, or an audience comprising many persons of limited education, cannot claim the same latitude. Hence the reason for that most valuable canon of preaching—to make use only of words in common circulation, and bearing clear and well-understood meanings. This is the true version of a rule often given, to use only words of Anglo-Saxon origin. Whether the words be of Saxon origin or not is of no consequence, provided they be in common use and bear well-defined meanings. Our language is a compound of many dialects, and though the Anglo-Saxon is doubtless the raciest and the most intelligible, it has no monopoly of these qualities. But that the words be in common use, and that they bear distinct meanings, is quite indispensable to a right pulpit style. Many an expression that would be quite in place in college essays, because it is the most correct expression of all, is out of place in a sermon, and the preacher must learn the self-denial which leads him to avoid it. It is hardly credible how anxiously some writers and preachers search for common and well-understood words. It is said that Archbishop Tillotson was in the habit of reading his sermons to an illiterate old woman that lived with him, and altering all the phrases till he had brought them down to the level of her capacity. Some authors will go over a paper again and again for no other purpose than to find out whether more common and intelligible words or phrases might be substituted for any that they have used. It is a mistake to suppose that a style on which no pains have been bestowed is necessarily a clear one. The probability rather is that it is quite the reverse.

There is a style of writing characterictic of half-educated persons, which no man of taste and training can too carefully avoid. It consists in the use of grand words instead of plain words ; in heaping gaudy tropes and other figures of speech on subjects that are in little need of illustration ; in accumulating long adjectives and other expletives, not for the purpose of conveying or elucidating thought, but of making a great blaze of oratorical fireworks. Such writers, some one has said—

> " Mistake the language of the nation
> For long-tailed words in -osity and -ation."

It is hardly possible to convey too strong a warning against any approach to this style. Words that convey no definite meaning ; expletives introduced merely to round a sentence, but not to express a thought; tawdry metaphors, heaped on each other with barbaric profusion ; ornamental expressions that draw attention to themselves but give no increase of vividness to the meaning—are all to be given to the pruning-hook, and remorselessly cast into the fire.

2. *Force.* That style has a certain *dynamical* power must be admitted by every one who considers how much more impression is usually made by a truth pithily and concisely put, than by the same truth expressed diffusely. The proverbial form of expression derives much of its force from this circumstance ; if you say, *e.g.*, " Fools and their money are soon parted," you send the truth further than if you put your meaning thus : " When persons of a facile disposition are in possession of funds, they show a tendency to disperse them rapidly." " The proper study of mankind is man " is more forcible than— " Among the studies which are most suitable for us, the constitution of the human mind, the development of human character, and indeed everything which bears on man's life and welfare, is one of the most important." But in respect of this quality, force, as of its predecessor, plainness, we remark a close connection between the thinking and the speaking. Intensity of thought and feeling gives birth to force of expression. It is the man that thinks deeply and feels strongly that expresses himself

forcibly. Without deep and strong action of the soul, there may be an affected strength of expression, there may be exaggeration and a copious use of superlative degrees, but there is not likely to be much of real force—not much of that dynamic power that sends truth far under the surface, and leaves it in full possession of the soul.

In particular, the quality of forcible style stands connected with *a penetrative habit of mind,* which, having gone itself to the heart of things, aims at communicating its own experience to others. Partly from mental indolence, or mental superficiality, and partly from the effects of a hurried mode of life, which leaves little time for acts requiring leisure, most men, and it is to be feared many preachers, content themselves with superficial views and impressions of truth. Let us take, for example, the truth of man's lost state by nature. The knowledge which many persons seem to have of this truth consists in what they have gathered up, here and there, as it were, around it ; they know something of its terrible aspect in this direction and in that—as involving punishment, perpetual inward disorder, the loss of all that one was created for, the annihilation of all hope and joy. But some have penetrated far deeper into this truth, and gained a much more intense experience of it. They have *felt* separation from God. They have felt like shipwrecked sailors in mid-ocean cast on a lonely rock, with all the agencies of destruction closing on them, and none but God in heaven to help them. They have looked, oh ! how wistfully, on this side and on that, and found no helper—for helper they cannot have but One ; and that, the displeased God, the angry Judge, whose gracious face they have not yet learned to look on. He who teaches this truth after such an experience, after so penetrating a knowledge of it, will teach it right forcibly. Taught himself by the Holy Spirit, his words will have the penetrative power —they will not play upon the surface, but go right to the core, and stick there. And this penetrative power may be exercised with a great absence of noise and fuss. Sometimes the calmest men have most of it. With little appearance of eloquence, they are enabled to find the surest avenues of the heart, and plant their weapon in its inmost citadel.

It may be remarked, further, that a forcible style does not harmonize with a speculative or a very subjective mode of thought.* It pertains to strongly objective truth, and associates

* See Shedd, p. 75.

itself with great realities. Rationalism, with its perpetual
atmosphere of doubt and uncertainty, is most unfavourable to
it. The message of God's Word, so objective, so momentous,
so solemn in all its bearings, is admirably adapted to it. He
that is enabled to penetrate to the heart of those stirring truths
which form that message, can hardly fail to become master of a
forcible mode of stating them. He that holds them superficially
and lightly cannot be expected to project them forcibly. In
point of fact, as has been well remarked by Dr. Shedd, "All the
high and commanding eloquence of the Christian Church has
sprung out of an intuition like that of Paul and Luther—a mode
of conceiving and speaking of God and man, and their mutual
relations, that resulted entirely from the study of the Hebrew
and Greek Scriptures."

3. *Fulness* or *Amplitude*. Even in written or printed composition this quality is desirable ; but for spoken or oral discourse it is indispensable. It is not enough that a thought be
correctly presented to an audience ; it ought to be presented in
such a manner that if possible all the audience shall have a full
perception of it. One of the greatest difficulties of a public
speaker is to make an enduring impression on the attention of
his audience ; it is comparatively easy to gain their attention
for the moment, it is much more difficult to get a truth to abide
in the mind, with its full measure of impression. To secure
such objects a measure of amplification is indispensable.

There is a rough analogy here between the process of bodily
and that of mental digestion. It is remarked by physiologists
that the stomach does not operate with advantage on the mere
essences of food. Any one trying to live on Liebig's essence of
meat, pure and simple, would be rendered helpless in an exceedingly short period. Horses, as Whately has remarked, cannot
be fed on oats and beans alone ; straw or hay must be added
to distend the stomach and enable it to act with advantage.
So also with the mental stomach. If thought be presented in
the most condensed form, the process of assimilating it is too
exhausting. Something corresponding to the straw or hay is
necessary to make it more easily digestible ; not, however, in
the Apostle's sense of " wood, hay, and stubble "—a metaphor
applicable to building but not to feeding. We have said that
fulness is especially needed in spoken discourse. When a reader
is dealing with what is written or printed he can go back, he
can read again and again, and this process of repetition furnishes
the needed assistance for mental digestion. But when you are

listening to spoken discourse you have no such resource. You lie at the mercy of the speaker, and if he be wholly destitute of the faculty of expansion, and try to hurry you on unrelieved from one general truth to another, the fatigue of following him will be found excessive, and the effort to attend will speedily be given up.

The greatest orators and most effective preachers have always been masters of the art of expansion. Our blessed Lord has set us a memorable example. It was not enough for him to say what we were to do if our right eye should offend us ; the same instruction is repeated *totidem verbis* with reference to the right hand. It was not enough, in rebuke of distrustful care, to point to the fowls of heaven; the same lesson is immediately enforced by a reference to the lilies of the field. The woe denounced on Chorazin and Bethsaida is followed by the woe against Capernaum ; the possibility of an impression being made on Tyre and Sidon, as a rebuke to the people, is paralleled by the same thing in the case of Sodom; and the example of Jonah is followed by that of the Queen of Sheba as a reproof of the blindness that failed to recognise the Son of God. The same thing may be readily traced in all the oratorical books of Scripture. " A man shall be as an hiding-place from the wind, and a covert from the tempest ; as rivers of water in a dry place, as the shadow of a great rock in a weary land " (Isa. xxxii. 2). One great fundamental truth is here, but with a fourfold diversity of aspect and application. Or let us go to St. Paul's wonderful account of the resurrection. " There is one glory of the sun, and another glory of the moon, and another glory of the stars : for one star differeth from another star in glory. *So also* is the resurrection of the dead. It is sown in corruption; it is raised in incorruption : it is sown in dishonour; it is raised in glory : it is sown in weakness ; it is raised in power : it is sown a natural body ; it is raised a spiritual body " (1 Cor. xv. 41—44).

Of modern orators, Burke, and of modern preachers, Chalmers, have shown most fertility in the quality of expansion. In the case of Chalmers the quality is so remarkable as to become oppressive. The door swings so much on its hinges that we become impatient for a forward motion. But the view presented of the truth in hand is very full and complete ; we cannot misunderstand it, and we can hardly forget it. The very exaggeration of the quality in Chalmers draws attention to its importance, as one of the chief attributes of really effec-

tive discourse ; while at the same time it serves to warn us of
the danger of the opposite extreme of pleonasm and verbosity.
Chalmers, however, often atones for excessive amplitude by a
happy instance of terseness. By means of a striking antithesis,
he sometimes gathers into a single line the substance of many
pages. The same thing may be noticed in Burke, and it has a
most happy effect on the hearer.

Of the various methods of expansion we cannot speak at
length. Resolving the general into the particulars which compose it ; putting the same truth in various forms (*e.g.* positive,
negative, interrogative, interrogative-negative); repetition with
variety ; examples and illustrations—are some of the methods
that will most naturally present themselves. The combination
of the various methods is obviously most desirable ; but in
this, as in most other matters, the best speakers will be guided
rather by their instincts, quickened by familiarity with the
best writers, than by any rules which can be given for their
direction.*

4. Last in the roll of the more important elements of pulpit
style we place *Beauty*. By assigning this place to it, we protest
equally against those who exalt it as if it were of supreme
importance, and those who depreciate it as unworthy of a
thought. Beauty, beyond all doubt, is a Divine creation, and,
though in quite different forms, it abounds equally in God's
revelation of himself in the book of Nature and in the books of
Scripture. It has a conspicuous place in the earth around us,
with all its manifold variety of form and colour, its tinted skies
and great vault of blue ; and it has a place not less conspicuous
in the Bible, with its Song of Solomon, its psalms and poems
innumerable, its gorgeous visions, and that wonderful music of
words which even a translation does not sweep away. And it
is on the basis of this style, in a form touched with a corresponding beauty, that devout souls love most to hear the lessons
of Divine truth from human lips. Where this beauty is wholly
wanting, there is no provision for that craving which is so
attracted by the allegories of John Bunyan, or the poems of
Milton or of Cowper. A tinge of beauty in style is like a streak
of colour in nature, and, without adding anything directly nutri-
tious, gives to truth a relish and to the mind a refreshment
that greatly increase the enjoyment of instruction. There are
undoubtedly preachers who have no conscious relish for it
themselves, and never take any pains to produce it. Let such

* See Appendix.

preachers, at the least, beware of the weakness of disparaging in others a quality of which they are destitute themselves. In any case beauty of style is rather the finishing touch, than an essential part of the process of uttering thought; but without it the expression of truth must be imperfect, deficient in one, though not the most important, of the elements of what the Psalmist calls "the beauty of the Lord" (Ps. xxvii. 4).

The subject which we have discussed in this chapter is sometimes exposed to disparaging strictures. A preacher who bestows pains on the style of his discourse is supposed to aim only at decking it out, or, as the phrase goes, "polishing his periods;" and to occupy one's self with such a task is represented as sheer trifling with the great truths of salvation. But in point of fact, there is no reason whatever why pains bestowed on style should be regarded as having no higher aim than that of polishing it on the one hand, or making it elaborate on the other. The true idea is precisely the reverse. Let pains be bestowed on the style in order to render it more simple and transparent—a more exact and faultless vehicle of truth ; to clear away redundancies, to strengthen what is weak and supply what is lacking ; to place the links of argument in the best possible order, and to find ways of entering the human heart by all the various avenues of approach with which God has furnished it. Certain it is that no small pains have been used for such ends by some of the highest masters of eloquence. Benjamin Franklin used to read the *Spectator*, and try to reproduce it from his notes in order to acquire the style of Addison ; William Pitt, by his father's advice, used to translate aloud into English from books written in other languages, in order to find readily the right English word. Mr. Bright, in the days of his finest speeches, was in the habit of studying carefully the great classical poets of England, finding that they helped him to correctness and fulness of diction. Gibbon is said to have written the first chapter of the " Decline and Fall " three times before he was pleased with it. Lord Brougham re-wrote the peroration of his speech on the Queen's trial eighteen times. Our habits have become so rapid, that such statements can hardly be believed by us. But such indications of the pains used by secular orators and authors to place their thoughts in the most impressive form, ought not to be lost on those whose office deals with the great truths of salvation.

With one other remark on this subject we must conclude ;

H

let it have all the weight of a closing counsel. Of the style of which we have spoken, the sacred Scriptures furnish the best and most striking examples ; nor can there be any better means of forming and enriching a pulpit style than familiarity with their contents, and that power of apt and graceful quotation of their language, which not only gives authority to a discourse, but makes it sparkle as with precious stones.

CHAPTER IX.

THE first business of the preacher, when commencing his preparation for a specific act of preaching, is to select his subject and his text. From time immemorial, sermons, or addresses to congregations on religious truth and duty, have usually been founded upon passages of Scripture. Our Lord himself may be said to have given his seal to this practice, when, in the synagogue of Nazareth, he founded his address on the passage which he had read from the prophet Isaiah. On the other hand, the Sermon on the Mount had no single text as its subject, although texts not a few were made use of in the course of it. St. Paul's address at Athens was founded on the inscription upon the altar " To the unknown God." It is not indispensable, therefore, that every address on religious topics should be founded on a Scripture text, especially in the case of audiences where the Divine authority of Scripture is not admitted. But where the Bible is accepted as God's revelation there are many considerations in favour of the practice, and as it has happily obtained the sanction of use and wont,* it is very desirable that it should be continued. Thus—

1. It is a perpetual recognition of the preacher's function as a preacher of the Word. It is a symbol of his office and his work—a token that he is there, not to set forth his own notions and fancies, but to declare God's message—that, in a stricter sense than was verified by Balaam, " he cannot go beyond the word of the Lord to say less or more."

2. The text is a perpetual reminder to the people of the

---

* The schoolmen in the Middle Ages occasionally selected a passage from Aristotle in their addresses to Christian assemblies (Riddle, " Christian Antiquities," p. 448). In a recent book called " Unorthodox London," a Comtian religious service is described in which the text was from Theodore Parker!

authority of Scripture. It is a testimony that the Word of God, as contained in the Old and New Testaments, is the only rule to direct us how we may glorify and enjoy him. The Bible is appealed to as the one fountain of truth regarding salvation : " To the law and to the testimony : if they speak not according to this word, it is because there is no light in them " (Isa. viii. 20).

3. Texts are adapted to be easily remembered by the people. They are the memorials as well as the subjects of sermons. They are the anchors which prevent the whole discourse from drifting away. And while the text suggests the sermon, the sermon often throws light on the text. Many a text seems to have a new force and brightness after a preacher has opened it up. It sticks to the conscience and to the heart, and sometimes becomes the kindling spark of new life in the soul. It recurs again and again to such a hearer amid the manifold changes and trials of life ; and as its light was the first gleam of heaven that fell upon its soul, so, peradventure, it is the last that gladdens and sustains him in his last conflict.

4. Texts are great helps to variety in preaching. It would be almost impossible without them to construct so many religious addresses as the preacher requires to deliver. They enable him to take up the various classes of topics embraced in " the whole counsel of God." And when viewed in their connections, they are not only suggestive of suitable topics, but of suitable modes of treatment ; they are guiding-posts to the preacher, guiding himself, and enabling him to guide others, to the full knowledge of God's will.

It is not meant that these objects are accomplished in all cases by the giving out of a verse of Scripture before beginning a religious discourse. Unless the preacher himself feels that in giving out his text he utters God's Word, and unless his use of it is in entire harmony with this thought, the text will no more end authority to the discourse than a cross over the door will give sacredness to a theatre.

If, however, the right use of a text be adapted to serve the purposes now enumerated, the choice of it should evidently be made with care. It ought not to be announced, as was said of Bourdaloue, merely that the preacher may show his skill in getting rid of it as soon as possible. And when it is announced as the authoritative subject of discourse, the preacher ought, with the most scrupulous conscientiousness, to attach to it no other meaning than that which he believes that the Holy Spirit

meant it to bear. Nothing can be more irreverent or inexcusable than the handling of texts after an odd or fantastic fashion.
Unfortunately there are various ways in which this has been
done. Some preachers have actually descended to punning
upon their text. Others again stretch the principle of accom-
modation so as to bring out of a text a lesson which there is not
the faintest reason to believe that the Holy Spirit intended it to
convey. Thus, the nine-and-twenty knives, which Ezra tells
us were restored by Cyrus to the Jews, have been taken to
represent nine-and-twenty kinds of Providential judgments ; the
old cast clouts and rotten rags which Jeremiah put under his
arm-holes have been made to stand for the stained righteousness of the sinner while Ebedmelech's words have been inter-
preted as showing that Christ's was the only true righteousness
for him.* The offence in such cases has not been lessened by
the fact that the preacher might have found other passages
expressly affirming his doctrine, and might have used some of
these words or incidents as ordinary illustrations ; whereas,
for mere fantastic and sensational purposes, he has given to
words of the Holy Spirit a sense unwarranted by the Spirit
himself.

The chief temptation in our time lies in the direction of unauthorised spiritualising. Passages in the Old Testament are
referred to Christ simply because they appear to fit Him, and
doctrines of the New Testament, developed only in the last
period of the later dispensation, are ingeniously discovered at
the very dawn of the earlier. Such a practice opens the door
to all the vagaries of Origen or Swedenborg, and is inconsistent
with the true purpose of texts—honouring God's Word as the
great fountain of authority and light, and showing that it is not
his own fancies that the preacher dispenses, but the message he
has received from his Master.

The choice of a text may surely be regarded as a suitable
matter on which to ask Divine direction by prayer. For if you
consider how a particular text may possibly become to some
hearer a message of life, it becomes awfully important that you
should take all possible care to choose the right one. The
answer to the prayer which you offer may come in the form of
a strong bright light cast upon some particular text, enabling
you to see how it may become the germ of a useful discourse ;
or in the form of a conviction that your people are for certain
reasons in need of a sermon on some particular subject ; or in

* Moore's "Thoughts on Preaching," p. 104.

the form of providential occurrences that give a definite direction to your mind. It is unsafe to rely on vague impressions, unsupported by reasons, as answers to prayer. Those who trust to such impressions are prone to the temptation of mistaking the mere fancies of their own hearts for intimations of the mind of God.

Divine direction having thus been sought, the preacher is not sent out to roam at large through the wide fields of Scripture in search of a text. A search begun in so hopeless a man er would probably consume a large share of the time available for the composition of the discourse. We suppose our preacher to have accumulated a store of texts—texts that in the course of his homiletical reading have struck him as the right keynotes for sermons, and on which, perhaps, he has already stored some thoughts of his own.* One caution, however, may be useful in reference to texts that have been stored in this manner. Very probably the flash that has brightened them, and made them suggestive to your mind of some useful train of thought, has fallen on them while you were meditating in the quiet of the evening, or while you were listening to a discourse, or while you were reading your English Bible. It may be that an examination of the original or of the context might somewhat modify your view of the passage. The caution to be offered is, that before proceeding to construct a sermon on it, you make sure that your view of its import is in accordance with the original and with the context.† It is not

---

* "'How do you obtain your texts?' said a friend on one occasion to the eminent young preacher, Thomas Spencer, of Liverpool. He replied, 'I keep a little book, in which I enter every text of Scripture that comes into my mind with power and sweetness. Were I to dream of a passage of Scripture I should enter it, and when I sit down to compose I look over the book, and have never found myself at a loss for a subject.'"— KIDDER's *Homiletics*, p. 83.

† It may be useful to give some instances of such mistakes :—Eccles. xii. 1, "Remember now thy Creator in the days of thy youth." One is apt to lay great emphasis on the *now* of this verse, whereas on turning to the Hebrew Bible we find merely the simple copulative " and "—" and remember thy Creator." 1 Tim. ii. 8, "I will that men pray everywhere," looks like an exhortation to prayer in all places, whereas on turning to the original we find it is τοὺς ἄνδρας, " *the* men," in opposition to the women ; it is the men who are always to offer prayer in public. Isa. i. 5, 6, "The whole head is sick, and the whole heart faint," &c.. sounds vaguely as a statement of universal corruption, and is often so used in confession ; whereas the context shows the meaning to be that chastisement has been so abundant as to leave no part of the body whole. 1 Cor. ii. 2, "For I determined not to know anything among you, save Jesus Christ and him

at all unlikely that you may find yourselves mistaken ; and in that case, painful though the sacrifice must be, your duty is plain and simple ; you must take no advantage of an ambiguity in our translation, since an error of translators can never give to a statement the authority of God's Spirit.

In the selection of texts a preacher will of course be guided largely by regard to the species of discourse which he purposes to deliver. For purposes of instruction, long texts may often be best ; but there is an obvious advantage of another kind in a short text. It falls on the people's ears with a sharp sound of authority ; it is easily remembered, and it can readily be introduced at suitable passages of the discourse to clinch the preacher's reasonings or appeals. The practice, once so much thought of, of preaching more than one sermon on the same text, is now almost wholly discarded, as it is obviously prejudicial to freshness and variety, and preachers of good sense would rather leave out something that might be said, than incur the risk, or rather the certainty, of wearying their hearers.

In the choice of his text, the preacher will do well to bear in mind the different objects which his preaching must contemplate, and the varied character which his sermons must accordingly bear. To probe the conscience, and thereby convince men of their sin and misery ; to guide the anxious to the Saviour ; to expound the great work of the Cross ; to set forth the whole circle of Christian doctrine ; to remove difficulties and objections ; to enforce the claims of holiness ; to elevate the standard of moral practice ; to furnish encouragement for serving God suited to the circumstances and temptations of his people ; to vindicate the ways of Providence ; to point out the various forms of Christian usefulness, and urge his audience to practise them—are among the objects which the preacher must aim at, and all require corresponding texts. Some sermons must be expository, some doctrinal, some argumentative, some practical, some experimental, some ethical, some hortatory, some minatory ; and texts must be equally varied. It is natural for preachers to preach much in some particular line to which

crucified." This is often explained as meaning that the Apostle determined to exclude every other subject, and has no doubt led many conscientious men to narrow very much the scope of their preaching ; whereas the original, "οὐ γὰρ ἔκρινά τι εἰδέναι ἐν ὑμῖν, εἰ μὴ," &c., "I did not resolve to know anything among you except," &c., shows the meaning to be that this was the only topic that he made the subject of a fixed resolution ; other topics might come in as occasion served, but to introduce " Jesus Christ and him crucified " he had fully and formally resolved.

their own minds have a strong affinity. Some are fond of rousing their hearers, and some of delineating the inner life or experience of the believer, and some of setting forth his moral obligations; in other words, the preaching of some is awakening, of others experimental, and of others practical. It would not be right to discourage preachers from going more than others into subjects on which they are particularly at home, and which they are specially qualified to handle. But, on the other hand, no preacher should confine himself to one class of subjects, and no preacher should be content to leave topics untouched which are essential to a full message, and to the full edification of a congregation.

More particularly, it is requisite that every preacher should be able to handle the fundamental doctrines of revelation, to set forth the glad news of the kingdom of God. Texts containing the substance of God's message to the sinner every Christian preacher ought to handle from time to time, although, as has already been said, such texts should not be the only texts which he does handle. "A man," says Dr. J. W. Alexander, "should begin early to grapple with great subjects. . . . The great themes are many. They are such as move the feelings; the great questions which have agitated the world, which agitate our own bosoms; which we should like to have settled before we die; which we should ask an apostle about if he were here. These are to general Scripture truth what great mountains are to geography. Some, anxious to avoid hackneyed topics, omit the greatest, just as if we should describe Switzerland and omit the Alps. Some ministers preach twenty years, and yet never preach on the judgment, hell, the crucifixion, nor on those great themes which in all ages affect children, and affect the common mind, such as the deluge, the intended sacrifice of Isaac, the death of Absalom, the parable of Lazarus. The Methodists constantly pick out these striking themes, and herein they gain a just advantage over us." *

Having selected his text, the next thing for the preacher is to mature the plan of his discourse. How is he to treat the text in question? What is to be his great aim in his sermon, and how is it to be accomplished? What topics is he to introduce, and in what order? What illustrations, elucidations, and applications of the text is he to embrace? How are the various topics to be arranged, so that not only a proper unity shall pervade the whole, but the effect shall be cumulative, each

* "Thoughts on Preaching," p. 7.

successive part of the discourse tending more and more to the desired result, and the impression being most powerful just as the discourse is brought to a close ?

Evidently it is no ordinary mental power that can really accomplish such an end as this. As Dr. Shedd remarks, " A powerful methodising ability implies severe tasking of the intellect, a severe exercise of its faculties, whereby it acquires the power of seizing the main points of a subject with the certainty of an instinct and then of holding them with the strength of a vice—and all this, too, while the feelings and the imagination, the rhetorical powers of the soul, are filling out and clothing the structure with the vitality, and warmth, and beauty of a living thing. This power of densely and quickly methodising can be acquired only by diligent and persevering discipline ; and hence it should be kept constantly before the eye of a preacher as an aim, from the beginning to the end of his educational and professional career. He cannot meet the demands which the public will make on him as its religious teacher unless he acquires something of this talent ; and he may be certain that, in proportion as he does acquire and employ it, he will be able to convey the greatest possible amount of instruction in the shortest possible space, and, what is of equal importance for the orator's purpose, he will be able to produce the strongest possible impression in the shortest possible amount of time."*

In view of the importance of the independent exercise of this methodising power, some writers object very strongly to the use by young preachers of skeletons prepared by others in the planning of their discourses. Such books as Simeon's " Horæ Homileticæ," which contains several thousand skeletons, may have been of service to many ill-trained preachers ; but, it is contended, they foster a habit of unwholesome dependence, and promote a most artificial and ineffective species of preaching. No preacher, with due independence of mind, who aims at something higher than the vocation of a huckster, who remembers that one of the chief reasons for a standing ministry in the Christian Church is that the truth may be ever poured into men's hearts through the living thoughts and feelings, the personal convictions and experiences, of the preacher, will condescend to be indebted to the machinery of others for what he ought to produce himself. But it does not follow that no use whatever is to be made of the plans or skeletons of others.

* " Homiletics and Pastoral Theology," pp. 57, 58.

There is no good reason why the same sort of use should not be made of skeletons that may be made of treatises and commentaries. The thing to be deprecated is, the preacher adopting another man's plan, or another man's anything, without passing it through the alembic of his own mind—without making it his own. The use to be made of commentaries and published sermons is similar. Every appearance of patchwork must be avoided. A unifying cement must give organic oneness and symmetry to the whole, otherwise it will be an old garment with a new patch—it will be new wine in old bottles.

On the subject of outlines or skeletons drawn up in preparation for any paper, Archbishop Whately remarks : " As a practical rule for all cases, whether it be an exercise that is written for practice sake, or a composition on some real occasion, it is necessary that an outline should be first drawn out—a *skeleton* as it is sometimes called—of the substance of what is to be said. The more *briefly* this is done, so that it does but exhibit the several heads of the composition, the better ; because it is important that the whole of it be placed before the eye and the mind in a small compass, and be taken in, as it were, at a glance ; and it should be written, therefore, not in *sentences*, but like a table of contents. Such an outline should not be allowed to *fetter* the writer, if in the course of the actual composition he find any reason for deviating from his original plan. It should serve merely as a *track* to mark out a path for him, not as a *groove* to confine him. But the practice of drawing out such a skeleton will give a coherence to the composition, a due *proportion* of its several parts, and a clear and easy arrangement of them, such as can rarely be attained if one begins by completing one portion of them before beginning the rest. And it will likewise be found a most useful exercise for a beginner to practise—if possible under the eye of a judicious lecturer—the drawing out of a great number of such skeletons, more than he subsequently fills up ; and likewise to practise the analysing in the same way the compositions of another, whether read or heard."*

It is hardly possible to exaggerate the importance of lucid order and symmetrical structure. This quality will often constitute one of the chief beauties of a discourse. Given a certain number of good thoughts—required the effect of two different methods of handling them. In one case they are taken up helter-skelter ; the preacher loses himself, goes abruptly from

* " Elements of Rhetoric," pp. 16, 17.

one topic to another, cuts the thread he is trying to unravel, produces a discourse to which might be applied the famous line of Pope, as once altered by Dr. Chalmers in reference to a celebrated controversial pamphlet—" a mighty maze, but *quite* without a plan." In the other case the whole of the thoughts have been worked into a harmonious whole ; bone has come to his bone and sinew to his sinew ; every thought and every sentence is dove-tailed into its predecessor, with tenon-and-mortice-like precision ; a symmetrical structure, like that of the human body, is produced ; a structure not only more beautiful in itself, but bearing a much closer resemblance to Divine structures of every kind. "Thoughts," says Theremin, " at first present themselves as hard, brittle, and separate particles ; the mind must seize them, and by grinding them incessantly upon each other crush them, until friction kindle the mass, and it resemble molten ore. The higher ideas, thrown as it were into this solution, take up the thoughts which belong to them, and which, now that they are fluid, obey the mystic power that attracts like to like, so that they form themselves into a firm chain." * " To attain the power," says another writer, " of readily fusing ideas, and combining them for oratorical effect, is an object worthy of the earnest endeavours of the public speaker. For this he should determine to put forth zealous and continued efforts.' †

In endeavouring to make the plan of a discourse more simple, orderly, and concise, the preacher may find it an advantage to leave out much that he has thought of introducing. Nor need he be afraid to do so. A sermon is not like a philosophical treatise, in which a subject must be viewed in all its length and breadth, and in all its aspects and relations. It is a persuasive address, in which, depending on the help of God, he tries to produce a particular impression. It is not necessary for this purpose to say everything at one time. It is not necessary, as Dr. Chalmers used to say, to take " a whole lift of theology " in every discourse. He may find use afterwards for materials that he cannot introduce now. It is quite true that at the commencement of his career a preacher is always afraid of a deficiency of material. He hardly knows how to fill up the time. But it is equally true that in practice the time *is* always filled up, and, as most hearers will tell you, more than the time. In this part of the island we seldom hear of our sermons being considered too short. We hear a great deal of their being too long.

* Kidder, "Homiletics," p. 112.   † Ibid., p. 112.

And this complaint is often well founded. It is important to find out when a sermon *is* too long, where the attention of hearers flags, what part of it might with most advantage have been abbreviated. And generally it will be found, in the case of sermons of average ability, that it is somewhere in the middle of the discourse that the redundancy lies. The introduction has excited some interest. But there was a somewhat barren region in the centre, and here eyes began to wander and heads began even to nod. As the preacher warmed towards the close, the hearers became more attentive again. But the body of the discourse was too much of a dead level. The preacher did not advance fast enough, and people cannot bear their preacher to think more slowly than themselves, any more than in a procession they can bear the leaders to walk at a snail's pace before them. So, by a sort of tacit arrangement, they lay down for a little in the middle of the sermon, but got up and rallied round the preacher as he pushed on more nimbly at the end. Tediousness is surely a fault that might be much more avoided than it is. It may surely be classed among preventible evils, and prevented it would be if preachers had more manliness and self-control.

Some years ago some experiments were made by certain inspectors of schools and others, with the view of ascertaining for how long a period young persons were capable of giving bright and undivided attention to an oral statement made to them by another. The results were somewhat curious, but generally it was found that the period was very short. Beginning with the age of ten or twelve, the number of minutes during which undivided attention could be given was ascertained to be ten or twelve, and for every year of addition to the age of the young person a minute had to be added to the length of the period, till you came to the age of twenty-five years, and the period of twenty-five minutes, which was believed to be the maximum period practicable. We do not attach much value to the so-called statistics, because they take no account of a very important element, the degree of interest which the statement contained for the minds of the listeners; it being obvious as an axiom that people can listen far longer, and far more intensely, to what is of profound interest to them than to matters of indifference. But it is well for preachers to bear in mind that the capacity of their hearers to give sustained attention is limited, and to try so to plan their discourses that that capacity shall not be unduly strained. Let the plan be simple, the arrangement natural, the style plain and forcible, the qualities that give interest to a discourse duly studied, and the length of the discourse suitably regulated. There are indeed preachers to whom any audience could listen for hours. It is said that when Jonathan Edwards preached on the unchangeableness of Christ, on the occasion of his installation at Princeton, though the sermon occupied a couple of hours, the people were so entranced that it seemed quite short. The late Dr. Thornwell, of South Carolina, at an early period of his ministry, was so carried on while preaching an earnest gospel sermon, that on looking at his watch, and finding he had preached and hour and a half, he apologized to the congregation, and proposed to stop, when he was met by cries, " Go on, go on; " and he did go on, holding his audience entranced for another hour. But it is not safe for any man, however high his estimate of himself, to assume, without proof, that he belongs to this order of preachers ; and as a general rule it will be better that the people should be sent away hungering for a little more rather than exhausted with too much.

The securing and sustaining the attention of the audience demands, at least on the part of ordinary preachers, continued care from first to last. Young preachers can have but a faint notion of the amount of inattention that prevails in an ordinary congregation. If men were as devout and earnest as they ought to be it would be otherwise ; but many persons are neither devout nor earnest. One class come into church with their minds preoccupied with the cares of this life. The farmer who has got his fields to sow in a few days, or whose cattle are about to be despatched to the fair, or who is on the eve of making a new offer for his farm, is not in the best mood for giving sustained attention to a serious discourse. I have been told of an eminent publisher that the idea of his most successful publishing schemes occurred to him in church. The merchant hard pushed for the bill that has to be met to-morrow has a serious rival to the preacher, however loud he may thunder from the pulpit. On the part of other hearers, well-disposed too, there is the tendency to dream. Alike in prayer, in praise, and in preaching, wandering thoughts are terrible foes to duty and edification. And it is quite wonderful how small a matter will send some persons off on the wings of reverie.*

---

* " Your hearer," says an American writer, " hears you say, ' Some fastidious persons are like the old Pharisees, of whom our blessed Saviour said, " Ye strain at a gnat and swallow a camel." ' ' Yes,' says he to him-

To remedy this wandering habit, some preachers resort to the method of scolding. It might be more effectual if it were addressed to themselves. It is vain to demand attention if we cannot command it. To secure the attention of our hearers, we must make ceaseless endeavours to give interest to our discourse. The idea of our audience, and of the infirmities of our audience, must be ever present to our minds. " Eloquence," says Vinet, " is the gift of feeling with others what they think and feel, and of adapting the words and the movements of one's discourse to speak the thought of another. Eloquence rests upon sympathy. One is never eloquent except on condition of writing or speaking under the dictation of those whom he is addressing ; it is our hearers who inspire us, and if this condition is not fulfilled, we may be profound and agreeable, but we shall not be eloquent. In order to be eloquent, we must feel the necessity of communicating our own life to others, and know intimately the chords which must be made to vibrate with them."*

Perhaps the result of all these suggestions may be to produce the impression that the due preparation of discourses is very difficult and very troublesome. But let me ask you to revert to what was said already on the benefit of a high ideal. Let me also ask you to remember that pains and trouble at the commencement of an enterprise are often represented not only by high success, but by ease and comfort, towards the close. And further, let me remind you of what is of no small practical importance, that the pulpit at the present day has not by any means so unchallenged a field as it once had, and that the army of trained preachers now engage in their work with an active and able body of volunteers at their side. Lay preachers and exhorters of various kinds have risen up—in some cases have been raised up—with a remarkable capacity, within certain limits, of plain, earnest, interesting address, so that some people are asking, What better are professional preachers, and what purpose is served by divinity halls, except to make them dull and heavy ? Such questions are not likely to be asked by

---

self, ' the boys at school used to read it, Strain at a gate and swallow a saw-mill. A great set of boys ! Bill Moore married his cousin. Bait got drowned, poor fellow ! Andy Snider went to Shenandoah to be a blacksmith. Bob M'Cowan is a poor bachelor.' And he chases these boys all over creation before he wakes up, arrests his reverie, and comes back to the subject of discourse."—TAYLOR's *Model Preacher*, p. 3.

* " Homiletics," p. 7.

thoughtful persons, for, with all the excellences of some lay preachers, the best of them are qualified to deal with but a slender portion of revealed truth; their power lies in but one kind of address. One may most cordially wish them God-speed, and yet be thankful for a trained and regular ministry, familiar with all the aberrations into which good as well as bad men have been led in the past, able to traverse the whole field of revealed truth, to bring forth out of their treasury things new and old, and to present in due balance and proportion all that bears upon the welfare of man. But just because the volunteers are so popular, the regular ministry must look well to their work. A minister must be more than a mere lay preacher. He must be capable of presenting God's message in all its breadth and fulness, as well as in its pointed and burning significance. He must be a skilled labourer, not merely a rough, though it may be vigorous, apprentice; and his skill must be the result of much intellectual discipline, combined with manifold grace and spiritual wisdom—a knowledge of man and a knowledge of God—chastened by the spirit of the little child, and an unfaltering dependence on the grace of God.

CHAPTER X.

THE different parts of a sermon correspond pretty nearly to the different parts of an oration, as they were long ago laid down by Aristotle—the introduction, the proposition, the proof, and the conclusion. The introduction, of course, prepares the way for the rest; the proposition announces the topic to be handled; the proof contains what it is deemed proper to say in the way of establishing it; and the conclusion is designed to rivet it on the attention of the hearer. The opening sentences of a sermon correspond to the introduction; then, more or less formally, the preacher announces the proposition, or subject to be handled; the divisions or heads, if such are needed, indicate the considerations which he brings forward in support of his proposition; and the conclusion is generally an endeavour to press the subject practically on the heart and conscience of his audience. In offering a few remarks on these several parts of a discourse, we do not commit ourselves to the position that they are all to be presented to the audience formally and specifically, as a logician would present the parts of a syllogism. On the contrary, they are often best treated when they are not formally enunciated; formality and uniformity being among the things which the preacher has most need to shun.

I. THE INTRODUCTION.—It is seldom wise to plunge, without introduction, into the heart of a religious discourse. Introductions are, perhaps, less needed in platform speeches or in political harangues; and in law-courts they can often be dispensed with altogether, especially if the pleader is addressing himself to a judge. The reason is, that the purpose of an introduction is to bring up the audience to a point of view suitable for considering the subject to be handled—to bring the hearers into sympathy with the speaker, and to get them to take an interest in the subject. In the case of platform and political speeches, and in the case of pleadings from the bar, this is less needed than in the case of sermons, because hearers usually are more ready to take an interest in the former than in the latter. Nevertheless, even in sermons, introductions ought to be brief. The limits of a sermon do not admit of a lengthened introduction. In all circumstances, indeed, anything which is only of a preliminary nature, when spun out unduly, becomes intolerably tedious, and exposes one to the criticism said to have been passed on John Howe by a good woman, one of his hearers : " He took so long to lay the cloth, that I despaired of the dinner."

The introduction to a sermon has been sometimes called the preacher's cross, being the part with which he has often most difficulty, and which he finds it hardest to do well. It will serve to lessen the difficulty if we notice some of the kinds of introductions used by preachers, and the principles on which they depend. These are very diversified, and what we now notice are rather samples than a complete enumeration.

1. Some begin by indicating the connection of their text with the context. This is what may be called the exegetical method ; it is the favourite method of scholarly minds, and the method to which students almost invariably resort. Canon Liddon, for example, hardly ever deviates from it. It is well suited for sermons of which instruction is the leading object, and almost indispensable in expository lectures ; and it is especially appropriate when the light thrown by the context on the text gives it a peculiar vividness and force, and thus makes it take hold of the attention and the interest of the hearers. Such a text, for example, as " Come now, and let us reason together, saith the Lord " (Isa. i. 18), has a striking light thrown on it from the fact that it follows an elaborate and frightful delineation of wickedness, which might have been expected to be followed up by a denunciation of doom rather than an offer of infinite mercy. So also the text, " Behold, I lay in Zion for a foundation a stone," &c. (Isa. xxviii. 16), follows a frightful representation of the reckless guilt of the men of Jerusalem, who were making a covenant with death and an agreement with hell. But for the most part, tracing the connection is not a very effective mode of introduction in the case of the majority of hearers. It is only the more advanced members of congregations, those who are habitually attentive, that care much either about context or connection. For ordinary hearers something more arresting is necessary. In the case of sermons, it is desirable, too, in general, that the text be *self-contained*—

I

flashing out clearly with its own bright light, and announcing its lesson with that clear definite ring which marks authority and commands attention.

2. Another form of introduction connects the topic of the text with some wider subject, the importance of which is universally admitted. It refers the species to the genus. It announces the general law of which the text furnishes an instance, exciting the interest which is usually connected with successful generalisation. Thus a sermon by a distinguished living preacher on Paul's words to King Agrippa, " I would to God, that not only thou, but also all that hear me this day, were both almost and altogether such as I am, except these bonds" (Acts xxvi. 29), begins by adverting to the power which Christianity has ever evinced of influencing all classes of society, the highest as well as the lowest, and notices the proof of its Divine origin and marvellous quality furnished in this, its all-pervading influence—its power to turn the world upside down, its influence on human laws, the tone it gives to literature, the features it imparts to the character even of its bitterest opponents, so that men who in heart have never bowed to Christ are constrained to glory in the very name of Christian. All this tends to throw interest on that approach to Christianity which Agrippa made, and which gave rise to the noble words of Paul. It may be remarked, however, that it is still only the more thoughtful class of minds that are impressed by this mode of introduction. It is only thoughtful minds that appreciate the principle of generalisation—the referring of the species to the genus, the indication of a kinship among facts or phenomena apparently unconnected.

3. Perhaps it is the same principle—the interest excited in resemblances among things apparently unlike—that makes an *analogy* a very popular and effective way of beginning a discourse. Thus John Knox, in a sermon on "The Source and Bounds of Kingly Power," founded on a passage in the 26th chapter of Isaiah (v. 13—21) in which the prophet seems sometimes to bow before the storm of judgment, and sometimes to resist it and lay hold of God's mercy, thus begins (in a sentence, however, which is too long and involved for an introduction) : " As the skilful mariner, being master, having his ship tossed with a vehement tempest and contrary winds, is compelled oft to traverse [tack], lest that, either by too much resisting to the violence of the waves, his vessel might be overwhelmed ; or, by too much liberty granted, might be carried

whither the fury of the tempest would, so that his ship should be driven upon the shore, and made shipwreck; even so doth the prophet Isaiah in this text, which now you have heard read."

4. A more popular way of employing analogy in the introduction is to start with an *anecdote*, or matter of fact. If it be really pertinent, and not introduced sensationally, it is very useful; only it makes it difficult to keep up the rest of the discourse at the same pitch of interest. Thus Dr. Arnold commences his sermon on the text, " The children of this world are in their generation wiser than the children of light " : " It is a remarkable story, told by the poet Cowper of himself, that when he was a young man, and living in London, where his companions were not only persons of profligate life, but of low and ungodly principles, they always had a great advantage over him, when arguing upon the truth of Christianity, by reproaching him with the badness of his own life. In fact, it appears that his life at that time was quite as bad as theirs; and they used to upbraid him for it, telling him that it would be well for him if they were right and he were wrong in their opinions respecting the truth of the gospel, for if it were true he certainly would be condemned on his own showing."

5. It may happen that an introduction is furnished not by indicating a hidden analogy, but a hidden difference. Instead of connecting the text with something to which it has an affinity, real though not obvious, it may be useful to separate it from something with which it seems to be identified, but is not. Thus Mr. Robertson of Brighton, preaching on the loneliness of Christ (John xvi. 31, 32): " There are two kinds of solitude ; the first consisting of insulation of space, the other of isolation of the spirit. The first is simply separation by distance. . . . The other is loneliness of soul."

So also a sermon by another preacher on Phil. i. 23, " I am in a strait betwixt two," &c. : " The two things that St. Paul was in a strait between are not those which most men are in a strait between. Most men who are in any strait in connection with religion are in a strait between Christ and the world, between earth and heaven, between the broad road that goes down to destruction, and the narrow path that leadeth to life. . . . But the things that St. Paul was in a strait between are quite different from these. His hesitation lay between the service of Christ here and the full enjoyment of Him hereafter ; between this life, with all its drawbacks, but its noble opportunity of Christian usefulness, and the life to come, so perfect in its blessedness, so glorious in its rewards."

6. In other cases, the introduction is furnished by some special and indisputable reason for giving attention to the lesson of the text. Tillotson, for example, begins the sermon on the Resurrection by a reference to the fact that the doctrine has been much opposed and run down : "The resurrection of the dead is one of the great articles of the Christian faith ; and yet it hath happened that this great article of our religion hath been made one of the chief objections against it. There is nothing that Christ anity hath been more upbraided withal, both by the heathens of old and by the infidels of later times, than the impossibility of this article. So that it is a matter of great consideration and consequence to vindicate our religion in this particular. For if the thing be evidently impossible, then it is highly unreasonable to propose it to the belief of mankind." A similar, but rather sharper instance may be given from Chillingworth, who rouses attention to his sermon on the perilous times of the last days by thus beginning : " To a discourse on these words, I cannot think of any fitter introduction than that wherewith our Saviour sometime began a sermon of his, ' This day is this Scripture fulfilled.' And I would to God that there were not great occasion to fear that a great part of it may be fulfilled in this place."

The circumstances that give special interest to a text, or to a subject, are extremely various. The very brevity of a text may be turned to account. The first of Dr. J. H. Newman's " Parochial Sermons," founded on the text, " Holiness, without which no man shall see the Lord," begins with the remark, " In this text it has seemed good to the Holy Spirit to convey a chief truth of religion in a few words. It is this circumstance which makes it peculiarly impressive ; for the truth itself is declared in one form or another in every part of Scripture." Whatever, then, may be fitted to give special interest to a text, either at all times or in the peculiar circumstances of the congregation, will furnish matter for an appropriate beginning.

7. Occasionally it is suitable to introduce a subject by referring to something strange or mysterious about it that excites curiosity and demands an explanation. If we may judge from the frequency with which it occurs in his volume of sermons, this would seem to be a favourite method with Dr. Ker. On the text, " He that increaseth knowledge increaseth sorrow " (Eccles. i. 18), he begins : " This is a very strange declaration

to come from the man who had made wisdom his choice as the
supreme thing in life, and who had been approved of by God
for the decision." A sermon on the burial of Moses begins :
"There is something strange and altogether singular in this,
that Moses, the greatest of all the Old Testament prophets,
should find a resting-place on the earth, and no man be able to
find it out." And on the young man whom Christ pronounced
not far from the kingdom of God, he begins : "If these had
not been the words of Jesus Christ, there would probably
have been some Christians found strongly objecting to them."
Whenever an interest is excited by this means in the strange or
unexpected feature of the text, attention is sure to be given to
the attempt that must follow to explain the matter and remove
the mystery.

8. Still another way of introducing sermons is the dramatic.
To be effective, this method requires more dash and boldness
than is common among our countrymen, or, except in a very
subdued form, very suitable for young preachers. But it often
comes with much effect from the great French preachers.
Thus Bourdaloue, on the Passion, taking for his text the words,
"Daughters of Jerusalem, weep not for me," &c., thus starts
at once : "Is it then true that the Passion of Jesus Christ, of
which we celebrate to-day the august but sorrowful mystery, is
not the most touching object that can occupy our minds and
excite our grief ? Is it true that our tears can be more holily
and more suitably employed than in weeping over the God-man,
and that another duty more pressing and more necessary
suspends, so to speak, the obligation which so just a gratitude
imposes upon us in another place, to sympathize, by sentiments
of tenderness, in the sufferings of our Divine Redeemer ?
Never could we have supposed it, Christians ; and yet it is
Jesus Christ who speaks to us, and who, as the last proof of
his love, the most generous and the most disinterested that ever
existed, on his way to Calvary, where He must die for us,
warns us not to weep at his death, and to weep over every
other thing rather than his death."

Although it may not often suit our quiet manner to begin in
a way so dramatical as this, something of this kind is often
highly appropriate. Dr. Guthrie begins his "Gospel in
Ezekiel" thus : "Having scattered over an open field the
bones of the human body, bring an anatomist to the scene.
Conduct him to the valley where Ezekiel stood, with his eye
on the skulls and dismembered skeletons of an unburied host.

Observe the man of science, how he fits bone to bone, and part to part, till from those disjointed members he constructs a framework which, apart from our horror at the eyeless sockets and fleshless form, appears perfectly, divinely beautiful. In hands which have the patience to collect and the skill to arrange these materials, how perfectly they fit!—bone to bone, and joint to joint, till the whole figure rises to the polished dome, and the dumb skeleton seems to say, ' I am fearfully and wonderfully made.' "

In many cases, the simplest form of dramatic writing, asking a question, makes a good beginning, as in Dr. Newman's sermon on ¿ " The kingdom of God is not in word, but in power" : " How are we the better for being members of the Christian Church ? What reason have we for thinking that our lives are very different from what they would have been if we had been heathens ? Have we, in the words of the text, received the kingdom of God in word or in power ? "

It is well to bear in view these different ways of beginning sermons, and the principles that underlie them. At the same time, it may be doubted whether it would be a wise thing for a preacher to get into the way of framing his introductions by rule. The ablest preachers have seldom done so, but have been guided by a kind of instinctive perception of the best way of catching up the attention of their hearers, giving them a just view of the text, and preparing them for the discourse that was to follow. In any case, it is not desirable that a preacher should have only one way of beginning, for different occasions and different subjects will demand different introductions. It may often happen, too, that a different introduction will suit the same sermon preached to a different audience, or on a different occasion ; the preacher may find something specially occupying the minds of the people that will enable him to make a more effective start. Experience, too, will help to guide young preachers. There is a hushed attention sometimes at the opening of a sermon, which not only shows that the preacher has struck a happy chord, but indicates that it would be well for him not to allow it to slumber, but appeal to it as often as he wisely may.

II. The second thing in a discourse is to announce the PRO-POSITION. This, however, is not always done formally, and does not always need to be. Sometimes it is self-evident—the text itself proclaims it. Texts like the following announce their own subject : " It is appointed unto men once to die ; " " We

must all appear before the judgment-seat of Christ ; " " The
blood of Jesus Christ cleanseth us from all sin." But in cases
where the exact topic to be handled is not self-evident, or
where the division will not bring it plainly out, there is an
undoubted advantage in distinctly stating it. Thus, Dr. Chalmers's celebrated sermon " On the Expulsive Power of a New
Affection," begins by expressly announcing the thing to be
shown. " There are two ways," he says, " in which a practical moralist may attempt to displace from the human heart
its love of the world—either by a demonstration of the world's
vanity, so as that the heart shall be prevailed upon simply to
withdraw its regards from an object that is not worthy of it ;
or by setting forth another object, even God, as more worthy
of its attachment, so as that the heart shall be prevailed upon,
not to resign an old affection which shall have nothing to succeed it, but to exchange an old affection for a new one. *My
purpose is to show* that from the constitution of our nature the
former method is altogether incompetent and ineffectual, and
that the latter method will alone suffice for the rescue and
recovery of the heart from the wrong affection that domineers
over it." Some of the old preachers made a practice of formally
announcing their subject. Jonathan Edwards commonly gives
it as a Proposition ; Ebenezer Erskine, and others of the same
school, as a Doctrine. This formality would now be embarrassing ; but in every case in which a statement must be given of
the object of the discourse, no common pains ought to be taken
to do it well. Clearness and conciseness must be earnestly
sought after, because the statement ought to be capable of
being readily remembered, and ought to remain before the
minds of the audience during the whole progress of the discourse.

III. We proceed to the third thing—the Proof ; and in connection with this we shall notice the divisions. The discourses of
our Lord and his apostles had not formal or announced divisions, and the preachers of the early Church, though they sometimes numbered their paragraphs, did not often enumerate their
heads. It would be foolish, therefore, to represent heads as
essential to a good sermón, or to condemn a preacher for not
using them, provided he could more effectively draw his remarks, each out of its predecessor, like the folds of a telescope,
and in this way he could keep up the attention of his audience,
and engage both their heads and their hearts. In platform
speeches one seldom makes use of heads, because on the plat-

form we are more conversational and less given to abstract treatises ; and when in the pulpit the conversational method is followed, and the preacher strives to speak *to* the people—right home to the actual feelings of their hearts—he is less disposed to resort to formal divisions. It is the heaviest style of preaching that needs most to be broken up into heads ; and there can be no doubt that in many cases the divisions that are so formally announced are little better than a disguise of heaviness. Yet in discourses which have the instruction of the audience as one of their leading objects, divisions of some sort are very desirable, both as guiding-posts to the preacher and stepping-stones to the audience. Only it must be seen to that instead of signals for inattention they really tend to increase the interest of the audience in the subject.

The celebrated essay of the French divine, Claude, " On the Composition of a Sermon," is chiefly occupied with the division of discourses. The subject is treated with remarkable fulness, both theoretically and by illustrative cases. Many modes of viewing texts and topics are suggested to show the best method of dividing, and likewise of bringing out in proper order and with great fulness all the views and lessons which the subjects embrace.

On whatever principle the division of a subject may be made, three general rules are always applicable : 1. The heads ought to be few in number ; 2. Logical in arrangement ; 3. They should be briefly, concisely, and attractively stated.

1. A great multiplicity of heads and divisions is simply bewildering, and is accepted by the bulk of hearers as a proof that, as no effort to remember the whole could be successful, no effort to remember them needs to be made. If it is really desired that the substance of the sermon be carried away by the hearers, the preacher must limit his points to the number which their average attention and memory may reasonably be expected to grasp. If the number of points that present themselves to him be much greater, it is absolutely essential that he make a selection of the most salient or important.* " Division," says Claude, " ought in general to be limited to a small number of parts :

---

* It is said' of a Puritan preacher that he once got the length of "seventy-sixthly." I have heard of a clever criticism of a Latin discourse delivered long ago in the Divinity Hall at Aberdeen, when, after a full hour, the discourser announced his last head, " undevigesimo et tandem ultimo," on which his critic remarked, that the only observation that occurred to him was, that he had never before heard the word *tandem* used with such singular propriety.

they should never exceed four or five at the most; the most admired sermons have only two or three parts."

2. In arrangement, divisions ought to be logical. Care must be taken not to put a division first which requires something to be explained belonging to a subsequent head. Care must also be taken, in any enumeration of points, to avoid repeating the same thing in different words, or making that a separate head which is properly a particular under a former division. Suppose, for example, that the text is, " Be ye also ready ; for in such an hour as ye think not, the Son of Man cometh." Here it would be natural to show what is implied in being ready. Suppose it should be laid down that to be ready is—1. To be at peace with God. 2. To be a sincere believer in Christ. 3. To be following peace with all men and holiness. 4. To be a partaker of the Holy Spirit. 5. To be using one's talents in the Master's service ;—it is evident that, though all of these are right separately, the enumeration is doubly faulty. The first particular is not only included in the second, but depends on it, as does also the third on the fourth. Union to Christ and participation in the Holy Ghost might be referred to as the fundamental requisites, and under these such special fruits of either as bear specially on the readiness in question.

3. The statement of the divisions ought to be clear, pithy, and concise. If possible, each ought to be expressed in a single word. If we would condescend to take a lesson from children's sermons we should see this very clearly, for every successful preacher to children expresses his divisions with wonderful conciseness. He knows how vain it would be to make their memories carry more. It is the conviction that but little attention is usually paid to divisions that makes some preachers omit them altogether, trusting more to the general effect of a number of thoughts bearing in the same direction than to a definite statement and illustration of each several particular.

To come now to the practical question, How ought we to divide ? The question really branches into two ; for there is one rule applicable to the division of texts, and another to the division of subjects.

Texts often contain their own division. " And now abideth faith, hope, charity, these three ; but the greatest of these is charity." The division obviously is—first, the three graces that *abide* or are permanent (the force of μένει must not be overlooked) ; and, second, the superiority of charity, and the grounds thereof. The corresponding passage in 1 Thess. i. 3, in which the apostle dwells on the grounds of his satisfaction with the Thessalonian Church, equally suggests its own division : " Remembering without ceasing your work of faith, and labour of love, and patience of hope in our Lord Jesus Christ." So also the three rules from the believer's daily life (Rom. xii.) : " Not slothful in business, fervent in spirit, serving the Lord."

It is often useful to announce the division by neatly indicating the topics contained in the several parts of the text. Thus, in Eph. vi. 18 the apostle exhorts to prayer : " Praying always with all prayer and supplication in the Spirit, and watching thereunto with all perseverance and supplication for all saints." Here we have a full view of the more important qualities of true prayer. (1.) *Incessant*—" praying always." (2.) *Manifold*— " with all prayer " (all kinds of prayer—secret, ejaculatory, domestic, public). (3.) *Spiritual*—" in the spirit." (4.) *Vigilant*—" watching thereunto." (5.) *Persevering*—" with all perseverance." (6.) *Intercessory*—" supplication for all saints." The following instances we take from Claude. It is founded on the text, Eph. i. 3, " Blessed be the God and Father of our Lord Jesus Christ, who hath blessed us with all spiritual blessings in heavenly places in Christ." (1.) A grateful acknowledgment—" blessed be God." (2.) The title under which the apostle blesses God—" the Father of our Lord Jesus Christ." (3.) The reason for this —" He hath blessed us." (4.) The fulness of this blessing—" with all blessings." (5.) The nature of the blessings—" spiritual." (6.) The place or sphere in which He hath blessed us—" in heavenly places." (7.) The person through whom—" in Christ Jesus." Discourses of this kind are among the most useful that one can preach, and they fulfil a celebrated canon of Chrysostom's in regard to sermons—" That God ought to speak much, and man little."

Texts that so obviously suggest their own division are not, however, the most numerous class, and in many instances it is more difficult to divide them. The preacher's great effort ought to be to find out the natural order of the topics, and, following that, to give to the subject all the unity of which it is capable. Great benefit will often be derived from carefully singling out the leading statement of the passage, and grouping the subordinate statements under it. Thus (2 Cor. iii. 18)— " We all, with open face beholding as in a glass the glory of the Lord, are changed into the same image from glory to glory, as by the Spirit of the Lord." It will be found that the leading statement here is, that under the gospel we behold the glory of the Lord as in a glass *with open face*, and that the subordinate statements are—1. By this process we are changed into the same image. 2. This change is gradual : "from glory to glory." 3. It is produced by the Spirit of the Lord.

There is a large class of texts which are not to be divided into their parts, but rather treated according to their aspects. They do not so much contain truths as they recognise and suggest them. Thus in the sermon already referred to on the text, "I would that not only thou, but also all that hear me, were both almost and altogether such as I am, except these bonds," the preacher finds two of the Christian graces, but in different modes of action—Faith in a state of *repose*, and Love in a state of *struggle*. Faith in a state of repose shows itself in its satisfaction with its condition ; and, though the text hardly suggests the particulars, the preacher shows how faith is satisfied—(*a*) with its *foundation*, (*b*) with its *experiences*, and (*c*) with its *expectations*. Love, on the other hand, is here seen in a state of struggle—it pants for the establishment of Christian brotherhood, "such as I am ; " for the *entire* blessedness of those that excite its interest, "both almost and altogether ; " for the entire blessedness of *all* men, "not only thou, but also all that hear me ; " and it pleads with God to make them so, "I would to God." There is a combination here of parts and aspects, or rather the parts are brought skilfully in under the aspects.

Sometimes the preacher proceeds by building upon the text a series of observations suggested by it. For example, the text (Acts ix. 4), "Saul, Saul, why persecutest thou me ? " has been treated thus after the observational manner : 1. Unconverted men generally are in a persecuting spirit towards earnest Christians. 2. Christ has his eye upon persecutors. 3. The kindness or injury done to his people Christ considers done to himself. 4. The conviction of sin is the first step to conversion. 5. The calls of Christ are earnest and particular— "Saul, Saul." 6. Christ condescends to reason with his enemies—"Why persecutest thou me ? "

Textual sermons may also be constructed by specifying the particular modes in which some general principle or statement finds its verification. Thus let the text be (Numb. xxxii. 23), "Be sure your sin will find you out," a useful discourse may be based on the different ways in which sin finds out the sinner —*e.g.*: 1. By remorse of conscience ; 2. By the power of natural law; 3. By the special working of Divine Providence; 4. By the awful revelations of the day of judgment. A very favourite and interesting species of textual discourses of this class are those which are founded on some figure or emblem of Scripture. The resemblances between the symbol and the thing symbolised always open an interesting field. For example (Rev. xxii. 16), " I am . . . the morning star:" 1. Christ's influence is as light after darkness; 2. Possesses for ever the freshness of the morning; 3. Is the pledge of a glorious future; 4. Even of the perfect day.

From the division of texts we should advance to the division of subjects; but we confess that we shrink from a matter on which so much has been written to so little purpose. It may be useful to study the twenty-eight topics of Aristotle, the twenty-seven of Claude, and the sixteen of Gresley; but we do not think that even after doing so the student will find himself in possession of very serviceable rules. In general it will be better for him to consult his own common sense, and in connection with each topic to consider what mode of presenting it is most likely to lodge the great truths which belong to it in the mind and heart of his hearers.

There is a danger of divisions becoming a hindrance instead of a help to the great end of preaching. When constructed too artificially and stated too formally, they break up the continuity of thought, and diminish instead of helping the final impression. Number two may lead the preacher into a line quite different from number one, and number three may lead apart from either. The true use of a division is to promote clearness, unity and continuity of thought, and to aid each part in increasing and intensifying the impression produced by the part preceding. If continuous thought and accumulated impression can be secured better without formal divisions, by all means let them be discarded. The most efficient discourses are those where the preacher's line is clear and simple, so that as he goes along he gets nearer to his audience, and forces them to give more heed to the great lessons of his sermon.

IV. The last part of a discourse is appropriately termed the CONCLUSION. Of the importance of this part it is hardly possible to speak too strongly. It ought to be the most vital of the whole, and if the preacher has been gradually warming, and accumulating force as the discourse has advanced, at the conclusion his spirit should be on fire, and the impression of his closing passages should be by far the strongest of any. Yet in practice the conclusion is often the weakest part. The preacher, perhaps, in preparing his discourse, gave up the labour of arranging his thoughts before coming to the close, so that, instead of being more concentrated at the end, his discourse lost itself in a marsh, or ended like the emptying of a pitcher, with a few poor drops and dregs.

In general, the conclusion of a discourse will assume the form either of inferences or of a direct appeal. The nature of the subject will determine which of these is preferable. If the subject has been chiefly of an expository nature, inferences will probably be needed to bring out its significance and importance, and its relation to the practical interests of the hearers. If no inferences are needed to show the practical bearing of the subject, the preacher's concluding remarks will naturally take the form of an appeal. But in any case the inferences ought to embody the spirit of an appeal, and the appeal ought to carry all the weight of inferences. The last effort of the preacher ought to be a signal one—like Samson's last achievement against the Philistines. It ought to be the concentration, as with a burning-glass, of all the rays that have been collected during the progress of the address. If during the sermon he has been bringing up his guns, at the close he should make their fire converge with resistless momentum. The rule " ut augeatur semper, et increscat oratio " reaches the climax of its application now. Considerations derived from the discourse fitted to move the will, conscience, and feelings of the hearer should be pressed with an earnestness that will take no denial. " Hic si unquam," says Quintilian, " totos eloquentiæ fontes aperire fas est." If the understanding has been gained in the earlier parts, the heart and the will must be gained in the later.

But let the preacher beware of trifling with this opportunity. Let him beware of the temptation to play off some highly rhetorical passage at the close of his discourse. The arts of a mere tinsel rhetoric are at all times sufficiently hateful in the pulpit, but most of all when the preacher is about to part with his audience, and utter the words that are to ring in their ears when his voice is silent. Let him also above all things avoid an artificial earnestness. There is no time when an earnest preacher can so readily forget himself and everything else, save the eternal interests which he represents. The last five minutes of the discourse, in point of real effect, ought to be worth all the thirty or thirty-five that have gone before them. It is great wisdom to know when to end. To spin out a discourse after the preacher has exhausted both his audience and himself, and leave them with no wish but that he would be done, is terrible. It is a sin to expose a Divine ordinance to the scornful treatment which such a proceeding provokes. If any summing up of the previous remarks is necessary, it ought to be brief. Preachers, no doubt, do well to aid their hearers in carrying away as much of their discourses as they can. But they will do better to remember that discourses are for a higher purpose than even to be remembered, and that no sermon accomplishes its end which does not bring the hearer into God's presence, and leave him under its holy influence.*

* It is said of a poor woman who worked in a wool-mill, and used to walk a long way to attend the services of a godly minister, but could not remember his sermons, that when her neighbours used to taunt her, she replied, with that happy art which can make ready use of common things for spiritual purposes, " Do you see the wool that I am washing ? It keeps none of the water, but it is always growing whiter. It is true I remember little of what I hear, but I would fain hope that I, too, am growing whiter."

CHAPTER XI.

EXPOSITORY LECTURES.

THE object of an expository lecture is to bring out the meaning and apply the teaching of longer passages of Scripture than are commonly used as the texts of sermons. The " lecture," as it is technically called in Scotland, is more didactic than the sermon. The element of teaching occupies a larger place than that of persuasion. Not that persuasion may be omitted, for the highest skill of the preacher, in the construction of a lecture, will be shown in making the whole converge in the way of persuasion. Only, by the nature of the case, he will have to bestow more time and pains on the exposition of the passage ; whereas in the sermon he will aim more directly and constantly at moving, guiding, and elevating the soul of his hearers.

In lecturing, you necessarily throw yourselves more thoroughly into the current of the thoughts of the sacred writer. You place yourselves as much as possible in his position, and you try to bring out precisely the whole circumstances of the case as they presented themselves to him. Hence arises one of the difficulties of the lecture. To expound the past is one thing, to move the present by means of it is another. The perfection of lecturing is, so to combine the past and the present, to make the past such a mirror of the present, that what is said of the one shall have a powerful influence in moving the other. Suppose, for example, that you are lecturing on the parable of the unfaithful steward. Naturally you bend your energies in the first instance towards expounding the parable—removing the difficulties and vindicating the teaching of our Lord. But to what effect will all this be if you do not come into contact with analogous things in the hearts and lives of your audience ? Your discourse will be little better than a piece of dry antiquarianism. And no doubt it is a fatal fault of many lectures, as of many sermons, that they keep at a great distance from present-day experiences, and aim only at throwing light on the remote past. To find out the representative principle that underlies the sacred Scriptures, to find in the past a type of the present, and so to expound what was said or done in that little patch of Syrian soil, the land of Canaan, that the hearer of the nineteenth century shall feel unmistakably, "Thou art the man," is the very perfection of an expository lecture. Scripture thus expounded is in little danger of being caricatured as " Hebrew old clothes." It then becomes plain that what things were written of old were written for our edification, and that the Bible, being God's revelation, is a book for all ages and for all men.

Since the lecture aims so much in the first instance at expounding the passage on which it is founded, the *introduction* may very fitly be of a more exegetical character than is commonly best for the sermon. Not that this is invariably the best form of introduction. The drift of the passage may be too obvious to require to be indicated, and many things may make it desirable to begin the lecture on the same principle as the sermon, with something that will arouse interest or draw attention. In lectures as in sermons, a monotonous or commonplace commencement—too often a mere signal to hearers to let their attention wander—is by every means to be avoided.

The advantages of expository preaching, especially when the lectures form a continued series, are numerous and important. The preacher finds his text ready to his hand. He is led to embrace a greater breadth of scriptural truth than he would take in if each text were chosen by itself. He is carried beyond the range of topics which he might naturally choose—borne out, as it were, more into the open sea   Details of duty and of sin, which otherwise might seem beyond the scope of the pulpit, may not only be brought within it, but the preacher may gain additional authority in handling these from the fact that it is a text coming in course that gives him the occasion. Thus in a course of lectures on the ten commandments, one may say things regarding the seventh which could not be said if the subject were approached without the protection which is afforded by its coming in course. To the people the practice of expository lecturing is very instructive ; they see more of the fulness and comprehensiveness of Scripture, and are trained to a more careful habit of reading it, and to an habitual endeavour to observe its scope and connection.

On the other hand, there are difficulties connected with the lecture, and especially the course of lectures, which not every preacher, not even every able preacher, can always overcome. Subjects may turn up into which the preacher cannot enter with much spirit, because no allied stream of thought has started up in his own mind. At the same time, there can be little doubt that if the preacher's attention be directed early to the passage, if pains be taken to find out its bearings, and if the fountain of all light be earnestly resorted to, the subject, whatever it may be, will become more interesting to him, and a suitable line of remark will open before him. A still greater trial to the preacher's powers, however, will be found in the effort to grasp the whole passage, ascertain its great central truth, group the subordinate lessons and details, pass from one to another without abruptness, and fuse the whole into a homogeneous mass. For a lecture, in the real sense of the term, is neither a paraphrase nor a commentary. It is not an easier mode of preaching, adopted by the preacher to save trouble. It is not a series of little sermons on half-a-dozen consecutive texts in place of one. The preacher must not suppose that he is to take up clause after clause, making a few unconnected remarks on each, passing rapidly from those which are unsuggestive, and dwelling at greater length on those on which it is easiest to hang a few commonplace remarks. The true lecture, as has been remarked, like the true sermon, should have a true unity, and all its parts ought to bear upon a definite object. Our Lord's parables, in the distinctness with which they present some great central truth, and the skill with which various related truths are attached to it, present the *beau-idéal* of the structure of an expository lecture. It is not necessary in lectures, any more than in sermons, to insert every remark that could be made upon the passage, but only such as have a bearing on its great lesson. A lecture is not a philosophical treatise, but an address designed to impress some truth or duty on the hearers. The topics of which it ought to consist are those most fitted, under God's Spirit, to accomplish this end.

" Even when a suitable passage has been selected," remarks Dr. Shedd, " the sermoniser will need to employ his strongest logical talent, and his best rhetorical ability, to impart sufficient of the rhetorical form and spirit to the expository sermon. He will need to watch his mind and his plan with great care, lest the discourse overflow its banks, and spread out in all directions, losing the current, and the deep, strong volume of eloquence.

K

This species of sermonising is very liable to be a diluting of Divine truth instead of an exposition. Perhaps, among modern preachers, Chalmers exhibits the best example of the expository sermon. The oratorical structure and spirit of his mind enabled him to create a current in almost every species of discourse which he undertook, and through his lectures on the Romans we find a strong unifying stream of eloquence constantly setting in, with an increasing and surging force, from the beginning to the end. The expository preaching of this distinguished sacred orator is well worth studying in the respect of which we are treating."*

In the well-known work on Preaching by the Rev. Daniel Moore, of the Church of England, special commendation is bestowed on some of the Puritan writers as excelling in expository discourse. "For power," says he, "to seize on the salient moral of a passage, or pick up the interlacing threads of several verses, and combine them into one strand of thought, the preachers of the period referred to are surpassed by few. Writers like Manton on St. James, or Adams on St. Peter, or Greenhill on Ezekiel, or Caryl on Job, will rarely be consulted by the expository preacher without profit. As greatly helpful to his purpose also, especially in affording examples of devout application, as well as dexterous and able grouping, he will not overlook the commentaries of Matthew Henry and the pious Burkitt." † To the older works here mentioned, let us add Archbishop Leighton's Exposition of First Peter. Fair in exegesis, excellent in arranging and grouping, rich and suggestive in commenting and applying, Leighton is moreover marked by a serenity of mind and a saintliness of tone that seem to carry us to the gate of heaven.

Some of the exegetical writers of Germany have contributed valuable materials for the expository lecture. Of Bengel's "Gnomon" it is not needful that we should speak. Hengstenberg, Tholuck, Stier, Olshausen, Besser, Krummacher, Delitzsch, and others, have done much towards enabling us to bring out of our treasuries things new and old. The commentaries edited by Lange are especially helpful; the "homiletical hints," if used simply as hints, being very valuable for enriching our expositions.

Let us now notice briefly a few of the different modes of treatment.

* Shedd's "Homiletics and Pastoral Theology," p. 155.
† "Thoughts on Preaching," pp. 307, 308.

1. Sometimes the passage suggests or even states its own divisions, and this is a great advantage both for perspicuity and unity. Suppose, for example, that the lecture is on the first Psalm. Not only the great salient truth of the psalm, the contrast between the godly and the ungodly, but the illustrative particulars under each great head, are expressly stated, and with something of the force and interest of a climax. It is of no small benefit to the lecturer to be able to devise a simple logical division, running parallel to the successive verses or paragraphs of his text. Thus the psalm describes—I. The blessedness of the godly man. II. The misery of the wicked. I. The godly man is delineated—1. In his character ; 2. In his condition. As to his *character*, there is first a series of negative particulars, showing what he is not ; then illustrations of what he is—(1) He walketh not in the counsel of the ungodly ; (2) he standeth not in the way of sinners ; (3) he sitteth not in the seat of the scornful. But, positively, (1) his delight is in the law of the Lord, and (2) he meditates therein day and night. His character being thus described, his *condition* corresponds. And here the poetry of the psalm comes out ; a figurative resemblance is chosen, giving animation and beauty to the description—" He is like a tree planted by the rivers of water, that (1) bringeth forth fruit in season ; (2) his leaf doth not wither ; and (3)—the figure being now dropped—whatsoever he doeth shall prosper. The case of the wicked man is then dwelt on. The *character* is not enlarged on—being the converse of the other. His *condition*, like that of the other, is described by a figure—he is like the chaff which the wind drives away. And this instability will come to its climax and its ruinous consequences will be seen on the day of judgment. This gives the preacher the opportunity of enlarging the contrast and deepening its colour. The certainty of these conclusions is confirmed in both cases by the Lord's omniscience—" For the Lord knoweth the way of the righteous : but the way of the ungodly shall perish."

It is plain that such a variety of topics admit of being handled in a single lecture only in the way of a running commentary, and that a different mode of treatment must be adopted if the preacher is to go deeper into the substance of the psalm. Such a treatment is the following : Two classes of men are here described by their appropriate law or rule of life. The one follow the law of the Lord, and the other follow the counsel of the ungodly. The fruits or results of these several rules of life are described—the stability and growing prosperity of the one, the instability and final destruction of the other.

2. In many cases, however, the passage does not suggest its own division, and pains must be taken to discover the natural order of the topics. Suppose that the subject of lecture is 2 Cor. v. 1—8, where the apostle contrasts the earthly house of the tabernacle with the house not made with hands. It is plain that, following the order of the passage, we should have to repeat the same topics: *e.g.*, v. 2, "we groan;" v. 4, "we groan, being burdened;" v. 2, "we earnestly desire to be clothed upon;" v. 4, "we would not be unclothed, but clothed upon." We must therefore endeavour to find a simple but comprehensive order of topics; laying hold, first, of the leading truth, and grouping the subordinate truths under it. The leading truth is, that in its future state the soul of the believer will be lodged in *a better dwelling* than here. In illustration of this four positions are laid down : I. The present dwelling is imperfect, the soul groans and is burdened in it, but still it desires a dwelling of some kind. II. The future dwelling has many advantages—(1) it is a house not made with hands ; (2) a building of God ; (3) in the heavens ; (4) eternal ; (5) in it mortality is swallowed up of life. III. Our fellowship with the Lord is different in the two buildings—in the one we are absent, in the other present with the Lord. IV. We are confidently assured that when the one is removed the other will come, for—(1) God hath given us the earnest of the Spirit; (2) we walk by faith and not by sight ; hence the joyful state of mind even of the suffering Christian, and the earnest desire with which he looks forward to the change when the body is dissolved by death.

3. Again, there are lectures, founded on passages of acknowledged difficulty, where a considerable share of labour must be devoted to the elucidation of the meaning. Of such passages the following are samples : Romans ix. 3—5, " For I could wish that myself were accursed from Christ for my brethren, my kinsmen according to the flesh," &c. ; Hebrews vi. 4—6, " For it is impossible for those who were once enlightened, and have tasted of the heavenly gift . . . if they fall away, to renew them again unto repentance." To ascertain the meaning, the context must be examined with unusual care. A careful comparison may be needed with other passages, either parallel or apparently opposed, and the exact meaning of particular expressions may have to be investigated. This process of exegetical inquiry being completed, all that remains will be to press home

the lessons of the passage. Much care must be taken, in handling such a text, to adapt one's self to one's audience—avoiding the extremes of excessive depth and excessive superficiality.

In lecturing on our Lord's parables there is not often occasion for grappling with difficulties or obscurities, but there is much need for ascertaining the precise point in hand, the single analogy with which our Lord deals. The remark has often been made that to represent the parables as containing analogies at every point would be to turn them to purposes the very opposite to what our Lord designed, inasmuch as it seems to have been his intention to make the one point of real analogy conspicuous by surrounding it with circumstances where there was opposition rather than agreement.

Historical passages have sometimes difficulties, but more commonly not. In general, a brief statement of the facts is desirable, avoiding tediousness. This statement should convey the preacher's idea of the light in which the facts are to be viewed, and prepare the way for the lessons derived from them. A delicate task is presented to the lecturer on historical passages; the sacred writer seldom states explicitly what is to be praised and what is to be blamed, either in the acts or the sayings of the person in question; the sifting of the character and life falls to the preacher. The successful treatment of history and biography in the way of lecture is extremely difficult to minds of the rigidly logical and dogmatic cast; where there is more of the discursive and imaginative quality, success is usually greater.

4. A *fourth* mode is that in which the lecturer proceeds by a series of observations. This, however, is less desirable than any of the other methods, because it affords less security for exhausting the whole teaching of the passage.

As a general rule, the practical and hortatory part will come most fully at the end; but it is not at all desirable to make a complete separation between the explanatory and the hortatory as you go along; there should be a practical vein all through. Whatever there is of an inferential kind at the close should rather be the summing up of what has been substantially brought out as you have gone along than new matter reserved to the end.

It may be useful here to offer a few observations regarding the portions of Scripture which may best be employed for a course of expository lectures. It is remarkable how intensely interested many of the better class of hearers become in such a course, when it is really thorough and satisfying—how great exertions they will often make not to miss any member of the series. When this is the case, the minds of preacher and hearer are bound together by links of singular strength. It is to be remarked, however, that a taste for expository preaching on the part of a congregation presupposes a more than ordinary measure of esteem for the Word of God, acquaintance with it, and interest in it. It is the more ignorant, easy-minded, and careless class to whom lecturing is distasteful. Robert Hall found that lecturing was relished by his well-trained congregation in Cambridge, but when he removed to Leicester he found the people less capable of appreciating it, and had to give up the practice. Where there is a profound sense of the authority of Scripture, a deep desire to be under its guidance, an earnest wish to know and follow all that the Lord has spoken, good expository lecturing cannot fail to be highly valued.

It is very common in Scotland for preachers to give expository lectures covering the whole of some book or books of the Bible. Preachers have been known to begin at Genesis and go right on—sometimes, however, selecting only portions—till they came to the end of Revelation. But for the most part the method of selecting certain books, as being better adapted than others for expository lecturing, has been followed. From its very varied historical, biographical, and general interest, the book of Genesis has been generally a favourite one. The only other books of the Old Testament that *as complete books* seem to be often attempted are the poetical books—the Psalms, the Song of Solomon, and, perhaps, we may add, the difficult book of Ecclesiastes. In regard to the New Testament, however, the case is almost precisely the reverse. There is hardly a book that is not often subjected to this process (with the exception, perhaps, of the pastoral Epistles). The Gospels, the Acts, the Epistles of Paul, the Hebrews, the general Epistles, and even the Apocalypse itself, though probably least frequently of all, are quite commonly made the subjects of exhaustive exposition. The preacher must determine for himself which of these he will adopt. According as he feels most at home in narrative, or in doctrine, or in experimental subjects, will probably and properly be his first choice. Thereafter he will be more guided, perhaps, by a regard to what he deems the spiritual necessities of his flock. He will endeavour, as a wise steward, to give to every one a portion of meat in due season. He will guard against monotony, and if once he has carried his people elaborately through one of the profounder books he will probably deem it wise to let the next book be somewhat more easy. Whatever other subjects a minister may select, it is hardly possible that, in these times, he should not feel it a duty, in some shape or other, to take up the life of our blessed Lord. Either in lectures on a single Gospel, or on a harmony of the Gospels, or on selected portions, he will try to bring that subject prominently before his people.

A less serious undertaking than lecturing over a whole book is to lecture on selected chapters. For, indeed, there are chapters, or groups of chapters, that have a character of their own, as much so as if they formed separate books. The Sermon on the Mount, the farewell discourse of our Lord, the 53rd chapter of Isaiah, certain of the Psalms, such as the 22nd or the 51st, the 8th or the 12th chapter of Romans, the 13th or the 15th of 1 Corinthians, the 2nd of Ephesians, the 11th of Hebrews, the 2nd and 3rd chapters of Revelation, and many other chapters that might be named, are admirably adapted for this purpose. The people get the benefit of the principle of continuity, without being kept too long in a single field of the Divine pastures. One thing the preacher must make up his mind to—when once he begins, to go on to the close. He must guard against a habit of fitfulness and irregularity, for people are quick to spy out a minister's infirmities, and it will be no advantage to his influence if his people are tempted to compare him to the man that began to build a tower, and was not able to finish it.

The biographies of Scripture furnish a very favourable field for expository lectures to those whose hand has the proper touch for such subjects. It needs something of the artist's power to grasp the striking features, portray them clearly and strongly, connect them with moral and spiritual truths, and point them easily and strongly to the great practical lessons of life. But the interest, the variety, and the charm of Scripture biography are so great, that no common effort should be made to cultivate this field.

Besides lecturing on particular books, or portions of books, it is a common practice to give courses on connected subjects. Our Lord's parables and miracles obviously form a most convenient and useful basis for this practice. The attributes of God have been made the subject of a celebrated series by Atterbury, as the Apostle's Creed has also been by Barrow. The Ten Commandments, the Beatitudes, the Lord's Prayer, the relative and social duties, the works of the flesh and the fruit of the Spirit, the whole armour of God, the several parts of the edifice which, in 2 Peter i., we are exhorted to build on faith, are also suitable. " Christ in the Old Testament" is the title of a long series of discourses by the late Dr. Gordon, his principle of selection being that of Christology—whatever passages seemed designed to bring up the Messiah. The late Dr. John Brown gave lectures on the sayings of our Lord. Dr. Goulburn's well-known treatise on " Personal Religion " is a series of lectures bearing on one subject, with texts selected from various places.

Another mode of exposition, " the running commentary," is sometimes made use of when a chapter is read for general instruction. Twice over, in his ministry at Chester, Matthew Henry in this way read and commented on the whole Scriptures. It is apparently a very simple thing, and yet to be well done it requires no little tact, neatness, and force. The object is to aid the hearer in perceiving the drift of the passage, and to link it on here and there to his heart and conscience, to aid him in making the application of it to his own circumstances and character. It is a mode of treatment that cannot so well be applied to the denser portions of Scripture ; it is more appropriate to the narrative parts. It wonderfully freshens the reading of a chapter when a few appropriate remarks are made here and there, either clearing the meaning or pointing the application. But it ought not to supersede the devout, uninterrupted, authoritative reading of the Holy Scriptures, as the Word of the living God, not depending on man's commentary or man's application, but itself appealing both to the understanding and the heart. In our zeal to edify we must take care lest we reverse the rule of Chrysostom, that God should speak much and man little.

There is still another species of expository discourse very rarely to be met with, but fitted to be most useful, namely, a discourse bearing on a whole book. The late Dean Alford, Dr. Fraser, and others, have very usefully done this through the press ; and why should not a pastor, in like manner, explain to his people the drift and purpose of a whole book, or group of books, and give them such information about them as may serve to facilitate their understanding of the whole ? Would it not be useful sometimes to hear a lecture on the Romans as a whole, or the Hebrews, or the Apocalypse ? It may be objected that it is difficult to combine with this what is especially characteristic of an oratorical discourse. A lecture of this sort, it is thought, must be almost wholly an address to the understanding. The hearers can have but little to rouse their consciences, to warm their feelings, to quicken their efforts after holiness, or to give them an impulse heavenward. But surely there must be a great defect in the preacher if he set forth the scope and bearing of any book of Scripture without finding material for spiritual counsels or appeals. For if, instead of gathering up the materials for impression as they are found in some small section of the sacred books, we should extract the great lesson of the whole writing, and bring it to bear on men's hearts and consciences, instead of the impression being feebler, might we not reasonably expect that it should be greatly stronger?

With reference to expository discourses of all kinds, it is no doubt true that they afford less scope for oratory than the sermon, and that they tie down the preacher more to a prescribed line of thought. But the time has not gone past when Christian preachers may be found who esteem it no drawback to have their message blocked out for them by the inspired writers, and who are willing to sacrifice something of the oratorical for the sake of the useful. The faithful exposition of Scripture was certainly the great business of the ministry in the early ages of the Christian Church, and those who strive to bring us back to primitive church usages could restore no more profitable practice. But the combination of the expository lecture and the ordinary sermon is the very best provision that can be made for the edification of congregations. The flock is led out to the green pastures and still waters of the Word; while the preacher has constant opportunities of placing the great points of faith and practice in every variety of light, and enforcing them with every consideration that can send them home.

CHAPTER XII.

THE merits and the demerits of the three different methods of delivering discourses from the pulpit—namely, reading, reciting from memory, and extemporising—have often been discussed during the last two centuries. In a closely printed appendix of twenty-five pages subjoined to Dr. Kidder's treatise on "Homiletics" (p. 351, English edition), we have a summary of opinions on the subject, *pro* and *con.*, beginning with Bishop Burnet, and coming down to the more eminent preachers of the present time.

In the first age of the Church sermons do not appear to have been written, far less read. The preachers of the first three centuries, though doubtless they may have availed themselves of the aids which help to give force and finish to extemporaneous addresses, do not appear to have committed their sermons to writing beforehand. About the time of Origen we hear of shorthand writers (ὀξυγράφοι), men licensed by authority who were employed in taking down public addresses, and who were expected to submit their manuscripts to the preacher before publication. Some of the discourses of the early preachers contain passages that seem to have been introduced on the spur of the moment, and that indicate the possession of a faculty of no small value—the power of turning to account slight passing events, and building on them suitable exhortations. One of Chrysostom's sermons on Genesis contains an extemporised passage suggested by the circumstance that, while the lamps in the building were being lit, the eyes of the people were following the lamplighter in place of the preacher : "Let me beg you to arouse yourselves, and to put away that sluggishness of mind. But why do I say this? At the very time when I am setting forth before you the Scriptures, you are turning your eyes away from me and fixing them on the lamps, and upon the man who is lighting the lamps. Oh, of what a sluggish soul is this the mark, to leave the preacher and turn to him! I too am kindling the fire of the Scriptures, and upon my tongue there is burning a taper, the taper of sound doctrine. Greater is this light and better than the light that is yonder. For, unlike that man, it is no wick steeped in oil that I am lighting up. I am rather inflaming souls, moistened with piety, by the desire of heavenly discourse."

Some critics will probably doubt whether this often-quoted passage from Chrysostom was purely *ex tempore*, or was not the result of premeditation. But there can be no doubt that this celebrated preacher did not usually write his sermons, since it was his habit, at certain times, to preach every day. In regard to Augustine, too, there can be little doubt that he dealt largely in the extemporaneous method, for he sometimes told his audience that when he entered the pulpit he had meant to pass over certain topics on which, nevertheless, he felt it his duty to enlarge. Yet we cannot suppose that all those wonderfully concise instances of antithesis and alliteration which stud the homilies of Augustine were entirely unpremeditated. Nor can there be much doubt that during that brilliant period when so many men that had studied rhetoric in the schools became Christian preachers, they were not content to trust themselves to extemporaneous speech. We are told of Cyril of Alexandria that some of his homilies were committed to memory by Greek bishops as models of Christian declamation. Augustine excuses those whose preaching ability was but slender for committing other men's discourses to memory, and reciting them to their flocks; though, for his part, he knew a more excellent way, and strongly urges the preacher " to read in the eyes and countenances of his hearers whether or not they understand him, and to repeat the same thing in different terms till he perceives that it is understood—an advantage which those cannot have who by a servile dependence on their memories learn their sermons by heart, and repeat them like so many lessons."

The practice of reading sermons from a manuscript does not seem to have been practised till after the Reformation, nor to have ever prevailed extensively in any other language than the English. Bishop Burnet traces the practice to the fewness of qualified preachers in England after the Reformation, and the necessity of getting the people instructed in religious truth by the best means that were available. The book of Homilies was accordingly prepared, and these were appointed to be read to

congregations one by one by some qualified reader. The practice of reading sermons from manuscript would very naturally
in process of time grow out of this arrangement. But it was
not a practice that met with approval either from the people or
from the authorities. In 1674, during the reign of Charles II.,
a royal decree was published against the custom, addressed to
the Vice-Chancellor of the University of Cambridge: " Whereas
his Majesty is informed that the practice of *reading* sermons is
generally taken up by the preachers before the University, and
is continued even before himself, his Majesty hath commanded
me to signify to you his pleasure that the said practice, which
took beginning with the disorders of the late times, be wholly
laid aside; and that the aforesaid preachers deliver their
sermons, both in Latin and English, by memory, or without
book, as being a way of preaching which his Majesty judgeth
most agreeable to the use of all foreign churches, to the custom
of the University heretofore, and to the nature and intendment
of that holy exercise. And that his Majesty's commands in the
premises may be duly regarded and observed, his further pleasure is, that the names of all such ecclesiastical persons as shall
continue the present supine and slothful way of preaching be
from time to time signified to me by the Vice-Chancellor for the
time being, upon pain of his Majesty's displeasure.—MONMOUTH."

In spite of the royal decree the practice of reading continued
to hold its ground in England. In the eighteenth century the
prevalent coldness and formality of the time encouraged it, until
the older method, sanctioned though it was by the example of
all Christian antiquity, came to be counted a token of fanaticism.
So rigorous did the rule become, that what is now called slavish
reading was the only style of delivery counted proper in a
gentlemanly preacher; and it is said of a clergyman of this
class that on one occasion he seriously compromised his character
because he ventured to raise his eyes from his manuscript during
the reading of his sermon. The practice of reading the published
sermons of the most eminent preachers, which in the *Spectator*
obtained the commendation of Sir Roger de Coverley, was a
natural consequence of this state of things. Then followed the
practice of clergymen borrowing sermons from one another,
and the still more handy custom of lithographed sermons sold
at so much the dozen. Under such practices, it need not be
said that the pulpit suffered fearfully.* The worst of them was,

* Congregations that groaned under its dulness and lifelessness might be
excused for making the most of the ludicrous incidents that sometimes

that the chief purpose for which the Head of the Church had organized a living ministry was entirely lost ; instead cf the truth falling with a deeper impression by coming warm from the hearts of men who felt it, and by being skilfully adapted to the circumstances and state of mind of the people who heard it, it fell like lumps of lead, serving no good end but that of exercising their patience. It would be very unfair, however, to represent the style of reading introduced by such preachers as corresponding to that which was practised by preachers like Jonathan Edwards or Thomas Chalmers ; or to overlook the conditions under which, but not without which, read sermons have not unfrequently been the means of much edification.

Let us endeavour, therefore, deliberately and fairly to consider the relative merits of the different modes of delivery, with a view to prepare the way for some practical counsels.

1. As to *reading* sermons. The advantages of this method are, that it secures more care in the planning and working out of the discourse, more exactness of thought and precision of language ; while it also protects the preacher from the effects of a nervous or timid temperament, from the danger of losing the thread of his discourse, and of giving it out confusedly or hurriedly, or with important omissions, or with alterations that are fatal to the sense. Where the effect of the discourse, or of any part of it, is *cumulative*—where it depends upon the skilful building up of clause upon clause or paragraph upon paragraph—reading, it is alleged, is quite essential to efficiency, unless at the expense of an amount of drudgery, in the way of committing to memory, which absorbs time, consumes nervous energy, and creates a constant anxiety, fatal to activity and efficiency in the other departments of the ministry.

On the other hand, it is objected to the practice of reading, that a certain monotony and unnaturalness of tone are almost inseparable from it ; that the preacher cannot, in reading, hold that real and close communication with the minds and souls of his audience which is necessary to their being thoroughly impressed ; that the effort to *seem* to be doing one thing, viz. speaking to them, while in reality he is doing another thing, viz. reading, must be awkward and enfeebling ; that it is extremely difficult for him to have his own heart exercised in

occurred, as when a preacher once surprised a quiet country congregation by mysterious allusions to the late terrible catastrophe, and it turned out that the sermon which he had read had been prepared several years befo e on the occasion of the earthquake at Lisbon.

unison with what he is reading; that where vivid emotion has to be expressed, or earnest appeals have to be made, the process must be sadly artificial; and that read sermons, however well they may be fitted to *instruct*, cannot be effective in *persuading* hearers.

2. The second method of preaching—that of *reciting*—has accordingly been devised with the view of securing the advantages, and at the same time remedying the evils, of reading. To a certain extent this object is accomplished. Consecutiveness of thought, exactness and even beauty of language, are secured by this method where it is properly carried into practice. But it is not so well fitted to secure ease, freedom, naturalness in delivery. The difference, as has been remarked, is, that the preacher reads from his memory in place of reading from his manuscript. The tendency on his part is to recite something before the people rather than speak to them. There is a somewhat similar awkwardness as when reading is practised, in seeming to be doing one thing—speaking—when in reality he is doing another thing—reciting. Nor is it much easier for a man reciting to enter into the feelings proper to what he is uttering. What he says is not very likely to come out with the freshness and naturalness of a working brain and a beating heart. If, in natural speaking, the tones of the voice are moulded by the molecular movements of the brain and nerves roused by the living soul, it follows that when the brain and nerves are not so roused, the tones of the voice will not be moulded naturally, but artificially. In such a case, the organs of speech do not spontaneously express the emotion; if they succeed in expressing it at all, it can only be in the way of imitation. In recited sermons, the tendency is rather to imitate the tones of emotion than spontaneously to express them. The rule of course is not without exceptions, as we shall presently see.

With recited sermons there is another difficulty : when the memory of the preacher fails him, his sole resource is gone. The difficulty and the awkwardness are extreme; there remains hardly an alternative but to pull the manuscript from his pocket, and try to find the forgotten sentence.

3. The third method of preaching—the *extempore* method—embraces many varieties of one species. It comprehends all that lies between two extremes—the practice of the man who chooses his text in the pulpit, or very shortly before going up to it, plunging into the wide sea without premeditation, and coming to land as best he may ; and the practice of the man

who carefully plans his discourse, lays out the trunk-line with great deliberation, arranges his thoughts and illustrations in careful order, and bestows pains on what may be called the joiner-work of his sermon, making each part fit naturally and readily to the rest. In all ordinary circumstances it is only this last variety, or something near to it, that can find acceptance with a conscientious extempore preacher. It is impossible to reprobate too strongly the adoption of the extempore method on the ground that it is *the least troublesome*—that it saves the preacher from the drudgery of careful writing or careful thinking. There is little doubt that preachers in remote parts of the country, with flocks small and obscure, and without the stimulus to mental effort which residence in a large and active town involves, are apt to become careless in preparation, and to fall into a style of extemporaneous preaching which is so vapid and pointless as to bring the pulpit into contempt. Young men, with all the lively impulses of youth upon them, and strong with the generous purpose "to scorn delights and live laborious days," are not likely to have any tolerance for such a habit. And yet one cannot be sure that if the fervour of youth has somewhat abated, and the sense of weariness that attends long and laborious efforts has begun to come upon you, some of you may not be tempted to resort to this as the easier method. Country life is often not very favourable to the sustained habits of mental exertion, which, under any plan whatever, are unquestionably indispensable not merely to an efficient, but even to a conscientious, ministry.

Of such extempore preaching as can thus alone be regarded as admissible, the great advantage is—the facility which it gives for freshness and naturalness of delivery, for arresting and maintaining the attention of the audience, for enabling the speaker to speak what he feels and to feel what he speaks, and thus, with God's help, carry his hearers with him, through all the varieties of thought and feeling to which he may give expression in his discourse. "Of such a speaker," says M. Bautain, * " the language will be more forcible and brilliant, more real and more apposite. Originating with the occasion, and at the very moment, it will bear more closely on the subject, and strike with greater force and precision. His words will be warmer, from their freshness ; they will in this manner communicate increased fervour to the audience, and will have all the energy

* " The Art of Extempore Speaking." By M. Bautain, Vicar-General and Professor of the Sorbonne. 1867.

of an instantaneous effort. The vitality of thought is singularly
stimulated by this necessity of instantaneous production, by this
actual necessity of self-expression and of communication to
other minds." It has the advantage, moreover, of not rigidly
confining the preacher to what has been premeditated, but
allowing him, like Chrysostom, to introduce remarks in the
literal sense *ex tempore*—thoughts which may either be flashed
into his mind with unusual vividness under the excitement of
preaching, or which may be suggested by what goes on at the
time. A preacher presents himself to an audience under a great
advantage when he stands up to *speak* to them—to enter into
that friendly relation which speaking implies. There is something in this, when modestly and respectfully done, that bespeaks
their favourable consideration—unless their consciences shrink
from plain faithful dealing, or unless their pride disdains the
compulsion to listen, or unless a painful experience of that
mode of preaching compels them to anticipate a mere outpouring
of vapour instead of a rich and solid repast.

Undoubtedly, the general judgment of the Christian Church is
against the reading of sermons. The practice is inconsistent
with the purpose of preaching; it interferes with it as a free,
living force ; preaching becomes a somewhat dull intellectual
operation, instead of a process in which every force and faculty
of the preacher is applied to move the entire nature of his
hearers. A young preacher deliberately adopting this method
publicly confesses his weakness—owns himself unable to preach
in the manner most in harmony with the nature of the ordinance and most fitted to accomplish its ends.

Yet there may be legitimate exceptions. In judging of such
cases some consideration requires to be had (1) of the *temperament* of individual preachers, (2) of the nature of the *subject*,
and (3) of the nature of the *audience* and the *occasion*.

1. In regard to individual temperament. There may in
individuals be qualities of temperament that divest the reading
of sermons of the faults that are commonly associated with it.
There may be unusual animation of spirit and of voice, and
unusual emotional susceptibility, so that the feelings of the
speaker cannot but go along with the thoughts expressed in the
discourse—his whole machinery, so to speak, being set in
motion together. If to this gift of temperament there be added
remarkable thinking power, and remarkable power of illustration
and application, a read discourse, instead of being from that
circumstance subject to drawbacks, will be an extraordinary

treat. Such, emphatically, was the case with Chalmers, and such is the case, too, with other preachers that could be named. As the countrywoman said of Chalmers, his was *fell* reading. The case of Chalmers was the more remarkable that the range of his emotion was so wide and its intensity so great. There are instances of preachers, however, with a smaller range, and a lower tone of emotion, to whose temperament reading is suitable, because, as they read, the emotion which they are wont to express is readily roused in them. Perhaps we may say that Jonathan Edwards was a man of this type. He had neither the blazing impetuosity nor the wide range of Chalmers. But under his calm self-possessed manner lay a deep fountain of feeling, and it welled out calmly but powerfully with his favourite subjects of preaching. In general, for *read* sermons, three things may be laid down as absolutely indispensable : first, lively tones of voice; second, vigorous style ; and third, interesting and rousing thoughts. If the preacher have a monotonous voice and a heavy style, if his thoughts are commonplace, and withal the sermon is long, it is no wonder if in popular estimation a read sermon becomes a synonym for dulness, a tax on the patience, and a temptation to sleep.

Again, there are temperaments to which the method of *reciting* seems well adapted. Such temperaments are not uncommon in France. The habitual liveliness of the French character, and the great amount of gesticulation with which the French speak, put the practice of reading sermons *hors de combat* in that country. On the other hand, their fondness for pointed, brilliant, epigrammatic diction, makes French orators unwilling to trust themselves to extemporaneous utterance. Recitation, therefore, has been the usual practice of the great French preachers. And, for the most part, they seem to have been able to do what is so difficult for English preachers—throw their soul into their recited sermons, feel intensely as they went along. But even they were not beyond that sense of bondage which is so apt to prevail when success depends on the memory. "Which was the best sermon you ever preached ? " some one once asked of Massillon. "That which I knew the best," was the significant reply. Bourdaloue, whose memory was less to be trusted, felt himself compelled to fall in with the practice ; although, it is said, afraid lest the sight of the congregation should make him forget his lesson, he was compelled to preach with closed eyes. At the present day, however, a strong feeling has begun to prevail in France in favour of more extem-

L

poraneous preaching. Adolphe Monod urged it as being the
best when the speaker had a natural facility and was well
prepared; without the last, he said, it was the worst of all
methods, both for matter and for form. And in the work
recently published by M. Bautain, Vicar-General and Professor
at the Sorbonne, the adoption of the practice is urged strongly
on the whole Roman Catholic clergy.

There are other temperaments, again, to which the extemporaneous method is the best adapted. Such, for example, was
Robert Hall. Finical though he was about his language, he
never wrote his sermons, and even the finest of them were
elaborated mentally while he lay on his back—the attitude in
which physical infirmity compelled him to study.* A faculty
of grasping a subject in its several dimensions and relations, a
facility in making one's thoughts fall into clear order and into
plain language, coupled with a power of deliberation and self-
possession, are indispensable to good extemporaneous preaching.
Such are, to a large degree, the gifts of Mr. Spurgeon, whose
sermons, though unwritten, exhibit a remarkable power of
clear thought and forcible expression within the mental range in
which he feels himself at home. Men who are apt to lose self-
possession, whose mental organs seem to be struck with
paralysis when they face an audience, and who are apt to
flounder from topic to topic without doing justice to any, are
not likely ever to feel at home with this method. And yet
even in such cases it is very wonderful what expertness may
come of beginning early and persevering steadily. As the Latin
proverb says, *Fit fabricando faber.* Some of the most striking
instances of failure in the attempt to preach extemporaneously
have been in the case of preachers who had long been accustomed
to another method. The " great clerks " that have been seen to—

> " Shiver and look pale,
> Make periods in the midst of sentences;
> Throttle their practised accents in their fear,
> And in conclusion dumbly have broke off "—

---

* When the proof-sheets of his celebrated sermon on Modern Infidelity
were submitted to him, and he came to the apostrophe, " Eternal God, on
what are thy enemies intent? What are those enterprises of guilt and
horror that, for the safety of their performers, require to be enveloped in
a darkness which the eye of heaven must not penetrate!" he asked, " Did
I say 'penetrate,' sir, when I preached it? Be so good as take your
pencil, and for 'penetrate' put 'pierce'; no man who considered the force
of the English language would use a word of three syllables there but
from absolute necessity. *Pierce* is the word, sir, and the only word to be
used there."

were probably accustomed to a different mode. Bishop Sanderson is said to have made an attempt before a village audience, that turned out a most mortifying and humbling failure. Tillotson once tried his powers in the same way, and after beating and buffeting about for nearly ten minutes, brought his discourse to a close, declaring that nothing would induce him to make the attempt again. And South, who was in the habit of committing his sermons to memory, on one occasion of trusting himself to an extempore attempt, broke down in the very opening of his sermon, and w.th the exclamation, " Lord, be merciful to our infirmities," rushed abruptly from the pulpit.* Such failures, however would probably not have occurred, and would certainly not have been so complete, had the method not been new to the preachers, and a great contrast to what they were accustomed to.

2. When we consider the *subjects* of sermons, as determining the right method of delivery, it becomes clear that writing and reading is the method best adapted to some. Such sermons, for example, as those of Bishop Butler, would never have seen the light as sermons, if the ordinance of King Charles II. had been rigidly enforced. But were they sermons ? Are they not rather theological treatises ? A preacher may sometimes see it his duty to go profoundly into certain subjects, in order to carry his people up to the higher reaches of Christian intelligence, or to help them to understand some of the more difficult aspects of divine truth. But if the practice of reading were wholly proscribed, such efforts would have to be abandoned. On other occasions a preacher may feel that he needs to use great discrimination and delicacy of language. He may find occasion to deal with forms of vice, all allusion to which is embarrassing before an audience embracing men, women, and children. Or he may have occasion to delineate some type of character belonging to some of his people, and requiring to be sketched both delicately and truthfully. Or he may be treading on some of those narrow ledges of truth,—navigating some narrow strait, as it were, between a Scylla and a Charybdis,—where he requires to be careful of every word, lest a false conception be conveyed. It would be hard to say that such topics are to be proscribed, as in most cases they virtually would be, if reading from a manuscript were to be totally banished.

3. In regard to *audiences*, it may happen that when the congregation is made up chiefly of professional men, or of

* *Quarterly Review,* cii. 491.

persons to whom the habit of attention is easy and common, a
read discourse will be the most suitable. But if read, it must
be well read, and good reading implies much practice and care;
so that if one who has never practised reading should on some
sudden occasion take to it, the likelihood is that the attempt
would be a failure.

To come now to the practical question—What method of
preaching ought to be adopted by the young ministers of our
day ?

First, in regard to the *preparation* of sermons, the advice
which used to be given by Dr. Chalmers is that which we
would humbly reiterate. Let every minister write out fully one
discourse in the week, and let him preach another, extempore,
or from notes more or less full. The habit of writing out one
discourse, at least during twenty years of one's ministry, is
attended with very many advantages. It disciplines one's own
mind; it ties one down by the conscience to at least one piece
of thorough work; it accustoms one to exactness of thinking
and writing; it gives one the opportunity of deliberately examining one's work, and of making systematic and continuous efforts
to improve it.

While thus giving heed to writing, the young preacher will
do well to accustom himself to deliver one discourse also from
less elaborate preparation. That discourse, however, will not
be an extempore effort, pure and simple. The subject will be
carefully studied as in the presence of his Master; the plan
will be systematically formed; the course of thought firmly
grasped; the illustrations and applications considered and arranged; and the transitions from point to point so managed as
to give unity to the whole, and save the discourse from the
character of a mere bundle of observations. How much of this
will be written is a question of detail, not to be settled by
another. Besides urging his students to cultivate both these
modes of preaching, it was the advice of Chalmers that once a
month, or at some such interval, they should prepare a more
than usually elaborate discourse on some topic of deep interest
—like his own on the Efficacy of Prayer and the Uniformity of
Nature, or M'Laurin's Glorying in the Cross of Christ, or
Jonathan Edwards's on Justification by Faith. He thought it
good for the preacher and good for the flock to have to rise
occasionally to the higher levels.

But when one discourse has been written and another
sketched, how are they to be delivered ? Is the written one to

be read, or committed to memory, or is an abstract of it to be made, and notes made use of in the pulpit, similar to those which form the preparation for the more extempore discourse ? To these questions the remarks already made on the several varieties of cases will furnish materials for the answer.   In every case the preacher is bound to decide the matter as in the presence of his Master, and as one lying under the most solemn obligations to present the truth in the most impressive form and with the largest amount of persuasive power.   Be his method what it may, his business is to *deliver* his message, and the right force of that word must never be evaded.   Ask the soldier what is meant by the delivery of a charge—ask the merchant what is meant by the delivery of a piece of merchandise—ask even the letter-carrier what is meant by the delivery of a letter : all will tell you that the thing in question must be lodged in the persons or in the premises of those for whom it is designed. The true delivery of a sermon, in like manner, means lodging it in the heads and hearts of the audience.   There are always two factors in the process—first, the clear presentation of the truth, and, second, the dynamical force sending it home.   For efficacy, both depend and both depend alike on a heavenly power.   But as no intelligent preacher dreams that, since it is the office of the Holy Spirit to enlighten, it matters not whether the truth be presented by him clearly or confusedly ; so no intelligent preacher dreams that, because it is the office of the Holy Spirit to apply truth savingly, he needs not to take any pains to make his message telling.   The best preacher is he who combines both, and in both seeks to be an instrument in the Spirit's hands.

In general we may say, that in proportion to the hold which the preacher has of his subject, or, better still, his subject of him, will be his hold on his hearers.   If he holds the truth feebly, his power over his audience will be feeble ; if he holds it firmly, and, still more, if he is possessed by it almost to the verge of enthusiasm, he will speak like one having authority, and his word will be with power.   The more that his own soul is exercised by the truth on which he prepares during the week to discourse, the more powerfully (other things being equal) will he be sure to preach.   In order that his soul may be duly moved, and in order that he may get the right tone and spirit, let him ever, as he is preparing, have his audience before him ; let him remember the utter deadness and worldliness of one section, the gross temptations of another, and the tremendous forces with which the devil, the world, and the flesh are ever opposing him and his work. Let him remember that the time which he occupies on the Lord's Day is the one golden hour of the week when the sin-driven and world-worn sinner is to get his glimpse of heaven, and to be plied with the truths that, if he is ever to be saved, must bear down the strongest tendencies of his carnal heart. There, in your audience, is a young man exposed all the week to the sneers and to the profane and filthy language of the other occupants of the counting-room ; yonder is a young woman persecuted by her family for her earnest efforts to serve the Lord ; there you have a working man driven the whole week in rough employments that develop little more than his animal nature ; yonder a mother heart-broken for her profligate husband or her reckless son ; there a student beset with sceptical doubts ; yonder a merchant haunted by the spectre of bankruptcy. Oh, what an art it is to arrest the attention of them all, and pour into their souls the living water, of which he that drinks shall never thirst again ! What a prayerful habit would the preacher need to have while brooding over his sermon, as well as on the eve of its delivery ! What power is needed to accompany every sentence, that it may be truly an engine for opening men's eyes, and for turning them from darkness to light, and from the power of Satan unto God !

CHAPTER XIII.

THE subject of public elocution, or, more properly, the right management of voice, gesture, and look in preaching, may seem to some a sorry and trifling one to be introduced in a course of theological instruction ; but a very slight consideration of some of the bearings of the subject will be enough to dissipate such an impression. The principle laid down by our Lord in his memorable command to the disciples, after the miracle of the loaves and fishes, to gather up the fragments that remained, *that nothing might be lost*, brings within the range of duty many things that might otherwise be ranked with trifles. A Christian conscience thoroughly disciplined will be careful to gather up every fragment of influence, seeing that the object is not to supply the body with the bread that perisheth, but immortal souls with the bread of life. Can it be maintained that no fragments of influence are ever lost in respect of inefficient management of the voice, the gesture, and the countenance in the pulpit ? It is said that the poet Thomson was once reading to a friend a part of " The Seasons " in his usual slovenly way, when his friend snatched the manuscript from his hands, declaring that he could not bear to hear good poetry so shamefully murdered. Was no such murder ever committed in the pulpit ? Was no admirable discourse, faultless in conception and composition, ever presented to a congregation in the condition of Hector's body after it had been dragged round the walls of Troy ? Is there no ground for one of the questions asked by Bishop Berkeley in his " Querist," " Whether half the learning and study of these kingdoms is not useless for want of a proper delivery and pronunciation being taught in our schools and colleges ? " It may be doubted whether the evil is ascribed wholly to the right cause, or whether teaching a proper delivery and elocution in our schools and colleges would alto-

gether remedy it ; but that there is a vast amount of remediable
inefficiency in the pulpit, through defective or vicious delivery,
is a fact that cannot be questioned. It may be true that
manner is but of secondary importance ; but it is equally true
that it is of some importance, nay, as the world goes, of great
importance. What Demosthenes said of action, or rather of
delivery, has passed into a household word—that it was the
first, and the second, and the third essential of true oratory.
We may not be disposed to estimate it so high ; but if any one
should talk of manner as a thing of no consequence, we would
ask him, Is there such absolute power in good and well-com-
posed thoughts, that in expressing them you can afford to
dispense with the aid of a suitable manner or an impressive
delivery ? Certainly it is not so in other departments. An
anecdote is greatly more impressive, in common conversation,
when it is well told ; the difference is marvellous when a story
comes haltingly and helplessly from a stammering tongue, and
fluently and heartily from one who has the *knack* of telling it.
Is there no real loss when solemn thoughts are expressed in a
sharp, shrill key ? or when matters pertaining to everyday life
are handled in the most solemn, sepulchral tones ? Is monotony no clog to delivery, no hindrance to impression ? Is it
not sometimes distressing to observe how little men appreciate
a substantial preacher whose manner is heavy, compared with
a superficial one whose manner is attractive and impressive ?
Are not men who shine at college for their intellectual gifts
like stars of the first magnitude, sometimes outstripped by
those of far inferior intellect but possessing a more popular
manner ? You say it is the fault of the stupid public. And
yet we ought not to be too hard on the public for its want
of appreciation. It is more appreciative in its own fashion
than is often thought. At least it is not slow to appreciate
anything like life in a preacher ; and it is not for the sake
of profound intellect, but for the sake of life, that our Lord
has constituted the ministry the chief means of perpetuating
his Church.

It is never to be forgotten that the ministry has been instituted because it is a *living* agency, and because the functions
which it has to discharge demand, above everything else, the
qualities of life. Had it not been for this, it would have been
easy to devise a better provision for the edification of the body
of Christ and the other purposes of the Church. For example,
without any ministry, there might have been a larger Bible, in

which every man might have found directly all that was necessary for his spiritual instruction. Or men might have been
appointed to collect the best theological treatises and the most
able discourses, and read these to the people. The few great
preachers of each successive age might thus have been set free
to labour among the heathen, extending the limits of the Christian Church. Handfuls of population in remote parts of the
country might have been provided for without the expensive
machinery of a settled ministry. Why, then, has the Head of
the Church preferred the method of the standing ministry?
Partly, doubtless, that provision may be made for adapting the
form in which the truth is presented to the ever-changing
necessities of times and seasons; but partly, also, that when
presented to men, the truth may have all the advantage derived
from the living heart and living voice, the living eye and the
living manner, of the person who communicates it. He who
preaches in a slovenly way not merely damages his own reputation and fails in his duty to his congregation, but he compro-
mises the wisdom of Christ in the institution of the ministry,
and especially of the ordinance of preaching; he makes his
Master appear to have acted foolishly. It is not merely the
intellect that should preach, but every organ and faculty of
the preacher. The voice, the face, the eye, the body, the
hands, must all (if possible) be pressed into the service. As
Luther said, there must be the "vividus vultus, vividi oculi,
vividæ manus, denique omnia vivida." The pulpit would
then vindicate itself, and stand no risk of losing its place
and its power amid the many rising intellectual instruments of
the age.

Yet let no one fancy for a moment that this state of things
can be brought about by a complicated array of artificial rules
for the management of the voice, the waving of the arms, the
twirling of the fingers, or the rolling of the eye. Though it
was said truly of Cicero that there was eloquence even in the
tips of his fingers, and of Garrick that by merely moving his
elbow he could produce an effect that no words could achieve,
it is not to be recommended to young preachers to move their
fingers like Cicero or their elbows like Garrick. Artificial rules
of this sort are the very bane of the pulpit and the ruin of
young preachers. They produce an affectation and a self-consciousness which, instead of a help, are a great hindrance to
efficiency. People justly lift up their voices against *acting* in
the pulpit—against everything that implies that the sermon,

and particularly the prayers, are *got-up* performances, and not the genuine utterances of the mind and soul.*

The simple general rule which we are concerned to press in reference to manner in the pulpit is—*be natural*. Feel what you say and say what you feel, and in saying it say it as you feel it, and let the feeling mould your voice, your gesture, and your countenance in the natural way. Simple though this advice is, it is not very easy. To some persons the most difficult thing in the world is to be natural. The model of a perfectly natural manner is to be found—some would say rather low down—in a little child. Who has not observed the perfect grace, freedom, naturalness, of a little child's whole manner? Its tones of voice are exactly adapted to the nature of its remarks; its eye and

---

* Goethe shows the difference between genuine production and artificial cooking :—

" *Wagner.*—I've often heard them boast, a preacher
Might profit with a player for his teacher.
Faust.—Yes, when the preacher is a player, granted
(As often happens in our modern ways).
Wagner.—Ah! when one with such love of study's haunted,
And scarcely sees the world on holidays,
And takes a spy-glass, as it were, to read it,
How can one by persuasion hope to lead it?
Faust.—What you don't feel, you'll never catch by hunting;
It must gush out spontaneous from the soul,
And, with a fresh delight enchanting
The hearts of all that hear control,
Sit there for ever! Thaw your glue-pot—
Blow up your ash-heap to a flame and brew,
With a dull fire, in your stew-pot
Of other men's leavings a ragout!
Children and apes will gaze delighted
If their critiques can pleasure impart,
But never a heart will be ignited
Comes not the spark from the speaker's heart.
Wagner.—Delivery makes the orator's success,
Tho' I'm still far behindhand, I confess.
Faust.—Seek honest gains, without pretence!
Be not a cymbal-tinkling fool!
Sound understanding and good sense
Speak out with little art or rule:
And when you've something earnest to utter,
Why hunt for words in such a flutter?
Yes, your discourses that are so refined,
In which humanity's poor shreds you frizzle,
Are unrefreshing as the mist and wind
That thro' the withered leaves of autumn whistle."
Faust (Brooke's Translation).

face are a perfect mirror of its heart; the movement of its
arms, the gesture of its whole body, is free and unrestrained.
If one would attain a good manner in the pulpit, one must in
a sense become a little child. If reasons be sought for the
faultlessness of a child's manner, they are to be found in its
guilelessness and reality, the transparency of its whole nature,
in its freedom from acquired habits, in the elasticity and vigour
of its muscular system, and, last not least, its want of self-
consciousness. If, on the other hand, you ask why so many
grown persons have an unnatural manner, the answer will
consist in reversing the conditions just enumerated. It is from
want of reality and guilelessness, from a desire to appear in
some way other than they are, from indolent habits, muscular
stiffness (arising from want of physical exercise), and, last not
least, an oppressive self-consciousness. Against all such things
you must resolutely contend.

Although no confidence is to be placed in artificial rules of
manner, yet, in order to give nature fair play, it becomes necessary to give some directions, chiefly for avoiding or correcting
faults unconsciously contracted. The great object is to give
free scope to nature, but for this purpose we must remove the
bandages and fetters that habit has thrown around her.

To three things in particular it is necessary to attend—
the voice, the gesture of the body, and the expression of the
face.

1. *The Voice.*—The rule which requires us to be natural is
highly necessary in dealing with the voice, but not in the sense
of forbidding any improvement or expansion of its original
capacity. On the contrary, the cultivation and mastery of the
voice is one of the most essential things to a good delivery.
" The voice," says Adolphe Monod, " ought to be exercised frequently and with care. Strive to render your voice at once
clear, strong, sonorous, and flexible ; nothing but practice will
accomplish this. Take pains to become master of your voice.
Whoever succeeds in this will discover many resources even in
a very poor voice, and will achieve wonders with little fatigue.
But the greater part of preachers are slaves to their voice ; it
controls them instead of them controlling it. The voice possesses wonderful capabilities, but it is a rebellious instrument.
We ought not to believe that the daily exercises which are
necessary for controlling it and making it flexible do harm to
the chest. If they are taken in moderation, they will rather
strengthen it ; hence some skilful physicians prescribe singing

and reading aloud for delicate persons. The time most favourable for these exercises is an hour or two after a meal; the stomach ought to be neither too full nor too empty." *

Of all men engaged in public speaking none needs to pay more attention to the culture of the voice than the Scottish minister. If it be true generally " that the Anglo-Saxon race are less gifted vocally, have the vocal apparatus naturally in less perfection and artificially in worse order, than any other variety of Indo-Europeans," † the remark, we fear, must be held to have a special application to Scotchmen. " As a rule," Mr. Hullah observes, " the English voice, if not always of inferior quality, is always almost in intensity or capacity inferior to (for instance) the Italian, the German, or the Welsh. No people give expression to their thoughts, *i.e. utter* (not choose) their words, so imperfectly and with such an absence of charm as our countrymen. To the foreign and unaccustomed ear the English language sounds, as to the foreign eye the Welsh language looks, made up of consonants, and these hardly distinguishable from one another." North of the Border we cannot be accused of so thoroughly neglecting our vowels, but we are apt to sound them as if it were a sin to make them liquid and musical; and what we do utter is often in a husky or drawling tone. Compared with the Englishman's the Scotchman's voice naturally has less of metallic ring, compared with the Irishman's less of musical fluency, and compared with the American's less of downright vehement emphasis. A theory has been hazarded that the muscles of the lower jaw are more feeble in the Scotchman than in the other sections of the family. If it be so, it must be because they are less exercised—he takes his speaking more easily. When the ventriloquist or the player wishes to speak as a typical Scotchman, it is with husky voice and muttered tones, a mouth that hardly opens and a jaw that scarcely moves.

In a church which makes no use of a liturgy, the whole business of edification depends on the voice of the officiating minister. If he be not distinctly heard, the whole service is a failure. In liturgical churches imperfect hearing is aided greatly by the use of the prayer-book. In other churches there is no such aid. Moreover, with the exception of the time taken up in singing, the voice of the minister is the only sound that is

---

* " Eloquence Sacrée." Discours par Adolphe Monod. (*Revue Théologique*, 1841, pp. 278-79.)

† " The Speaking Voice." By John Hullah, p. 1.

heard from first to last. It would really need to be a pleasant one. One of the secret but most effectual causes of weariness in church is to be found in the roughness, harshness, or monotony that sometimes characterizes the preacher's voice. An hour and a half is a long time for a child to listen to a sound resembling the barking of a dog, the croaking of a raven, the cooing of a wood-pigeon, or the rasping of a corn-crake.* On the other hand, a voice of good quality and compass is an element of enjoyment, and obviates the rise of a craving for artificial embellishments of worship. And still further, on another ground, viz. the preacher's own health and comfort, the cultivation and expansion of the vocal organs is of high importance. The undue straining of these organs is apt to produce what is popularly known as the *morbus clericus*, or minister's throat, a disorder which usually requires for its cure a long suspension of labour, and entails much anxiety, the loss of, perhaps, a year of the best part of ministerial life, and no small inconvenience and expense. Even where no disease is gendered, the fight in the pulpit with a feeble voice produces a discomfort resembling that which attends the fight of a traveller with a blustering wind. It produces, too, a self-consciousness, a painful tendency to think about himself, when his mind should be filled with his subject. On the other hand, where the voice is easy and efficient, and readily obeys all the movements of the preacher's heart and mind, his own enjoyment in the exercise is so much the greater, and so also, *ceteris paribus*, is the efficiency of his ministrations.

Some of the false modes of speaking into which preachers have been apt to fall arise from overstraining, while others arise from nervousness, or from an affectation to appear different from what they are. The falsetto tone, the high key in which some preachers speak, is probably due to overstraining, the habit being formed of confining themselves to the one note which penetrates furthest, and is most distinctly heard. The oratorical roll which others affect is in some cases the result of the idea that it is dignified and impressive, and in other cases it arises from nervousness and timidity; it is a sort of protec-

---

* Even a superior voice is apt to become wearisome when unrelieved for a long time. Revival preachers resort to the device of singing a hymn, as a solo, in the middle of the sermon. I have observed that even one of our finest lady readers of Shakespeare, in reading *Hamlet*, greatly relieved and enlivened the reading by *singing* the little lyrical pieces that occur here and there.

tion to a timid man. It enables him to keep at a certain distance from the people, though this, of course, just diminishes his efficiency. Another false tone, a sort of persuasive whine, arises from an overstraining after simplicity and affectionateness, and sometimes it is the result of imitation. In many cases all these unnatural modes of speaking are the effect of unreality, the words not coming from the heart, or at least not coming from a heart exercised at the time in accordance with the words. Undoubtedly, this unreality is one of the greatest enemies of efficiency in the pulpit; nor could any motto be suggested more thoroughly useful and appropriate to guide the young preacher than the Apostle's words, " *We believe, therefore have we spoken.*"

For remedying these and similar evils, much heed should be taken to the starting words of a discourse. In preparing the sermon, as the preacher is settling what the first words of it ought to be, it may be useful for him to consider whether they are thoroughly real, whether he will be able to speak these words to the people, and not merely to deliver them before them. Will he be able to *enter their minds* with them? will they establish a real communication between his mind and theirs? He must begin as much as possible on the ordinary key of his voice—the bell-note, as it is sometimes called—rising and falling from it as the occasion may require. By this means his voice is less likely to become unmanageable; he will be able to preserve its natural inflections, to the great saving of his own strength and the great advantage of his hearers. While thus striving to be real and natural, and to get as near to his audience as possible, he will be kept from unsuitable familiarity of tone or manner by remembering that he is the ambassador of the Lord Jesus Christ, and that he is speaking of the most important things that can engage the attention of immortal men.

In the details included in the due management of the voice, there is none of more importance than *distinctness of articulation.* Very many young preachers err in fancying that loudness is the quality most necessary in order to their being heard, whereas loudness is far inferior to distinctness. In order to distinctness, the habit of running many words together must be avoided, and the endeavour made to give to every syllable, and as far as possible to every letter, its own proper sound. Of course, the habit of distinct articulation may be carried the length of a poor pedantry, and there may be such a conspicuous effort after this as to defeat its own end, by drawing attention not to what the speaker is saying but to the way in which he is saying it. But here we may again listen to the practical counsels of the late Adolphe Monod, whose eminence both as a preacher and as a man of the highest spirituality of character gives him a special claim to our attention.

"You must learn," he says, "to give to each vowel the sound which belongs to it, and to make for each consonant the appropriate movement. This latter point is the more important of the two. If the purity of the vowel sounds contributes much to the beauty of speaking, it is mainly the articulation of the consonants that gives it distinctness, vigour, and expression. One who articulates distinctly can be heard a long way off without shouting, and even without sounding the vowels much ; and this is the method to which actors have recourse on the stage when representing the undertones of persons dying ; they lay stress on the consonants and suppress the vowel sounds. But he who articulates indistinctly will never be heard at a distance, and in making his vowels emphatic, he will only add to the confusion." We have here the explanation of what is often regarded as a mystery—preachers with powerful voices being less distinctly heard in large buildings than men with feebler pipe, but more deliberate articulation. The only thing that it seems necessary to add to Mr. Monod's instructions on this point is, that special respect ought to be paid to the last letter of every word, on the principle that if you do justice to it, you are likely to do justice to all that go before it. But no one should begin to practise such rules as these in the pulpit. They should be mastered in youth, in the course of those practisings and rehearsings which ought to precede pulpit efforts, so that by the time the pulpit is reached they may have become a second nature, neither giving trouble to the preacher nor diverting the attention of the hearer.

Pronunciation is another matter which claims some attention. Though proverbially uncertain, and incapable of being reduced to definite rules, it demands considerable care, for uncouth pronunciation hurts one's influence greatly with educated people, and one is apt to fall unconsciously into many a barbarism. The elocution class serves to correct errors and to give a purer accent ; but intercourse with correct speakers is by far the best education in the art of pronunciation.

Another matter to be attended to in speaking is respiration. When the lungs are well filled at the beginning of each sentence, the words come out both more easily and more distinctly, being floated out as it were on a current of air, instead of squeezed out by sheer muscular force. In such a case, too, public speaking is far less fatiguing. All that is necessary is to get into a habit of inflating the lungs during the momentary pauses in speaking. It is a simple rule, but one that carries very large results. As Monod points out, it corrects an error as serious as it is common, of letting the voice droop at the end of a sentence. " This is the abuse of a rule which nature indicates. It is natural to let the voice fall quickly the moment of finishing a clause, at least in most cases ; for there are some thoughts that require the voice to be raised at the end. But some speakers make the fall too great, and there are often three or four words at the close which are heard with difficulty, or not heard at all. As a general rule, the voice must be kept up to the end of the sentence, except to make the slight fall that denotes the completion of the sense. But for this, timely respiration is requisite ; it is the exhaustion of the lungs that makes the voice droop ; when there is no breath in the lungs there can be no sound from the lips."

2. *Gesture or Action of the Body.*—On this, little more can be said than that we should try to avoid or correct bad habits, and to give nature fair play. Let a man's bodily parts be free to follow the impulse of his heart, it is not likely that he will make the offer of the gospel, as Dr. James Hamilton said he had known preachers do, with clenched fists; that he will bend over the pulpit in depicting the horrors of perdition, or gaze up to the ceiling while remonstrating with the erring and the careless.

Two causes, however, must be mentioned which tend to interfere with the free movements of the body in correspondence with the emotions of the soul. One is *muscular stiffness*, arising from want of exercise, from the sedentary habits that are common in the case of students and preachers, and from their not taking much part in those games and sports which, accompanied though they often are with various evils and drawbacks, do certainly give ease, strength, and development to the bodily frame. The other cause of inefficient action is *timidity*. A nervous man is afraid to suit the action to the word—to raise his arm or move his body, thinking it better not to try it at all, than run the risk of doing it badly. But in any case, temperament has much to do with action. A man of very still temperament will find it much more difficult to use action than one to whom nature has given great vivacity. To a French preacher action is as natural and as indispensable as to many a Scotchman it is difficult, if not impossible. Yet when the Scotchman listens to the Frenchman, and observes how much help he derives in keeping hold of his audience from the quick movements of his body, the ease and fearlessness with which he can throw it into any suitable attitude, the wide compass of his voice, and the elasticity of his countenance, he cannot but feel that it is a great disadvantage for him to be unable to wield this instrument of impression. Where discourses are read from the pulpit, the amount of action, in all ordinary cases, must be but small. There can be but few Chalmerses, who, though reading every word, accompany the discourse with an over-whelming vehemence. In general, the best counsel as to manner for young preachers in this country would seem to be, to attempt but little at the beginning, but, as they gather experience and confidence, try to let their soul out more and more through the various bodily organs ; looking well to this, that it is the soul that works through the body, and not the body that merely apes the working of the soul.

3. *Expression of the Face.*—That the face may become a very powerful helper to the preacher is evident from the fact that in most cases its expression is so thoroughly under the influence of the soul. Of ·course, there are great differences here, from the proverbially impassive and unchanging countenance of a Disraeli, which defies the most skilful physiognomist to find in its features the slightest clue to his thoughts or feelings, to those open and transparent faces in which the soul is seen in all its varied moods of joy or sorrow, hope and fear, disgust and delight. It is not to be expected that the defect of nature in this respect can altogether be supplied. We know that some natures are demonstrative, and some are not. The demonstrative are generally the more popular, but not always the most trustworthy. But there is no merit in being undemonstrative. In the pulpit, on the contrary, it is a positive defect. Why should a preacher suppress the emotion which is working in his heart, and which his words express ? Why should he be ashamed to speak by his countenance the very thing that he is uttering by his tongue ? Is it more likely that he will be believed when one of the organs of expression is silent ? A preacher ought to feel that he is bound to preach with his face as well as with his voice. And the people expect it. Why do they always prefer a seat where they can have a full view of the preacher ? Because they know that if

M

he be what he ought to be, it will be an advantage to them to see his face as well as to hear his voice. They at least know that nature has adapted the eye and the other features for preaching purposes. Sometimes those who hear but indifferently are able to gather a good deal from watching the speaker's face. There is something quite remarkable in the way in which some of the features express the soul. The eye, for example. What a var ety of emotions the eye can appropriately represent! It sparkles with intelligence, flashes with indignation, melts with grief, trembles with pity, languishes with love, twinkles with humour, starts with amazement, or shrinks with horror, according to the impulse given to it by the soul within. A dog knows from his master's eye whether he is about to be caressed or kicked. Gamblers are said to be able to judge of the hand of their opponents from their eye and countenance. Wild animals, like the lion, are said to quail before the steady gaze of a fearless man. And God himself uses the eye as the symbol of his influence : " I will guide thee with mine eye." Why should such an organ not be pressed into the service of the pulpit ? Or why should it be thought that God's effectual power goes solely with the voice, and not with any other organ ?

It is to be remarked that to those who are not overpowered by the aspect of a great public assembly, there is something in its very appearance, and in its eager waiting on the ministrations of the preacher, that greatly helps impression. Audiences like those gathered in St. Paul's or in Westminster Abbey have a wonderfully stimulating power. The whole energies work more vigorously and more fearlessly : a sympathy is created between the preacher and the audience that imparts a power and a pleasure of a kingly order.

This subject has at least one great practical issue : we must feel deeply and truly, if our voice, our face, and our manner are to be right. The heart must be the prime regulator of all. Emotion must be gendered there, and then flow out through tongue, eyes, arms, face, and everything. Once more let us hear Adolphe Monod. " The tones of the soul are the tones of nature. It is these tones that tend to reproduce themselves. The hearer must recognise himself—must feel that the tones are genuine. For us it is requisite that we speak, not declaim. I have said before, Elevate, ennoble the tone of conversation and of common life ; but in raising it, do not abandon it. An able painter does not slavishly copy all the features of his model; he idealises them, he does not commit them to the

canvas without having subjected them to a kind of transfigura-
tion under his brain ; but by idealising, he retains so much of
them that they may be readily recognised, and it is in this way
that a portrait is a perfect likeness and often more beautiful than
nature. The process is similar in a good delivery. The tones
of ordinary life are improved, and yet they are easily to be
recognised because the essential parts of them are carefully
preserved. But to declaim, to assume a new tone because
you have entered a pulpit, to speak, in short, as people never
speak, is a great fault, and, what is very singular, a very
common one, and hard to conquer, and never, perhaps, to be
altogether eradicated. It is because it is easier to keep the
tone sustained and always equal than to follow step by step the
thought and the feeling in their endless changes, and because
one is never without some hearers of bad taste, who are im-
posed upon by a pompous utterance.

"Nevertheless, gentlemen, if you consider merely the human
effect of your preaching, you will find that the man who
speaks in the pulpit will in the end carry the day over the
man who declaims. Even those hearers who are dazzled by
the cadences of fine periods and the tricks of the voice yet
weary in the end, and prefer to the noisy preacher one whose
tone alone constrains them to feel that he thinks all that he
says. And what shall I say of the difference of real results in
the case of the two preachers ? How much more surely will
the latter find the way to the heart and conscience ! How his
moments of earnestness will be relieved by his calm tone and
simple ordinary delivery ! How much more will he be what
he ought to be, before God and before man, being himself, and
not violating truth in order to proclaim truth ! Yes, gentlemen, if you wish to reach a worthy, Christian, impressive style
of preaching, speak always with simplicity. Utter things as
you feel. Put no more warmth in your utterance than there is
in your heart. This honesty of expression (if I may so call it),
far from making your discourse cold, will constrain you to
throw into it a warmth more real, more profound, than you will
reach by any other way. It will react on your composition
and even on your soul in a wholesome way. For in showing
things as they are, it will expose your faults, and urge you to
correct them.

"I have spoken of the pulpit. If this were the place to
speak of the stage, there would be many things to be said to
the point. Great actors never declaim, they speak. Talma,

whom I have named so often, began, like others, with declaiming. An interesting circumstance made him feel the necessity of adopting a new manner, more in conformity with nature; and from that day he became in his profession a new man, and produced a prodigious impression. Those who have heard him will tell you that the extreme simplicity of his play astounded them, and that they were tempted to think of him as an ordinary man, who had no advantage over others except his magnificent voice; but ere long the natural subdued them, and the vivid impressions made on them compelled them to see that it was from its simplicity that his manner derived both its force and its originality."*

* "We were rhetoricians," said Talma, "not men. What fine academic discourses upon the theatre! how few simple words! But one evening, chance led me to a saloon where I was in company with the chiefs of the Girondists; their sombre, uneasy appearance arrested my attention. There were there, in visible representation, interests both great and powerful. They were far too sincere to be blinded by egotism—in that I found a plain proof of the dangers of the country. They proceeded to discuss and to touch questions of burning interest. It was very fine. I fancied myself present at one of the secret deliberations of the Roman Senate. 'One ought to speak in that manner,' I said to myself. 'A country—be it France or Rome—expresses itself in the same tone, the same language; if these men are not declaiming now, there could have been no declamation in the olden time; that is plain.' I became more attentive. My impressions, though produced by a conversation free from any excitement, became profound. 'A calm appearance in men deeply moved stirs up the soul,' I remarked; 'eloquence may then produce its effect without the body being distorted by disorderly movements!' I perceived that the speech, though produced without effort and excitement, made the effect more decided, and the countenance more expressive. All the deputies that happened to be present appeared to me more powerful by their simplicity than on the tribune, where, being in public, they thought it necessary to deliver harangues after the manner of actors, such actors as we were then, that is, declaimers full of bombastic nonsense. From that hour I got a new light, and the regeneration of my art flashed upon me."

CHAPTER XIV.

DEVOTIONAL SERVICES.

ALTHOUGH it is no part of our business in this place to
discuss the question of liturgies or free prayer, it may be
useful to state the substance of the leading arguments *pro* and
con., to help us to obtain a full view of the subject, and have
under our eye all that is to be aimed at on the one hand, and
avoided on the other, in our devotional services. All who
consider the question candidly will admit that on both sides
of the question there are not a few arguments of considerable
weight.

On the side of liturgies it may be urged that the Psalms are
essentially a liturgy ; that it is a great advantage for worshippers to know beforehand what prayers are to be offered,
that they may be able to join in them intelligently and heartily;
that a liturgy affords facilities unknown to free prayer for combining the whole congregation in the service, and drawing out
their responses to the petitions ; that the fact of their offering
the same great petitions which have risen from the Church in
all past ages, and are at the time rising from their brethren
throughout the whole world, stirs the heart and stimulates
devotion ; that by the use of a liturgy it is comparatively easy
for small companies to unite in public worship, even where no
ordained minister is present ; that congregations in general are
not left in absolute dependence for devotional help on the
officiating minister, who may be sadly deficient both in the gifts
and grace of prayer; and that liturgies admit of a conciseness
in the substance, and a beauty and finish in the language of
prayer, fitted to impress the worshipper and promote reverential
feeling.

On the other hand, on behalf of free prayer it may be urged
that it diminishes the risk of that cold, lifeless formality which
the continual use of the same form of words is apt to produce ;

that more encouragement is given to seek the guidance of the
Holy Spirit, who alone can enable us to offer acceptable prayer;
that by these means the gift and the grace of prayer may be
greatly developed ; that graceless and prayerless men are less
tempted to enter the ministry ; that abundant and very precious
opportunities are afforded for adapting the prayer either to the
special state and wants of the congregation, or to events in providence occurring *ex tempore;* that though the worshippers may
not know beforehand the precise particulars of the prayers to be
offered in public, they are generally well aware what their
purport will be, especially if the Spirit of grace and supplication
is poured out ; and that if the congregation will but give attention, they will be at no loss for opportunities of making responses
in their hearts—the only true responses—to the petitions that
are offered.

Into the controversy on this subject, we say, we do not mean
to enter ; partly because we do not see any good reason for
pitting the one method so exclusively against the other as is
done in controversy, or for refusing to entertain the question of
a combination of both.   It is an advantage we gain in quiet
times, when the catholic rather than the controversial spirit is
in the ascendant, that such questions can be studied calmly,
and without that controversial bitterness and vehemence which
goes so often to widen and perpetuate differences.   But the
question more immediately before us at present is, in what
manner we may best conduct the public devotions of our congregations according to the method in use among us.   The fact
that in neighbouring churches liturgies are much used, and are
often greatly prized by the devout for their special advantages,
may serve to illustrate our responsibility in this department of
service, and the duty thence arising to qualify ourselves for it
in the best possible manner.

It is undoubtedly a grave charge, for which there is but too
much occasion, that in our churches the devotional part of the
service is often conducted with little care and preparation.   It
may happen that if a preacher has fluency enough in the language of prayer to carry him on for the usual time without
difficulty, he does not think what he is to pray for, until he
rises with the congregation to begin the exercise.   The prayer
which he offers may have many faults, or it may have few ; it
may possibly be an excellent prayer ; but is it conscientious, is
it respectful to God, is it fair to the congregation, for the man
who is to be their mouthpiece at the throne of grace to rush

into so solemn and momentous a service with hardly a thought
of it beforehand ? He may do it well enough, remarkably well
in the circumstances, but can it be that he will do it in *the
best possible manner?* And is this a service that a conscientious
servant of God should be content to do except in the best
possible way ? Is it likely that he will be able to represent the
wants and feelings of the congregation in the most correct and
comprehensive manner? Will the selection of topics be the
very best ? Will nothing be left out that ought to be included ?
Will his soul not be somewhat slow of kindling into fervour,
beginning perhaps to glow only when it is time to stop ? Will
he be able to combine fervour of spirit and absorption of soul in
the exercise, with an orderly regard to all that his prayer is to
embrace ? Will the language be of that transparent, direct,
simple, yet beautiful order, of which the psalms and all the
prayers and anthems of Scripture are so remarkable examples?
Will the prayer be free from repetitions, clumsinesses, circumlocutions, and other incumbrances, which Bible prayers never
contain ? Who can say that it will ? Or who can say that it
is right to trust all to the Spirit helping our infirmities at the
moment, if we neglect what we might do beforehand towards
the more thorough performance of the duty ?

It is often thrown out as a reproach against our services,
that the preaching is everything and the devotional exercises
little or nothing. Our people do not hesitate to say that they
go to church to hear their minister, subordinating to this the
thought of worshipping God. When they have listened to a
discourse which has pleased them, they are said to be more in
the spirit of glorifying their pastor than exalting their God and
Saviour. To a certain extent there is truth in this charge, but
not so much as is often alleged. We *do* lay great stress on
preaching; it *is* the most prominent part of our service ; but it
is a great error to suppose that right preaching has no direct
bearing upon right worship. Without a great deal of right
preaching there will be little or no right worship. Worship
will become pervaded by the spirit of formalism, or sacramenta-
rianism, or superstition. Our altars will be altars to an unknown
God. Intelligent and evangelical preaching lies at the very
foundation of intelligent and evangelical worship. Men must
know GOD before they can understand what worship he requires.
They must know THEMSELVES to understand the footing on
which they stand to God and their miserable shortcomings in
his sight. They must know the MEDIATOR, in order to get near

to God by the new and living way, and have confidence towards
Him. They must know the HOLY SPIRIT, the only author of
spiritual worship. They must know the SCRIPTURES, where
alone they have the revelation of God, of themselves, of Jesus
Christ, and of the Holy Spirit.

Further, preaching is not merely adapted to communicate the
knowledge, but also to rouse the *feelings* that are connected with
true worship. Very miserable and inefficient preaching truly it
will be if it have no tendency to rouse these feelings. Whatever
tends to convince men of their sins, and humble them before
God—whatever serves to exalt the grace of God in Christ, to
commend His love, to impress the infinitude of His mercy on
the one hand, and the strength of His claims on the other—
whatever goes to deepen our sense of responsibility, to kindle
longings after purity and progress, to intensify our Christian
interest in the welfare of those about us, and of the world at
large—all tends to promote the spirit of worship. How will
such feelings get an outlet but in worship ? The very cherishing
of them, the consciousness of them, is of the essence of worship ;
they are the living soul of which the forms of worship are the
body. We utterly deny, therefore, that there is any essential
contrariety, and we maintain that there is the closest connection,
between preaching of the right sort and worship. At the same
time, we believe that there is commonly too little regard had to
this connection, too little endeavour to make preaching conduce
to the formation and development of a spirit of worship, and to
stir up and exercise the spirit thus developed in the devotional
services.

The truth is, that the whole prevalent theory of public
worship, not in Scotland or the Presbyterian Church alone,
but throughout Christendom generally, is narrowed by tradition
and formality, and stands in need of rekindling and expansion.
The true ideal of united worship is for the most part buried.
People go to church and chapel alike with hardly an attempt
to enter into the spirit of *common* worship—that is, to have
their hearts filled with a Christian and brotherly feeling towards
all their fellow-worshippers, and to try to embrace them along
with themselves in their thanksgivings, confessions, and supplications. The grand scriptural conception of public worship
was presented when the tribes of Israel assembled for their
festivals at Jerusalem. A man's individuality was all but lost
in the great public spirit of these occasions—in the sense of
the vast brotherhood with which he united in his devotional

services, every member of it having a brotherly interest in him, while he had a brotherly interest in every one of them. How vastly would it enlarge our hearts to feel thus with the congregation with whom we worship! Instead of merely bearing in mind our individual sins or mercies, burdens or temptations, to open our hearts wide enough for all our fellow-worshippers, so far as we know or can fancy their circumstances, and to go before God with our arms round them, as it were, and our hearts full of them. How much more acceptable a service should we in this way offer to God! How much more of the sweet influence of his presence should we feel, and what a vindication should we have of our assemblies for public worship, associated as they would be directly, and in the highest sense, with glory to God in the highest, on earth peace, goodwill to men!

The parts of public service which have now to be considered in detail are three—1st. The selection of psalms or hymns for public singing; 2nd. The selection of portions of Scripture for public reading; and, 3rd. The offering up of the common prayer of the congregation.

I. If three or four portions are to be sung during a meeting for public worship, the first is most suitably a direct invocation of God, to be sung as an act of homage, and an expression of longing desire and trust, of humility, faith, and love; the last is selected to follow up the discourse; and the intermediate piece or pieces may either be adapted to the prayers, or to the portions of Scripture that have preceded, or to the discourse that is to follow. The practice, still kept up in Scotland, though not usually elsewhere, of reading out in full the words of the psalm or hymn to be sung, which seems to have come down from times when psalm-books and hymn-books were less common, gives to the officiating minister the opportunity of associating it with the proper expression of feeling, and may help to bring the hearts of the people into tune with what their voices are to sing. In a congregation just assembled, or hardly assembled (as unhappily is too often the case when worship begins), there is a vast amount of dispersed or rather ungathered feeling—minds not concentrated on the act of worship, not at all in accord with the service to be begun. Anything that the officiating minister can do at the beginning to bring the hearts of the people up to the right starting-point is of real value. The devout but unaffected reading of the verses, as expressing emo-

tions which *he* feels, and which *they* ought to feel, is at least a
contribution, though a small one, towards this end ; and at
prayer-meetings, where there is less formality, a few simple
words indicating the character of the feeling expressed, and
calling on the people to endeavour to secure it, may have a
favourable effect.   Certainly there is something particularly
delightful and encouraging when from the very first the singing
denotes a *worshipping* people—when it is a genuine burst of
feeling, gathering together even the hearts that are least united,
and warming in some sense those which are most cold.   And
very much will depend on the example set by the minister
himself.   It is not right for him to give out such words as
these—

> " O thou my soul, bless God the Lord ;
> And all that in me is
> Be stirred up His holy name
> To magnify and bless "—

and then fling off the business on the people as if it were no
concern of his.   And it will be found that the minister who joins
most heartily in the opening psalm is in the best spirit for the
opening prayer.

For all that concerns the most direct and immediate fellowship which the soul can hold with God, the Psalms are unap-
proached and unapproachable ; and it will be a degenerate day
in the spiritual life of our country that sees them pass into dis-
use as materials for praise.   With hardly an exception, the
Christian Church now joins hymns and spiritual songs with
psalms in public worship ; and in order that a pure taste and
a pure theology may be combined in those selected for this
purpose, it is of no small importance, for those especially whose
taste lies in this direction, to cultivate an acquaintance with
lyrical poetry generally, and especially with religious lyrics.
It is a very charming study ; extremely refreshing in hours of
weariness ; touching up the dreary places of life with the
gold of heaven ; giving waters in the wilderness and rivers in
the desert.   Besides, it is by comparison that the peculiar
power and beauty of lyrical poetry comes to be known, and
the songs that are best adapted to foster a truly Christian spirit
are recognised.   A false taste in hymns is unfortunately too
prevalent ; and it rests mainly with Christian ministers and in-
fluential Christian laymen whose taste is cultivated to correct
and improve it.

In these days when *psalmody* rightly occupies so prominent a place among the things that we desire to improve, and when there is such scope for improvement in psalmody, such masses of improvable material in our congregations, it is a great advantage for a minister to be able to take part personally in this matter. For wherever he possesses the great spiritual influence that he ought to have, it will be found that no important movement thrives so well when he stands aloof as when he gives it his personal countenance and aid. And nothing is more valuable than his personal influence in this matter, in order to prevent the more *æsthetic* element from becoming too prominent, and from pushing the more *spiritual* element aside. In an ordinary congregation there are usually some persons interested in the psalmody, whose regard for the musical element preponderates; while there are others whose sympathy is almost exclusively with the spiritual. A certain measure of antagonism is liable to arise between them, and there is often a difficulty in bringing them together. It lies with the minister and officebearers to supply the uniting medium, by trying to get the musical element to become the handmaid of the *spiritual*, and the spiritual to give life, consecration, and elevation to the musical.

There are few matters connected with public worship on which there is more need for enlightening our congregations than the true purpose of music in devotion. If the question were asked of any congregation, Why, or for what spiritual ends, musical sound has been divinely ordained as a vehicle of worship? we should probably obtain in most cases a very bald and imperfect answer. Some would say, Because it affords opportunity to all to join; others, Because it relieves and freshens the minds of the worshippers; and others, Because man's enjoyment of music must be a reflection of God's. All so far true; yet there is a deeper reason which these answers do not touch. Musical sound is capable of being made a more powerful organ both of expression and impression than plain sound. It has a faculty of *expressing* thought and feeling. We see this in the case of all great singers. It is the depth, or the tenderness, or the sublimity, or the wildness, or the sweetness of the feeling they express that is the highest quality of their singing. Of this kind, too, devotional singing ought surely to be. But inasmuch as devotional emotions are so much more intense than most other emotions, the degree of feeling expressed in devotional singing ought to be correspondingly greater. It is for ministers, in superintending singing classes, to urge that the singing should be the expression, the manifest expression, of feeling. Professional teachers of psalmody are too little in the way of attending to this. When the singing does express feeling powerfully, there comes into operation the other power of good music, that of aiding *impression*. The act of singing reacts on the singer; his soul is moved, his whole being penetrated with emotion; a thrill passes through him. Still more is this reaction produced in the case of a great body of devotional singers; a glow passes over them; they appear to stand at the gate of heaven.

We seem, however, to be but beginning to apprehend the full use of which this part of Divine service is capable. The next generation is more likely to enter into this view, if the rising race of ministers will strive to instruct and guide them towards it. Imagination can hardly set bounds to the spiritual gain that would come to congregations if the singing could be brought up to its proper level—if every psalm and hymn were a real cardiphonia, the appropriate utterance of the heart, and if the utterance were so rich and full that the feelings of the worshippers would kindle into holy fervour, and sweep and circle up to heaven like a cloud of incense.

The use of music in worship is so apt to be abused, that care must ever be taken to make it and keep it the handmaid of true spiritual devotion. But where this is done, a considerably larger amount of time may profitably be set apart for singing in our public services. Specially attractive and interesting to the young, the service of lively song breaks the monotony otherwise so apt to be felt, while it is peculiarly suitable for the expression and development of that joyous hearty spirit in which the praises of a public assembly ought to rise to God.

II. For regulating the selecting of portions of Scripture for public reading the principles applicable will naturally occur to every one. Two considerations, of a general nature, may influence the selections, according as the aim is to help the devotional or the didactic part of the service. Where the object is devotional, the Psalms present themselves as the ready and incomparable means of accomplishing the end. And, indeed, it is a general conviction that great and manifold use should be made of the Psalms. It is one of the excellencies of the service of the Church of England that it fulfils this important condition. The method so common among us of singing the Psalms in little bits certainly does not enable us to get the full benefit of that many-stringed harp of David, with its wonderful richness and variety of feeling, sweeping over the whole field of religious experience. Very often, therefore, the Psalms ought to be resorted to for part at least of the public readings.

The art of reading the Scriptures well is one greatly to be coveted. To some the gift is given in a wonderful degree; their reading is like the perfection of music. The voice—easy, flexible, musical, adapting itself so readily to every shade of feeling; the subdued solemn tone, as if in speaking God's words one dared not let one's self fully out; the under-current of earnest feeling that shows itself by no boisterous eruption, but by the subdued spirit which seeks to be silent before God —may well be ranked among the "best gifts" which the Apostle has told us to covet earnestly. For the attainment of such a power there is needed a marvellous combination of mechanical skill and spiritual feeling.

III. We come now to public prayer. In adverting to this part of public worship it were difficult to find a better starting-point than the definition in the Catechism—"Prayer is the offering up of our desires unto God." Let this be kept in mind, in public and in private prayer, and almost without further direction it will guide to a right view of the mode of performing the exercise. Prayer is a transaction *with God*— as really, though not as palpably, as Abraham's intercession for the men of Sodom was a transaction with God, or Jacob's night of wrestling at Peniel. Let the minister feel himself face to face with God, speaking no word, expressing no feeling, harbouring no imagination from which he would recoil if he stood before the throne, and saw the Mighty One in visible form bending his ear. Prayer is the offering up of *the desires of the heart*. It is a presenting to God of certain spiritual offerings—the longings of the heart. Therefore it is neither a devout meditation, nor a sacred disquisition. There are prayers, so called, which in reality are little dissertations, or " preaching-prayers."* But public prayer is no prayer unless it represent and express the desires of the heart.

* The following enumeration of this class of prayers has been given by an American writer :—" (1.) *Doctrinal* prayers, or prayers designed to inculcate certain doctrines which are regarded by the speaker as essential or important. (2.) *Historical* prayers, in which are compressed long narratives for the information of persons not acquainted with the details of the facts referred to. (3.) *Hortatory* prayers, intended to stir up the zeal of the congregation in regard to some particular subject or enterprise which at the moment may be thought interesting. (4.) *Denunciatory*

Then "prayer is the offering up of *our* desires to God;" not of the desires of the minister as an individual—an exercise for which his closet is the appropriate place—but of the minister and flock together, of the minister as the representative of the flock, speaking with them and speaking for them. He is the head and mouthpiece, as it were, of a deputation at the throne of grace, and ought to feel that he is there as a representative, quite as much as the head of any deputation that ever went to present petition or memorial to a prime minister. It is his having this representative character in prayer that makes it so necessary for him to consider beforehand what his prayers are to consist of. Great individuality in public prayer, dwelling on things appropriate to his own condition, but not theirs, is an impertinence and a wrong. Common prayer should have as its substratum what belongs to all God's children; its starting-point, man's guilt, demerit, want, and misery; its attitude, towards the Cross; and its fundamental petitions, for the great evangelical gifts. Thus, even if the sermon should not be on the way of salvation, the prayers by their very structure, though not in formal words, would indicate that way—since the consciously lost sinner, in the person of the minster, would be seen looking up to the Cross, and asking the grace which guides to heaven.

In prayer, as in preaching, a very close bond is formed between the minister and his people when he enters sympathetically into their circumstances, and at the throne of grace shows that he is mindful of the very temptations, wants, difficulties, and perplexities of which they feel the pressure every day. Living as the minister does, and ought to do, out of the world, out of the sphere at all events where the world's most characteristic spirit reigns, it is not easy for him to know the real obstructions to a godly life, without and within, to which

prayers, designed to warn the audience against certain errors or practices, to put down certain sentiments, or to awaken towards them indignant feelings; being appeals to men, not addresses to God. (5.) *Personal* prayers, which spring from a desire to administer a secret rebuke, or to bestow condemnation, some individual being expressly in the mind of the person praying. (6). *Eloquent* prayers, in which there is a display of a brilliant fancy, and of polished and elegant language, compelling the hearer to say, 'What a fine prayer that was!' (7.) *Familiar* prayers, in which there is an evident absence of that sacred awe and reverence which should fill the mind in every approach to God. (8.) *Sectarian* prayers, indicating very clearly an attachment to a particular sect among the multitude of Christian denominations. (9.) *Long* prayers, which weary and exhaust the spirit of devotion."

the mass of people are exposed. That which is peculiar to the spiritual life he may and ought to know better than any; but the action of the ordinary conditions of the outer life upon the inner he must take some trouble to discover. When his prayers show an acquaintance both with the outward and the inward obstructions, and grace is sought suitable to this state of things, the drawing together of hearts is very wonderful. It is a good sign, both of minister and people, when he is much prized for his prayers—when the people feel that his words express all their hearts, and that in his company they are borne up close to the very footstool of the throne.

But if in public prayer the minister sustains this representative character, and is bound to take the godly part of his flock along with him to the throne of grace, the absence of all premeditation or preparation for public prayer must necessarily lead, as Dr. C. J. Brown has remarked, to one or other of two evils : " either he must slide gradually into a form of his own, a repetition of substantially the same things Sabbath after Sabbath (to which would not a good liturgy be preferable ?) ; or else, in trying to avoid this, he must wander up and down, as some ship at sea, without compass or rudder, at the mercy of every wind that blows." It is to avoid both these evils that premeditation is so necessary to the right discharge of this duty.

Three points require special attention in connection with public prayer—1. The topics or substance. 2. The language or style. 3. The tone and utterance.

1. Ever since the days of Origen, who wrote the earliest treatise on prayer (De Oratione), four divisions have usually been specified—adoration, confession, thanksgiving, and supplication. All public prayers must embrace more or less of these several divisions. But obviously no single prayer can include more than a few fragments of each. For a minister to attempt on a single occasion to go round the whole and embrace everything is out of the question. It is one of the points on which premeditation must be exercised—What topics are to be selected for each occasion, and how are they to be distributed so that within a suitable period all may be included ? While a certain character of unity will mark the public prayers of every thoughtful minister, there will at the same time be an ample field for variety. The same great subjects of thanksgiving, confession, and supplication ever occurring ; the details connected with each varying from time to time. In fact, it is one of the points

in which a holy skill requires to be exercised, to combine
brevity, unity, and definiteness. In Foster's remarks on Robert
Hall's Character as a Preacher, he adverts to a failure in this
respect by which the great orator was characterized.* While
the devotional spirit was admirable—"the greatest seriousness
and simplicity, the plainest character of genuine piety, humble
and prostrate before the Almighty"—there was often in the
petitions a vagueness and want of unity, a kind of random combination not to have been looked for in so great a preacher.
"Prayers," says Mr. Foster very justly, "which do not detain
the thoughts on any certain things in particular, take very slight
hold of the auditors."

2. *Language or Style.*—Instinctively, every devout heart will
express itself in prayer in simple language. Figures of speech
in prayer, except they be so simple as to have lost the semblance
of figures, are utterly out of the question. Elaborate rhetorical
periods are simply an abomination. What are described as
"eloquent prayers" must ever be regarded with suspicion. An
eloquent prayer is calculated to raise the question, Was it
designed for the ear of God or for the ear of man? The
reporter of an American newspaper revealed more than he
probably intended when he described "the most eloquent prayer
that was ever addressed to a Boston audience."

While artificial rhetoric is ever to be shunned, a certain neatness and conciseness of style is highly suitable. All uncouth-
ness, flabbiness, clumsiness, is especially disagreeable in prayer,
and no doubt it is the frequent occurrence of such things that
affords ground for objection to extempore public prayer. Attention at the beginning of his course to neatness of expression in
the language of prayer will be of the greatest service to the
young preacher. By and by his ordinary language will assume
somewhat of the point, precision, and finish of a liturgy.

The copious use of Scriptural expressions in prayer is of
essential importance. The remark of Addison has often been
quoted on this subject, although it is not very profound or
exhaustive. "There is a certain coldness," he says, "in the
phrases of European languages compared with the oriental
form of speech. The English tongue has received innumerable
improvements from an infusion of Hebraisms, derived out of the
practical passages in Holy Writ. They warm and animate our
language, give it force and energy, and convey our thoughts in
ardent and intense phrases. There is something in this kind
* "Hall's Works," i. 207.

of diction that often sets the mind in a flame, and makes our hearts burn within us. How cold and dead is a prayer composed in the most elegant form of speech, when it is not heightened by that solemnity of phrase which may be drawn from the sacred writings."

The use of the Lord's Prayer, provided it be not carelessly rhymed over, but uttered devoutly and thoughtfully, is to many devout minds a great comfort. Preachers can hardly understand with what delight some of their people welcome that part of the service where they are led in prayer, not in the words of man, but in the words of the blessed Lord himself. It is not merely that in every petition of the Lord's Prayer there is such infinite depth and fulness, but the language is such a model of clearness, directness, and simplicity. It were well if the Lord's Prayer were taken as a model for all prayer more than it is. The other prayers of Scripture are constructed on the same principle. Those of St. Paul are wonderful examples of brevity and richness, and are usually constructed with a fine musical cadence. It is no wonder if those whose ear is accustomed to such prayers are offended by the loose, rambling, flabby performances they sometimes hear. There is a language suitable for prayer equally removed from the grandiloquence of the rhetorician and from the careless clumsiness of the impromptu orator. David or rather Moses began it, and John, who quotes Moses in the Apocalypse, crowned it. Nothing higher or better ever has been or ever can be achieved.

To train himself to make skilful use of suitable passages of Scripture in prayer is one of the most indispensable exercises of the young preacher. To achieve this power ought to be one of his most earnest endeavours ; for not to be able to throw his petitions into the language of the Holy Spirit is to fail in one of the most important means of edification which a Christian congregation can enjoy.

3. *The Tone and Utterance.*—One rule, well observed, will make all other rules superfluous : let prayer be uttered as in the very presence of God—poured into his ear as from a miserable sinner who deserves his wrath, but to whom for Christ's sake He extends his infinite mercy. In prayer so uttered there will always be an undertone of felt unworthiness, the voice will have a touch of contrition, while a plaintive, fervent tone of entreaty will characterize the prayer throughout. The absence of this tone raises a great objection to many extempore prayers, and no other qualities can make up for it. The prayer of one

N

who does not seem to feel that he is in God's presence, or who, if he does, has none of that subdued air which is so appropriate to sinners standing before God, has a vital want. How can we expect to conduct our people into God's presence if we do not enter it ourselves, or to lead them to stand in awe before Him if our own air is that of self-satisfied indifference ?

The undertone of contrition need not hinder the right expression of that gladness and serene satisfaction which the experience of God's grace is fitted to bring. Our confidence indeed will be all the greater, that we can draw the line so clearly between our deserts and God's grace—can say, " Thou wast angry with us, but thine anger is turned away, and thou comfortest us."

It may be useful, with equal brevity, to advert to some of the most common faults in public prayer.

One of these is excessive length. Nothing is more clearly shown by experience than the impossibility of continuing to join heartily in very long prayers. For people to throw themselves into the current of another man's devotions involves a great mental effort, and in proportion to the greatness of the effort is their liability to fatigue. It is quite certain that attention cannot be given beyond a certain point, and when attention fails devotion ends. Whitefield is said to have remarked to an excellent minister, whose prayer was unreasonably long, " You prayed me into a good frame, and you prayed me out of it." A minister is not, of course, to have regard to the outcry of every worldly-minded person who sighs for short prayers, short sermons, short services, and, as some one proposed to add, short religion in general. But if it be the case that from five to ten minutes is the longest period during which the average capacity of a congregation can join in prayer, let him accommodate himself to their capacity, and if more time for prayer should be deemed necessary, let him rather increase the number of prayers than lengthen out any to an undue degree. It is to be observed that long prayers are not the usual characteristic of a very vital condition of Christianity, but rather of a time when formal services are substituted for true spiritual worship.

Another evil to be avoided is inaccurate quotation. We mean, of course, quotation from Scripture, for hardly any other quotation is endurable in public prayer. How many erroneous quotations, as from Scripture, have become stereotyped, and are reproduced by minister after minister taking them up

thoughtlessly from some one whom he has been in the habit
of hearing, would be almost incredible, if the facts were not
very clear. Dr. Brown has called attention to the extraordinary
physical attitude in which the minister sometimes proposes to
place himself and his people by a blending of no fewer than
four several passages : " We would put our hand on our mouth,
and our mouth in the dust, and cry out, Unclean, unclean!
God be merciful to us sinners." Often we hear it said, "There
is forgiveness with thee that thou mayest be feared, and plen-
teous redemption *that thou mayest be sought unto*"—these last
words being an unwarranted addition. So it is often said,
"Thou art of purer eyes than to behold iniquity, and canst not
look on sin *without abhorrence*," the last two words, which are
meant to strengthen, really serving to dilute and weaken the
sense. God is called " the hearer *and answerer* of prayer ; "
"the dark places of the earth are full of the habitations of
horrid cruelty ; " and where two or three are met together,
God is asked to be " in the midst of them, *to bless them and to
do them good*," as if God could bless them without doing them
good.

Expletives, repetitions, and redundancies are blemishes in
prayer. It is not seemly to be throwing in Oh's and Ah's at
all points ; they have at least an artificial look, and it is far
better that the earnestness of the heart should show itself by
the deep soul-fervour of the tones, than by words which are
certainly an offence to many, and probably an advantage to none.

The Catechism gives another instruction, admirably adapted
to public as well as private prayer, when it exhorts us " to draw
near to God with all holy reverence and confidence, as children
to a father." To *draw near ;* to be intimate, close, fearless, as
is the privilege of children ; yet reverential, as in presence of
the Infinite, before whom the seraphim cover their faces with
their wings. Let our dealings with God be direct and simple,
and such as to invite the co-operation of our people and almost
constrain them to utter their responsive " Amen." Let the
voice be equally removed from the cold tone of indifference and
the sharp notes of excitement; let our tone be neither an
affected whine nor a thundering roar ; but the humble, plaintive
tone of earnest appeal, in which the sense of unworthiness and
our confidence in God's grace blend in a kind of heavenly music.
The strength of prayer is not in the earthquake nor in the
thunder, but in the still small voice. " In quietness and in
confidence shall be your strength."

Nor must we forget that to qualify us for prayer in public, we need much experience of it in secret. The preparation of our own spirit, the exciting of earnest thoughts and feelings there, the appeal, " Awake, O north wind, and come, thou south," are indispensable to the right discharge of this duty. How can one be a leader in anything, if one is not even a doer? How can one lead the devotions of a congregation, if one has no devotion of one's own?

CHAPTER XV.

HITHERTO we have considered the Christian minister mainly as a preacher, a public teacher, addressing his people from the pulpit, or leading their devotions when they are assembled to worship God. It must be remembered, however, that ordinarily the minister is a pastor as well as a preacher. He is called to deal with individual souls, as well as to proclaim to an assembled congregation the message of the gospel. Between these two functions of the ministry there need be no opposition, though sometimes the impression prevails that diligence in the one is incompatible with success in the other. The fact, however, is, that where this has seemed to be the case, it has generally been due to the fact of the minister giving himself too exclusively to that department of work for which he has the greatest aptitude and inclination.

Some have a liking for society ; it is pleasant for them to be with their fellows, conversation is their element, they like to move about among their people ; and owing to this inclination they are led to devote to this branch of duty a disproportionate amount of time, and to leave too little for pulpit preparation. To others, again, owing to difference of temperament, it is difficult and irksome to pay visits ; conversation with uncongenial minds is a toil that oppresses them ; the communication of thought and feeling by that channel is always consciously feeble, if not consciously a failure ; it suits them better to address large numbers of persons ; for that they can summon up and concentrate their powers of thought and feeling ; consequently their temptation is to neglect the duties of the pastorate, and confine themselves to those of the pulpit.

But in point of fact there is no real antagonism between the pastorate and the pulpit, nor does it appear a very impracticable achievement that the one should be made the useful, happy handmaid of the other. The pastoral duty of the minister may easily be made a most valuable auxiliary to his pulpit work, and the pulpit duty, rightly performed, will seek its natural outlet and application in the pastoral. It is only by personal intercourse with his people that the minister can gain a true knowledge of them, their errors, sins, temptations, difficulties, the kind of guidance which they need, and the style of preaching that comes home to them and helps them. It is only by this means, too, that he can thoroughly learn the effect of his preaching—who are awakened, who are perplexed, who are at rest. Often, in pastoral intercourse, he will have texts and topics suggested to him, on which his preaching will have a life-like earnestness and power ; nay, like Paul at Athens, he will sometimes have his spirit stirred within him, and feel God's Word working like a fire in his bosom, which will not endure to be restrained. On the other hand, when the preacher is earnest in his pulpit, when, looking round, he sees unwonted interest expressed in this face or in that, some young person evidently arrested and beginning to look wistfully towards the gate of the kingdom of heaven, or some careworn countenance relaxing under the dawn of Christian hope, it is impossible not to desire to watch the change at a nearer point, and endeavour to be more immediately helpful to those who seem as if they would enter into the kingdom, if only some one would take them by the hand.

The pastoral functions of the Christian minister are not only fully recognised in Scripture, but are placed in a light at once interesting and beautiful. The emblems which shadow it forth are those which are most expressive of a relation of great affection, such as a nurse, a shepherd, a physician, a father. "We were gentle among you, even as a nurse cherisheth her children : so being affectionately desirous of you, we were willing to have imparted unto you, not the Gospel of God only, but also our own souls, because ye were dear unto us" (1 Thess. ii. 7, 8). The model of the faithful and affectionate pastor is presented to us by God in his own person : "I will seek that which was lost, and bring again that which was driven away, and will bind up that which was broken, and will strengthen that which was sick : but I will destroy the fat and the strong ; I will feed them with judgment" (Ezek. xxxiv. 16). In the New Testament the same figure recurs, applied by Christ, the good Shepherd, to denote the relation between Him and his flock : "My sheep hear my voice, and I know them, and they follow mc;" "but a stranger will they not follow, but will flee from him : for they know not the voice of strangers" (John x. 27 and 5). In Paul the Apostle we have the model at once of the great preacher and the affectionate and painstaking pastor. He could remind the Ephesian elders how he had taught them not only "publicly," but "from house to house" (Acts xx. 20) ; and in writing to the Church of Rome he fills a whole chapter with personal messages, showing not only his interest in individuals, but his acquaintance with the spiritual history of each (Rom. xvi.). If we seek in modern times for an instance of a great preacher moulded after the same type, we find it in our own Chalmers, so incomparable in the pulpit, and yet the founder of territorial missions, the reviver, in a great degree, of the parochial organization, and the unwearied searcher out of the lost and fallen.

The practice of pastoral intercourse between a minister and his people has received the strongest commendations from the earliest to the latest times. Ignatius, in his epistle to Polycarp, urges his friend to be the protector and friend of the widows; not to despise male or female slaves ; to speak to the sisters, exhorting them to love the Lord and to be satisfied with their husbands both in flesh and spirit; in like manner to exhort the brothers to love their wives ; and to seek after all *by name.**
Archbishop Leighton in his last retirement remarked, "Had I again to be a parish minister, I must follow sinners to their homes and even to their alehouse." Dr. Doddridge said that his heart did not upbraid him with having kept back anything that might be profitable to his people, but he feared that he had not followed them sufficiently with domestic and personal exhortations. † There are few earnest men who, on a review of their ministry from the close of life, will not in some degree share this feeling. Archbishop Whately begins his lectures to "The Parish Pastor" by strenuously urging the diligent and unwearied performance of this branch of duty.

Even in the lowest point of view, the advantages to a minister of a personal acquaintance with the flock to whom he preaches are remarkably great. It is in every way a benefit to the shepherd to know his sheep, and to call them each by name. A subtle but powerful sympathy is established between them, especially in the case of the young and the less edu-

* "Epist. to Polycarp," ch. iv. v.
† See Bridge's "Christian Ministry," part v.

cated classes. No one can well estimate the benefit which
a young person derives, in a religious point of view, from
personal acquaintance with his minister, if the minister be not
only a good but a friendly man. A young man who has no
religious parents, no religious associates, and no personal acquaintance with a Christian minister, is extremely apt to fall
under the impression that religion is a matter with which
personally he has little or nothing to do. But should a minister
know him, show an interest in him, speak to him seriously but
kindly, and urge on him his personal responsibility in regard to
the gospel, he is far more likely to respond to his appeals.
The subtlest and strongest human bond that draws the feelings
of men is that of sympathy. Now, friendly knowledge of a
person, the habit of speaking to him and inquiring for his
welfare when you meet, or of calling at his house with a friendly
purpose, is a contribution, though not a very large one, towards
the establishment of sympathy. So long as you labour to do
good from the pulpit among those whom you do not know, you
labour under the manifest disadvantage of having little or no
hold, at least no necessary hold, on their sympathies. Get
acquainted with them and interested in them ; a new force
begins to operate on your side.

We are not, therefore, to set down the craving which some
worthy people have for frequent visits from their minister as
wholly unreasonable and without foundation. No doubt there
are cases in which it arises from a low motive, from the love of
attention, from a poor desire to be made much of; but, on the
other hand, it may be the expression of that craving for sympathy and personal interest which makes the relation between
minister and people so much more pleasant and so much more
profitable. If, therefore, in the course of visitation, you can
do no more than get into personal sympathy with your people,
an important end is gained, provided the time you spend
together is not spent in a quite frivolous way. But this is
very far from the only benefit that pastoral visitation may
confer. If it can be made subservient to spiritual acquaintance,
if by means of it, whether directly or indirectly, the pastor can
learn what is passing in the hearts of his people and adapt his
instruction accordingly, its benefits will plainly be of a far
higher kind.

We have no hesitation, therefore, in pressing upon you,
when you are settled as ministers of congregations, and especially if they be small charges in the country, to give its due

place to pastoral visiting. If, in the course of time, you are translated to large towns, or call to minister to large flocks, and are compelled to engage in a large amount of miscellaneous work, your duty in pastoral visitation may not be so pressing. But in other circumstances it is quite necessary. And in order that you may do it effectually and thoroughly, the first requisite is that you do it *systematically*.

There are two kinds of pastoral visits to be kept in view, namely, the regular visitation of the whole families and adherents of a congregation or a territory, and the visitation of the sick and afflicted. For each of these purposes it is desirable to have an allotted time, but especially for the first—the visitation of families. The other cases will in a sense assert their own claims ; but without a fixed time set apart for it, the general visitation, as it may be called, is apt to be neglected. It is surely not too much to devote to this purpose the chief part of at least one day in the week. If so, let it be the same day. It is an advantage to the minister and an advantage to the people when it is known that one particular day is devoted by him to this purpose. To facilitate the work as much as possible, let a plan of visitation be constructed, indicating the order in which the people are to be taken, and the time in which it may be expected that the work will be completed, leaving a margin for possible interruptions. Let the minister be careful to have full lists of the people, containing the names, residences, and employments of all, and the ages of the young. He will find it, too, very desirable to keep a *record* of his visits. If he trust his memory to recall in future years the topics on which he addressed them on former occasions, he will probably find that he has been leaning on a broken reed. Such a record will become a most valuable document as a reminiscence of his work, and will greatly help the pastor in planning his visits after a few years have elapsed, when some fresh difficulties are apt to present themselves.

We are the more earnest in insisting on the systematic prosecution of the work of visitation, because many country charges are small, and in the case of these the necessity of system is less obvious, but not less real, than where the flock is large. In fact, it is one of the greatest snares of a small charge, and one that demands to be guarded against with extraordinary vigilance, that, being small, it seems as if there were no need for system in the working of it. There are certain apparent anomalies in life and habit that must be taken into account in connection with such matters. The philosopher could say that he was never less idle than when at leisure, nor less lonely than when alone. In like manner it may be said of some men, that they never do things so successfully as when they are busy, and that they never do them so ill as when they have little to do. There is something in the mental stimulus, the fillip given to the whole energies by abundant occupation, that causes everything that is undertaken by busy energetic men to be done with vigour, if they are not absolutely crushed by their labours ; and, on the other hand, there is something in the unconcentrated, unknit-up condition of a mind having little to do, that often causes that little to be done ill. Who has not felt in holiday time, when he was visiting a friend in the country, or spending his time in rambles or picnic tours, that it was an effort to write a single letter, whereas in his ordinary working mood he might throw off a dozen letters and do four times as much other work without any irksome feeling ? This indicates the danger men incur of turning lazy, mentally as well as physically, in small charges. System is needed in its own way in the small as well as in the large ; the two talents are to be diligently improved as well as the five ; and the rule of the kingdom is, " He that is faithful in that which is least is faithful also in much " (Luke xvi. 10) ; " Unto every one that hath shall be given, and he shall have abundance : but from him that hath not shall be taken away even that which he hath " (Matt. xxv. 29).

There is another great recommendation of system. It has a wonderful effect in reconciling one to what at first is irksome, and even causing one to do it with pleasure. If the work of visitation be naturally irksome, and no systematic method of prosecuting it be adopted, each time that it is attempted the sense of irksomeness will be renewed. But if a system be adopted, and conscientiously followed, it will be otherwise. The preliminary struggle with inclination will hardly be felt. This is the advantage of making up your mind to anything naturally disagreeable. You have settled that the thing must be, and inclination, as if it were a sentient being, seems to shrink from a contest in which defeat is inevitable ; so, when you work faithfully upon a plan, the fact that it is a settled plan seems to scatter your enemies. And this is not all. " There is no fact," says Dr. Shedd, " in the Christian experience better established than that faithful performance of labour, from conscience, ends in its being performed with relish and pleasure. Conscience is finally wrought into the will in a vital synthesis.

Law in the end becomes an impulse instead of a commandment." *

A few observations may now be offered on the practical following out of pastoral visitation.

First, of the regular visitation of families. How this can be best accomplished in all cases it hardly becomes any one man to attempt to determine.

It is one of the points on which every minister must become wise through his own experience and the teaching of God's Spirit, and on which brethren who are accustomed to speak often one to another will advantageously exchange thoughts and experience when they have been for some time engaged in the work.

If notice has been given of the minister's intention to visit at a certain hour, it is evident that something more than a mere visit of friendship or courtesy will be looked for. The minister, it will be felt, has come for the purpose of promoting the spiritual and eternal welfare of the family, and therefore the sooner he addresses himself to his errand the better. Some ministers are willing to prolong the preliminary conversation, in the hope that they will be able, after a time, to lead off the minds of the family to more serious thoughts, by building on something that comes up casually. And no doubt, if one has skill enough, this is the best method, provided the members of the family are not struck with silence the moment one touches what is serious, but are willing to continue the conversation. For, as Archbishop Whately remarks, the true idea of pastoral intercourse implies that the pastor is " not merely to speak, but to listen, and to encourage his people to open their minds freely to him, and that too, not on their spiritual concerns only, but on any others also on which they naturally and allowably feel much interest, and have a craving for sympathy." † But when once he gets into the current of temporal things, there is a great risk of his being so carried along, that it is only by an abrupt and awkward jerk that he can cross over to the spiritual region ; and in that case whatever he may say or do is apt to be set down as a mere homage to professional propriety, not the spontaneous outcome of a heart charged with its message. To avoid this risk it is often desirable for a minister, after a brief salutation and kindly inquiry after the welfare of the household, to proceed at once, like Abraham's servant at Padan-aram, to tell his errand, to do

* " Pastoral Theology," p. 393.
† " The Parish Pastor," p. 9.

what he has come to do. In speaking to the household he may
find a point of departure by saying why he has come, adverting
to the exceeding solemnity of spiritual things, and to the importance not of a mere general but of a special application of what
is said from the pulpit, so that no one may suffer the appeal to
go past him, or think he does right while he fails personally to
receive the message of God. Something may be said applicable
to the circumstances of the different portions of the family—
the parents, the children, older and younger, the servants when
there are such. Of the children questions may be asked, and
are probably expected to be asked ; but, let this be done in the
kindly manner of a friend, not in the stern tone of a task-master.
Generally, too, it will be well to bear in mind that there
is a tendency on the part of people to think of ministers as
beings awfully solemn, with but little of human sympathy—men
to be dreaded as stern reprovers, instead of respected and loved
as affectionate and sympathetic guides. In pastoral visitation,
therefore, let there be shown a frankness, a cordiality, a humility
of spirit, a winning brotherly-kindness that shall dissipate such
an impression and tend to gain the confidence of all.

All pastors will admit that to draw out the members of a
family into frank conversation on religious subjects is one of the
most difficult and rare achievements. It is so difficult that most
give it up in despair. It is not mere earnestness that succeeds
here. There is needed much tact and knowledge of the human
heart, especially of what on the one hand sends it shrinking
into its shell, and of what on the other draws it out, like a
flower opening to the sun. Among those things which are
most useful in drawing men out, the records of other men's
struggles and experiences have an important place. Suppose
you speak on the duty of the devout daily reading of the
Scriptures, you may get no response. But suppose you speak
of Luther, and his best hours given to reading and prayer, or of
John Knox reading the whole Psalter once every month, and a
daily portion of the Bible besides, you introduce a medium
which makes conversation easier. It is a sort of thread round
which it may crystallize. A memory stored with facts derived
from Christian biography and similar sources is of great value
in promoting pastoral conversation, and making it at once profitable and easy.

It must be owned, at the same time, that there is sometimes
a crass stolidity about the people whom a pastor visits, on
which it is impossible to make an impression. While some

families exert themselves to meet their minister half-way, and make it both easy and pleasant for him to deal with them in his pastoral capacity, others are singularly apathetic and chilling, responding in heartless monosyllables to his efforts to engage them in conversation, as if it were their very object to keep him as far from their hearts as possible. If people generally knew something of the minister's difficulties in pastoral visitation, they would think more how they might practically help to remove them.

It may be remarked here in passing, that the art of conversation, and social intercourse at large, is one to which students have need to give special attention. They are so accustomed to conversation within their own circle, that when thrown into social contact with others they find it difficult to get common ground and suitable materials. The art of social intercourse is one of the most important parts of unconventional education, being the art of getting into contact with minds unlike our own, and forming a bond between them and us that shall dispose them to look more favourably upon our views of spiritual things.

To return to pastoral visitation. Indispensable though we hold this practice to be in small congregations, and desirable, where practicable, in large, it is obviously to be regarded at the same time as a duty inferior to that of the pulpit, and not to be allowed to interfere with its efficiency. Some preachers of great mark and efficiency have deliberately, and from a sense of duty, abstained from undertaking much work of this kind. Among these was President Edwards. His reason for not engaging in it was, not that he did not feel its importance, but that he deemed himself unqualified for it, and considered that his time was spent to greater advantage in his study, to which he usually gave twelve hours a day.* A preacher of a very different type, the late Mr. Jay of Bath, in like manner restricted his pastoral visitation within much narrower limits than was agreeable to his flock. In his autobiography, Mr. Jay, without wholly justifying himself, says that to some extent this omission was voluntary, as he thought that much more was expected of him than was reasonable, and that it was *consequence* rather than *improvement* that was affected by disappointment. He says that he deliberately abstained from following the example of *three* classes of pastoral visitors. " 1. The *smokers*, or smoking ministers, who were furnished with a pretty pipe and

* Dwight's " Life of Edwards."

its usual concomitant at every house of call [thereby setting their people the example of an act of self-indulgence, which is certainly not the spirit that the minister of Christ is called to foster]. 2. The listless, who like to lounge about people's houses ra her than bind themselves down to diligent study. 3. The truly pious, who wished to do good, but were often less useful than they wished or imagined. Many of these have not the oily slang of religious phrases; they are not apt at free and appropriate address or turning all incidents to profitable account; yet they might preach to advantage had they time and leisure for reading and meditation.* Mr. Jay saw likewise that the visits of ministers were not always convenient, and, therefore, not always acceptable. As to set dinner and tea entertainments, his observation was, that it was almost impossible to commence or maintain discourse by which one could either gain good or do good. Social meetings he deemed useful enough for social purposes, for promoting good neighbourhood and social pleasure, but beyond that he had little faith in them.

2. The visitation of the *sick* and *afflicted* is one of the most interesting, one of the most blessed, and one of the most precious of the duties of a minister. It affords rare opportunities for the formation of most affectionate bonds—ties hallowed by the tenderest associations. He who has ever b en attracted to their dwellings by the intelligence of any kind of distress or sorrow; he on whose face they have ever seen the expression of a brother's sympathy and eagerness to help; he to whom they have always felt encouraged to tell of their sorrows and their burdens, knowing that his heart would be open to the doleful tale; he who has led them to the throne of grace on every occasion of distress, and sought for them the oil of joy for mourning and the garment of praise for the spirit of heaviness; he by whose ministrations the deathbed of a dear parent or partner has been cheered, the eye of a stricken son or daughter turned to the Cross, and the chill terror of death has given place to the calm joy and confidence of faith—can never be an object of indifference to those to whom, in the darkest passages of life, he has been the instrument of so much blessing. Let a minister have an affectionate Christian heart, and be ready at all times to show his warm sympathy for those of his flock who are in trouble—such a man will be loved by his people, and will have a degree of influence with them inexpli-

* "Autobiography of Rev. Wm. Jay," p. 154.

cable to those who do not know how the burdened heart appreciates sympathy in dark and cloudy days.

But there is a snare to be guarded against in this very fact. The object of the minister in visiting the sick is not merely to express his sympathy or to show them ordinary kindness. It is to turn the occasion into one of spiritual good. It is to show them how God is dealing with them and to cause them to hear the voice of the rod. It is his duty to remind them of the opportunity of meditation and self-examination which the sickness affords, and to urge them to improve it in the way of considering whether their hearts have ever responded to the call of God, and whether they have been making a business of their sanctification, following peace with all men, and holiness, without which no man shall see the Lord.

Where the sickness is likely to be mortal, and there is no evidence of due preparation, the duty of the minister is solemn and delicate. How to let the sick person know of the bodily danger, and the still greater danger of the soul; how to guide his mind during the few weeks, or it may be only days or hours, of life that remain to him, so that by God's blessing the great change may be wrought; how to get other influences to conspire best with that of the minister himself in order to the securing of this glorious result—are questions of awful solemnity, only to be resolved in the spirit of most earnest prayer. What magnifies the difficulty is the terror in which relatives often stand lest anything be said fitted to agitate the sufferer, and the injunctions to the same effect of some medical advisers, who, in their anxiety for the recovery of the body, do not always think of the eternal welfare of the soul. To attain the utmost faithfulness and yet the utmost tenderness in such a case—to leave nothing unsaid that, by God's blessing, may be of use to the soul, and nothing undone in respect of tenderness and gentleness of tone and manner that may prevent undue agitation or opposition—involves a strain upon our best and holiest energies, under which we could not but sink if we did not fall back on words like these : " My grace is sufficient for thee, for my strength is made perfect in weakness."

And there is still another difficulty. It is the glorious doctrine of our religion that the door of mercy is ever open, and that the finished work of Christ is ever available for the sinner. But there is a way of exhibiting this glorious truth that is objectionable. The atonement of Christ is sometimes presented to the Protestant in much the same way as the crucifix is presented to the Papist. The impression is apt to be produced, either on the dying man or on his friends, that there is in that truth a kind of talismanic virtue ; that it forms a sort of " open sesame " to let one into heaven. One needs to be very careful to let it be understood that what you offer the sinner is not a charm, but a living Saviour ; and that what gives value to that "looking unto Jesus" which you urge is, that spiritually the sinner becomes one with him, and, being emptied of self and filled with Christ, becomes inwardly as well as formally a child of God. The utmost care must be taken not to let the impression be formed, especially on ignorant minds, that salvation turns on something like a mechanical act, something like the signing of a paper, only done with the head instead of the hand. To counteract this, the fulness and spirituality of the Christian salvation needs to be earnestly dwelt on.

It is no doubt an exceeding great privilege for a minister to be the means of saving a dying sinner from the second death, and yet his harvest work should be regarded only as beginning when the tomb has closed over the departed one. The bereaved family, for the next few weeks or months, will afford a most interesting and hopeful field for his Christian efforts ; for when death enters the family circle and carries off one with whom all our lives have been intertwined, there is left on the survivors a peculiarly strong sense of desolation—the vanity of earth, the realities of eternity, the odiousness of sin, the preciousness of redemption, come home with unusual force, and the heart is peculiarly susceptible of impressions that may issue in conversion. This is just to say that the Holy Spirit is dealing with the heart ; a divine Visitor is at hand : " Behold, I stand at the door and knock." To try to have these impressions confirmed, so as to issue in true and final decision for Christ—to urge a course of Christian habits, of reading and prayer, and, perhaps, some species of Christian work—is the natural direction of the minister's efforts and prayers after some great bereavement. For in point of fact it is commonly found that even those who have been well brought up need the discipline of trial to bring them to decision, and that it is out of such discipline that the greater part of the piety among us actually springs.

Besides sickness and death, there are many other kinds of distress of which the Christian minister may and probably ought to take notice. Sometimes he is made the *confidant* of his people, and sorrows are poured into his ear preying upon

* See Appendix A, Section II.

their very vitals, all the more hard to bear because they have to be locked up in their own bosoms. Sometimes he hears a tale of domestic unfaithfulness or of family strife ; in trying to be at once tender and faithful, and not make things worse in the attempt to make them better, his tact and wisdom are taxed to the uttermost. And sometimes a revelation unsuspected and most horrible is made to him : he is told how a fatal plague-spot has shown itself in the character of the fine young man that promised to be the joy and pride of his family, and the anguish-stricken parents appeal to him for help. Possibly he has the still more terrible task of being called to comfort in a case where no comfort, but only submission, is possible—where sudden death has cut off a loved but erring one in the midst of his sins, and the desolate parents are prostrated under the burden of their very faith—when their clear vivid view of the eternal world, instead of brightening their hopes, is like to drive them to distraction.

It may not be often that the Christian minister is brought into contact with such tragedies ; it is not every day that one so tender-hearted as David is called to mourn for a son killed in the act of rebellion, or that the air is rent with the cry, " Would God that I had died for thee, O Absalom, my son, my son ! " But experience teaches us that the world is very full of disappointment. Many is the heart where that lump of lead lies at the bottom, though it may not be allowed to show itself. Many is the crushed affection, many are the withered leaves that strew life's common paths. Many is the parental disappointment, although, perhaps, the parent hardly remembers that at one time brighter dreams floated before his fancy, now gone for ever. Many a leafless branch waves in the cold north wind, and the time has gone past for fresh buds of hope to form and unfold in tufts of living green. Experience of life compels us to look abroad on our people with a more tender, a more sympathetic spirit ; we think how much disappointment has to do with the harsher and sterner features that disfigure their character. It were miserable if this experience did not also intensify our desires for their Christian good ; if, seeing them hovering disappointed about the broken cisterns, we did not try more earnestly to bring them to the fountain of living water, cheering them with words more potent than any charm : " He that drinketh of this water shall thirst again ; but he that drinketh of the water that I shall give him shall never thirst ; but the water that I shall give him shall be in him a well of water, springing up into everlasting life."

CHAPTER XVI.

IT may be a question whether the memorable charge of our
Lord to Peter, " Feed my lambs," had reference to the case
of children, or whether the class indicated was not rather that
of young disciples, babes in Christ, imperfectly instructed in his
doctrine. But there is no question that the case of the young
demands very special attention from every faithful pastor ; and
as little is there a question that holy effort in this direction is
for the most part eminently useful and amply blessed. Many
is the pastor and many the missionary, who, when disheartened
by the settled indifference or the settled wickedness of the older
section of their people, have turned wistfully to the young ; as
if there was nothing for it but that the carcasses of the older
generation should fall in the wilderness, and their children only,
with their more soft and tender hearts, should receive God's
grace and possess the land.

The Christian Church in our age has awaked to a sense of its
relation to the young. What is the precise standing of baptized
children in the Christian Church is a question that has caused
not a little speculation, and that is still involved in considerable
mist. This is not the place to consider the bearing of baptism
on the spiritual state of the children, or on the duties or the
hopes of parents who have dedicated them in that ordinance to
Christ ; but it is quite suitable that we should advert to the
relation in which baptism places children to the minister and to
the church. Baptized children become members of the visible
church. They are an integral part of our congregations, and it
is our duty to look on them as such, especially when we meet
for worship. They ought to be present to our minds as a part
of that large family with whom and for whom we unite in the
worship of God. Their sins and infirmities, as well as those of
the older members, ought to be in our thought in our public

confessions; their preservation, health, and well-being generally ought to swell our thanksgivings; and their difficulties, temptations, and trials, especially in connection with the service of God, ought to be before us in our supplications at the throne. Their edification, too, ought to be considered in our preaching, in so far as that can be secured without loss to others; and the winning of them to Christ, and their confirmation and establishment as living members of the church, ought constantly to be contemplated both by office-bearers and members in their intercourse with them. It is quite true that our feelings and actings ought to be very much the same towards all children, whether they have been baptized or not; the difference in the case of baptized children being, that the obligation has been formally acknowledged by us in a public ordinance, so that baptized children may claim from us as a right those Christian attentions which come to others simply in the way of favour.

The young persons in an ordinary congregation fall into two classes according to their age—children, and young men and women. The pastoral methods applicable to each are somewhat different.

I. CHILDREN.—Confining our attention to the duties of the *minister*, we may inquire, first, what regard ought to be had to the case of children in the ordinary services of the congregation; and second, whether any special services or meetings ought to be held for their behoof.

1. As to the ordinary services. It is the custom of some ministers to assign a particular part of each discourse to the children, or to conclude with an application to them of the subject on which they have been preaching. But if either of these methods is adopted *as a stated practice*, it can hardly fail to have the effect of leading the children to believe that there is little or no obligation on them to give attention to the other parts of the sermon. An occasional appeal to the children in the middle or at the close of an ordinary sermon, in the winning tone of voice by which children are usually addressed, may be exceedingly useful; but, as a rule, it is hard upon a preacher to be obliged abruptly to change his level and come down to the capacity of little children, as well as undesirable both for the children and the congregation generally. Would it not be better that discourses generally were constructed in such a way as not to be wholly beyond the reach of children? If the structure were simple, the style clear, and the delivery natural, if the lines of Scripture were followed closely, if illustrations

abounded, and other faculties besides the reason were habitually appealed to, an intelligent child might very soon find much to interest him in an ordinary sermon. The habit of attention would then be formed, and though there would be much in the sermon beyond his grasp, his capacity of understanding would be constantly growing. Our Lord's parables, for example, in their literal sense, were as easily followed by the young as by the old ; nor does He appear to have found it necessary to address grown people at one time and children at another. He appears to have had a wonderful power of arresting both ; and had we been present when He delivered such a discourse as that of the sheep and the goats, we should probably have found that the eye was as closely riveted and the attention as thoroughly secured in the case of the children as in that of the grey-bearded men or careworn women that pressed so eagerly to hear Him.

2. Separate services for children may assume various forms. In the first place, there may be occasional sermons expressly addressed to them. Where there are two regular meetings of the congregation for public worship, there can be no reasonable objection to one of these being occasionally appropriated to the children. If we are to deal with children effectually on spiritual subjects, two physical conditions are indispensable : first, that the minds of the children be fresh ; and second, that the same be true of the preacher. An exhausted preacher or an exhausted audience will be associated with wandering attention on the part of the children, ending, most probably, in their falling asleep. There is more likelihood of having a fresh preacher and a fresh audience if the sermon to the young is at an ordinary hour, and not at a supernumerary meeting.

Successful preachers to the young place themselves at once, by an instinctive process, *en rapport* with their audience ; find the level of their thoughts and feelings ; lay hold and keep hold of their attention through avenues that they know to be open ; and press them with the degree and kind of force which they feel to be likely to succeed. The process hardly admits of specific rules. A good preacher to the young, however, will be careful to choose a text short, bright, striking ; the arrangement will be simple, and the heads as obvious and as easily to be remembered as possible ; a large part of his sermon will be illustration ; and he will be specially careful to make a specific and not a vague application. In his delivery he will study to speak in a natural tone of voice. His performance will be at the furthest possible remove from that of an essay read before an audience ; most emphatically it will be a word spoken to them. In preaching to children, one can easily get rid of the fear of man which bringeth a snare, and without dread of offence say things which one might shrink from uttering face to face with the old. There is a directness and point in such preaching that often contrasts very favourably with the unnatural tones and vague circumlocutions of ordinary discourses. Many a grown-up person feels that his mind gets instruction from the simple explanations of doctrine given to the children, and that his conscience is quickened by the direct appeals made to them on duty. The relish for " bairns' hymns " which marked the dying hours of Dr. Guthrie is often paralleled by a relish for " bairns' sermons," even in the healthy hours of grown-up men. A successful preacher to the young rouses in older persons feelings that never grow old, and brings back to them something of the consciousness of childhood—the happy seasons of golden dreams, which, though dashed in the meantime, are nevertheless destined to a fulfilment more glorious than this life could ever have given.

In preaching to the young, some American ministers have been highly successful ; such men as Dr. Todd of Pittsville and Dr. Newton of Philadelphia have attained the first rank in this department of work. The American mind has such a proclivity to sharp, terse forms of expression, clever analogies and illustrations, keen analysis of feelings, vivid description and warm colouring, that we do not wonder that it should excel in addresses to which such qualities contribute so largely.

Another form of service or exercise for children adopted by some ministers is that of an examination, occurring about once a month, and based on the sermon which precedes it or on some subject that has been prescribed. While this method is exposed to the drawback of necessarily finding the children somewhat exhausted if they have given attention to the public service that has preceded it, it possesses the advantage, on the other hand, of allowing the minister to ascertain how far the discourse or the subject of examination has been understood by them. It gives him the opportunity of finding out what amount of knowledge they have actually attained, and, though with less certainty, what impression has been made on their hearts.

We do not enter in this place into the subject of Sunday-schools, or into that of " children's churches," as those meetings have been called which, being held at the hour of public worship, come in its place to the children for whom they are designed. Our subject is the work of the minister, and it is evident that except in the way of general oversight, the minister can take no more than an occasional part in these. The children's church is an interesting experiment in the art of attaching to Sabbath ordinances masses of children who would not otherwise acquire the habit of church-going, and in the art of framing services in which there is a fair prospect of children taking an intelligent and lively part. The experiment has been too short to enable us to judge as to its permanent effects. One thing, however, is obvious; the pleas sometimes advanced in its favour cast a somewhat painful reflection on the prevailing dulness of the pulpit. If the children's church can be expected to have the result of permanently introducing many children, otherwise sure to neglect them, to the ordinary services of the sanctuary, these services must receive a new element of liveliness, otherwise children trained at the livelier meetings will not attend them. And this is but one of many considerations that go to prove what a great desideratum liveliness is in our public services at the present day; no danger to which they are exposed is so great as that of becoming useless through their own heaviness.

Whatever plan may be followed by the minister, it is very desirable that, without taking any heavy burden upon him, he should have some mode of coming occasionally into contact with the children. It is of great importance that he should come to know and to love them, that they too should come to know and to love him, and that both should feel that they have to do with each other. It is worth while, too, to consider whether the old law of the Scotch Church might not be revived, by which all the children of a congregation were required to be examined by the minister at the several ages of nine, twelve, and fourteen. The Scotch Church has always been most desirous to secure the godly up-bringing of the young. If the older methods were marked by more authoritative strictness, and the modern possess more of affection and attraction, it is well to remember that each element has its own place, and that a judicious combination of both is the consummation most to be desired.

II. While the detailed religious instruction of the children must be carried on chiefly by their parents and others in the congregation, the case of young men and young women ought to engage much more of the minister's own time and energies. The practice of catechizing the young is coeval with the dawn of Christianity. St. Luke in the introduction to his Gospel refers to the catechetical training of Theophilus—"that thou mightest know the certainity of the things wherein thou hast been catechetically instructed (κατηχήθης)." Catechetical lectures, as we have seen, formed an important feature of the public services of the patristic Church, the process of question and answer probably following the delivery of the discourse. The skilful use of the question is beyond all doubt what gives most value to the Bible-class.

The benefits of this mode of instruction, when conducted with skill and animation, are many. (1.) It furnishes a backbone to the religious training of the young, so that the truths of Christianity shall be apprehended in their relations and connections, and not lie in a confused heap in the mind. (2.) It gives the minister an opportunity of perceiving what is apprehended and what is misunderstood by those whom he has to instruct. (3.) It sets in motion the mental faculties of the young—trains them to digest their spiritual food. (4.) It brings the minister and his young people into close, interesting, and most profitable contact at the period of life when they are most susceptible of being influenced by him. (5.) And it secures to him, in the course of a generation, a trained and instructed audience, by whom the ordinary pulpit ministrations will be much more appreciated, and who will be carried much further on in the knowledge of Divine truth.

So manifold are the benefits of catechizing, that in the olden time, when the authority of the Church was more fully and readily recognised than it is now, the catechizing of all the people in detachments or districts was one of the regular duties of the ministry. In some parts of the country the practice is still maintained. But as it might not now be practicable, even if it were wise, and as it would not be wise even if it were practicable, to unite persons of all ages and ranks in one promiscuous catechizing, we shall speak of the practice only in connection with that part of his people whom a minister may reckon on to take part in it—young men and young women.

In country congregations, and where the people are engaged in hard manual labour, it is commonly difficult to form Bible-classes except on the Lord's Day. While this doubtless entails a heavy task on a minister's strength, it has an advantage on the other hand, for the minds of the young persons are more likely to be in a suitable frame for taking part in the exercises of the class than they probably would be in a week-day evening.

Let it be understood at the same time that well-taught classes will attract a considerable attendance on any evening, and that sometimes the reason why a Bible-class collapses is, that it is so poorly conducted as to be hardly worth attending.

The question now presents itself—What is the best mode of conducting a Bible-class ? To this question the very name of the class furnishes the first part of the answer. Undoubtedly the Word of God should have prominence here as in the public services of the sanctuary. The opening up of the Scriptures in a somewhat more analytical way than the pulpit admits of, affords an admirable opportunity to the minister to adapt himself to the cravings and capacities of the young. So many subjects present themselves that the difficulty lies in selecting. The life of Christ ; the Miracles ; the Parables ; the Acts of the Apostles ; an Epistle, like Romans or Hebrews ; Bible biography; Bible history ; Bible geography; Bible typology ; Bible prophecy—are all susceptible of most interesting treatment in a Bible-class. The ease and familiarity with which such a class is conducted admits of many things being introduced in the way of illustration and in the way of application which could hardly be spoken from the pulpit. And a minister may be very plain and very earnest in pressing truth on the conscience of individual members of the class.

In a Church which possesses such a summary of doctrine and duty as the Shorter Catechism, the exposition of that symbol ought surely to have a leading place in classes for young men and women. We say this deliberately, without being indiscriminate admirers of the Catechism. Undoubtedly its tone is somewhat hard and cold, and we cannot but regret the absence of allusion to the free offer of the gospel, or of that view of redemption indicated in the glorious words of our Lord, " God so loved the world, that He gave his only begotten Son, that whosoever believeth in Him should not perish, but have everlasting life " (John iii. 16). But, notwithstanding its defects, we question if any treatise of the size ever contained a larger measure of truth, expressed in clear and careful language. Its bold announcement of man's chief end impresses us like a great stroke of genius at the beginning. Its definitions of effectual calling, justification, the offices of Christ, faith, repentance, the sacraments, and prayer, are in themselves theological treatises, each a *multum in parvo*, like those hardly visible photographs to which the microscope may be applied at its highest magnifying power, without the discovery of a trace of what is superfluous or unmeaning. Helps for elucidating its meaning are abundant. Thomas Vincent's explanation, though two hundred years old, is not yet antiquated, nor Richard Watson's, with its ample store of illustration, furnished liberally from the resources of a well-read and well-equipped mind. Matthew Henry's questions are so constructed as to be all answered in the language of Scripture—ingenious, but of little use for real catechizing. Fisher, one of the early Seceders, goes deep into questions of doctrine, while Paterson sets the example of analytical treatment, which is more in accordance with the modern idea in teaching. Such helps may be used as helps, chiefly in one's own study; the teacher who uses them in his class will find that he gets but lamely along. The great thing in opening up a question is to state clearly and strongly its main proposition or subject; then to indicate the various particulars which enter into the statement regarding it; then to establish, illustrate, and apply each; and finally, to show how they all converge on the proposition affirmed. While you thus deal with the subject, care must be taken to interest your class; let the attempt be made to stimulate thought and get them to exercise their minds; give them points to explain and difficulties to investigate; ask them the reason for this and the meaning of that; let the drier work of the class be relieved by copious illustration; and let the minister study to be animated and cheerful in his manner and interesting in his style.*

There are other subjects which have often been introduced with advantage in Bible-classes. Books have been used like the "Pilgrim's Progress," Paley's "Natural Theology," Keith's "Evidence of Prophecy," Hodge's "Way of Life," and even, in very select cases, Butler's "Analogy," and the "Philosophy of the Plan of Salvation." But such subjects, or at least the majority of them, are suitable only in particular cases; and the minister must exercise his own judgment as to the fit circumstances in which to resort to them.

Occasional written exercises are a most useful appendage to a Bible-class, and are contributed readily when the scholars have had a tolerable education. On the other hand, if writing and spelling are a terror to them, such exercises cannot be expected, except peculiar encouragement be given to make the trial.

It needs hardly to be observed that for the business of such a class, careful preparation is indispensable on the part of the minister. Nay, something in the form of written preparation

* See Appendix A, Section III.

may be urged. To write out the leading questions, and make jottings of the explanations and illustrations employed, will commonly be of very great service. It will be found to freshen the business very materially if he can introduce incidents of the day or passages from miscellaneous reading to throw light on the matter in hand. The trouble that may be taken at first in preparation for such a class will be amply repaid in the subsequent years of his ministry.

Under such a scheme of instruction, with the blessing of God, a minister can hardly fail to train a superior order of young people. Only he must beware of thinking or of leading them to think that his chief object is to instruct. In opening such a class it ought to be announced broadly that the great aim is to secure not their instruction merely, but their salvation. All through, this aim must be kept in mind. The opening prayer must ever recognise it, and the young persons should be made to feel that this is looked for. Personal and kindly dealing, one by one, with the members of a class so conducted is usually of the greatest avail. Decision for Christ is often the blessed consequence, and at an early period the young minister is often permitted to reap the first-fruits of the coming harvest.

When thus conducted, the Bible-class becomes the natural forerunner of a second meeting for Christian instruction and influence—that for young communicants.

Properly speaking, this is rather a class for Christian influence than instruction. The candidate for communion ought to be already well versed in the fundamental truths of the gospel ; and the special business of the communion class, if there are so many as to require a class, should be that of dealing with the conscience and the heart—with a view not only to prevent unworthy communicating, but to promote an enlightened, happy, and most profitable fellowship with Christ at his table. But it is not easy to secure that no persons shall offer themselves as communicants but those who have passed through Bible-classes. In such a case it seems desirable that the minister should explain the more vital questions in the Catechism—such as effectual calling, justification, faith in Jesus Christ—making sure in this way that the doctrinal foundation is firmly laid. Thereafter, it will be well to go over, fully and carefully, the questions on the sacraments in general, and that on the Lord's Supper in particular, supplementing the Shorter Catechism by the additional questions in the Larger ; to open up very search-ingly the words of institution, dwelling on the two acts, first the *taking* and then the *eating* and *drinking*, as the key to the whole ; to read along with this certain very practical chapters, such as John iii. or Ephesians ii., where the heavenly origin and inward nature of the Christian life are clearly set forth, closing with a portion of the Song of Solomon or with the 45th Psalm, to illustrate the more fragrant aspects of fellowship with Christ.

It is right not only to aim at rousing the conscience and the heart all through, but specially by conversation and prayer with every candidate, both at the beginning and the close of the class, to endeavour to influence them aright. It is a time of remarkable dealing of the Holy Spirit with the hearts of young persons ; the conscience is tender ; they will bear any amount of earnest dealing ; it is a sort of high-tide in their spiritual history, a time of peculiar sensibility, on the improvement of which the most precious results depend. A short printed paper, expressing the nature of the profession made and the obligations incurred by communicants, may be put into the hands of each ; and when the consent of all parties involved has been obtained to their admission, the minister and elders will admit them, commending them by solemn prayer to the grace of God.

Manuals for young communicants are abundant, but most are apt to bewilder the novice, and to distract his attention from the one great business of the Lord's Supper—receiving Christ and feeding on him. The best manual is the words of institution (Matt. xxvi. 26 ; 1 Cor. xi. 24). Perhaps the best commentary on these words is the question, " What is the Lord's Supper ? " * The best form of self-examination, " What is required of them that would worthily partake of the Lord's Supper ? " † The best help for solving the doubts of the timid, " May one who doubteth of his being a Christian, or of his due preparation, come to the Lord's table ? " ‡ And the best directory for the subsequent

* "The Lord's Supper is a sacrament wherein, by giving and receiving bread and wine according to Christ's appointment, his death is showed forth ; and the worthy receivers are, not after a corporal and carnal manner, but by faith, made partakers of Christ's body and blood, with all his benefits, to their spiritual nourishment and growth in grace."

† "It is required of them that would worthily partake of the Lord's Supper that they examine themselves of their knowledge to discern the Lord's body, of their faith to feed upon Him, of their repentance, love, and new obedience ; lest, coming unworthily, they eat and drink judgment to themselves."

‡ "One who doubteth of his being in Christ, or of his due preparation to the sacrament of the Lord's Supper, may have true interest in Christ,

improvement of the ordinance is the answer in the Larger
Catechism to the question, "What is the duty of Christians
after they have received the sacrament of the Lord's Supper?"*
But it may happen that persons peculiarly situated offer
themselves, particularly to the missionary-minister, in whose
case some modifications of the ordinary method must be resorted
to. When grown-up persons well advanced in life make application, the minister's duty is often most difficult. It is peculiarly difficult if there be a want of spiritual perception in the
applicants, an inability to comprehend the very meaning of the
new birth, accompanied, as that often is, by the feeling that the
reluctance of the minister to admit them is based on some
suspicion that they are living in wickedness, or on some
personal dislike to themselves. A tender-hearted minister,
placed in this dilemma, is most deeply to be felt for. If
possible, let him co-operate with the elders, and get them to
share the responsibility, for it is not right that he should bear
it alone. If even elders have not spirituality enough to sympa-
thise with him, what can remain for him but to throw himself
more unreservedly than ever upon his Master, and from Him
seek not only direction, but also the spirit of a mingled tenderness and faithfulness?

In general, considerable allowance ought to be made for
persons in mature life. Allowance should be made for that
feeling of reserve which holds so many in bondage and keeps
their hearts so close; for that *nervous excitement* which, even
under a stolid look and manner, may be embarrassing and
bewildering them; and for that *sense of shame* which is gendered
by the fact of their coming comparatively so late in life—

though he be not yet assured thereof, and in God's account hath it, if he
be duly affected with the apprehension of the want of it, and unfeignedly
desires to be found in Christ, and to depart from all iniquity, in which
case (because promises are made, and this sacrament is appointed for the
relief even of weak and doubting Christions) he is to bewail his unbelief,
and labour to have doubts resolved; and so doing, he may and ought to
come to the Lord's Supper, that he may be further strengthened."

* "The duty of Christians . . . is seriously to consider how they have
behaved themselves therein, and with what success: if they find quickening and comfort, to bless God for it, beg the continuance of it, watch
against relapses. fulfil their vows, and encourage themselves to a frequent
attendance on that ordinance: but if they find no present benefit, more
exactly to review their preparation to, and carriage at, the sacrament: in
both which if they can approve themselves to God and their own consciences, they are to wait for the fruit of it in due time: but if they see
they have failed in either, they are to be humbled, and to attend upon it
afterwards with more care and diligence."

acknowledging thereby their past remissness. When we read the accounts of the baptism of John the Baptist, or of the admissions into the Church by the Apostles, we perceive that they acted on the principle of seldom shutting the door against those who applied. The circumstances of the times are not quite parallel; to make application in those times was more of a test than it is now. But without sanctioning the practice of indiscriminate admission to the Lord's Supper, in all cases where the desire to become a communicant is expressed with apparent honesty by an adult, it ought, we think, to be treated with the largest measure of charity. Let the dealings with the conscience be as earnest and faithful as possible; but let an absolute refusal be the result only of a clear and insuperable sense of duty. It were a hard thing to keep from the Supper some sin-worn soul, that can say but little about itself except that it is hungry and would fain taste the bread of life.

The question is often put with eagerness, On what grounds ought the minister to decide whether or not to recommend the admission of applicants to the Supper? The answer to this question is virtually to be found in the province which our Church assigns to each of the three parties who ought to take part in examining him, previous to his admission—the minister, the elders, and the applicant himself. It is the duty of the minister to examine into his knowledge; it is the province of the elders to examine into his life and conversation; and it is the province of the applicant himself to examine into the state of his heart. "Examine yourselves whether ye be in the faith." The minister is not, therefore, called on to come to a decision in favour of the applicant grounded on the state of his heart. But though not entitled to decide this question authoritatively, as the ground of his admission, he is both entitled and bound in a friendly way to warn and exhort all not to come to the table unless they believe that they have in their hearts accepted the offer of the gospel. More particularly in the case of the young; having watched over them as a nurse watches over her children, he cannot but have formed an opinion on the state of their hearts, and it is seldom that a young candidate would be so reckless as to press forward in opposition to the friendly counsel of the minister. There is no duty in the discharge of which faithful and loving ministers have more searchings of heart, or are more powerfully reminded of the source of true preparation —"Not by might, nor by power, but by my Spirit, saith the Lord of hosts" (Zech. iv. 6).

CHAPTER XVII.

UNDER this head we purpose to embrace three classes of pastoral duties : 1. Those connected with marriages, bap-tisms, deaths, and similar occasions. 2. Week-day meetings for prayer, exposition of Scripture, and promotion of an interest in missions. 3. Occasional special meetings for promoting a revival of religion and elevating the standard of Christian life and practice.

I. It is a noteworthy fact that the duty of the minister brings him into special contact with his people at every im-portant crisis in their family history. If their minds be too dull and sluggish in their ordinary moods, they are shaken up into more activity on these unusual occasions, and present to an earnest minister a greater susceptibility of impression. He who watches for souls will be careful of these opportunities, and try much to turn them to profitable account.

To begin with *Marriage*. The minister has not only a right to be present, but his services are indispensable, except on those rare occasions when people are satisfied with the ministry of the Registrar. In Scotland, where marriages are commonly celebrated in private houses, some pains needed on the part of the officiating minister to give to the service its proper tone. Met on occasion of a marriage festivity, people like to dwell on its brightsome aspect, and were a minister to set himself right in opposition to the festive current in which their feelings flow, he would only provoke an unprofitable and unpopular collision. Yet, on the other hand, even marriage has a grave and solemn side ; the commencement of life's journey, even by the first pair in Eden, was a solemn as well as a gladsome event. It is so even still ; and the skilful minister will find, beneath the festive current that bubbles and glitters on the surface, a deeper feeling that will awake to his call. To this more solemn spirit he makes his appeal during the formal service; and it will not only not be out of place for him, but actually in keeping with the purpose of his presence, if he endeavours to keep it from being trampled on all the time he is there. The view thus brought out may operate as a check on that excess of frivolity which such occasions are apt to breed, and tend to secure that chastening of joy with a more solemn feeling which is appropriate to a life so short and so chequered as this, where even they that have wives must be as though they had not, and they that rejoice as though they rejoiced not, because the fashion of this world passeth away.

The performance of marriage is one of the occasions in the Scottish Church when, missing something of a liturgical form, the minister is led to construct one for himself. The necessity of brevity, neatness, and point makes this almost indispensable. A lumbering address and lumbering prayers are never more completely out of keeping. The service ought to begin with a short prayer, acknowledging God as the God alike of providence and of grace, casting ourselves as sinners on his mercy, and imploring his blessing, especially in connection with his own ordinance of marriage. The address ought to be founded on the passage in the Old Testament where marriage is instituted, and one or other of the passages in the New which lay down the duties of the Christian husband and wife. Whatever counsels are founded on these ought to be brief, and may probably be best directed to impress the importance of seeking God's blessing, as the one indispensable condition of all true happiness, prosperity, and peace. The question to the bride and bridegroom ought to be put in a solemn tone, and with a specific recognition of their being in the presence of God; and when they are declared to be married persons, the declaration ought to be made in his name and by his authority. The concluding prayer will invoke the Divine blessing on the married couple in all their interests, on soul and body, on their basket and on their store, on their going out and on their coming in; and will specially recognise the families of both, as well as the other families represented by those present. The apostolic benediction will appropriately conclude the service, the whole of which need not occupy more than a few minutes.

Baptisms, as conducted in the Presbyterian Church, afford an opportunity to the minister to stir his people up on one of the most important of practical duties, reaching out to an extent to which no limits can be assigned. The only parties whose responsibility is publicly recognised being the parents, the minister is called, both in private dealings and in public exhortations, to press their consciences with their obligation and privilege to bring up their children in the nurture and admonition of the Lord. In the baptismal address something of uniformity is almost indispensable, the parents having a right to know beforehand the obligations that are to be laid upon them. This address ought to be avowedly founded on Scripture, and may be rendered more impressive by reference both to the beacons and examples which Scripture contains. In our churches it is usual to address the father alone, but if would be an improvement, as in some other churches, if the father and the mother were together ; and in any case, health permitting, the presence of the mother also is most desirable, as her heart is usually more susceptible on the subject of her infant's welfare, and her influence in training him is far more constant and usually more powerful.

At *Funerals* the official services of the minister are again required. The policy of the Scottish Reformers to tear up, root and branch, those practices of Popery which had proved most mischievous in fostering superstition, and leading people away from the true ground of salvation, led them to discourage all religious services at the burial of the dead. Gradually, however, we have been receding from this extreme position, and now it is customary to have reading of the Scriptures and prayer when the mourners are met, occasionally prayer at the grave, and not unfrequently, when the persons are of mark in the congregation, funeral sermons or allusions to the departed. Nor do we see any danger in these practices, so long as we keep up sound teaching in our pulpits on all the great matters of the faith. There is no difficulty in the selection of appropriate passages from Scripture. But there is some danger of letting the prayer become an *éloge* on the dead ; and here the greatest caution must be used. In the case of persons well known for their consistent Christian character, the company are prepared to join in thanksgiving for grace bestowed by God upon them. In the case of others they can only hesitate, and should the officiating minister be too pronounced, they will be perplexed, but they will not be able to join in such a prayer. Even at funerals the minister must pray as the mouthpiece of the company, and abstain from expressing views in which it is not reasonable to expect that they shall be able to join.

The delivery of funeral sermons, or the making of allusions to deceased members from the pulpit, ought to be carefully restricted to the case of persons who by loftiness of Christian character or by eminent services to the church will be generally admitted to deserve the recognition. When such a practice becomes promiscuous, or when it is extended to all persons in a high social position, it loses its effect; jealousy is apt to be roused when any are passed over, and men of very mixed character are liable to be canonized, about whom, perhaps, the less that is said the better.

When death occurs in a house, the minister is expected to be in close communication with the bereaved family, comforting them as he may be able, and urging them to take those solemn views of life, death, and eternity, which such an event is fitted to urge. But the true servant of God will never be satisfied with the performance of his mere official service on such occasions. Regarding them as seasons when special access is afforded to the hearts of his people, and when the door is opened by Providence for near and earnest dealings with the soul, he will strive to press the truth home with peculiar fervour. The fact that the minister is so closely related to every occasion of joy and especially of sorrow in the history of his flock, while it is greatly fitted to endear him to them, gives him a hold and a power of usefulness which ought never to be overlooked.

Nor ought he to confine his Christian offices to the more recognised and open occasions of this kind. The watchful eye and the watchful heart of the true minister will notice when a son or a daughter is about to leave home for school, or college, or business, or it may be to settle in a distant colony; and regarding that occasion as not less really a crisis in the history of the family than a birth or a death, will take the opportunity to offer his friendly counsel to the departing member, and carry them all to the mercy-seat to implore the guidance and the blessing of the God of Bethel. In public prayer, too, without obtruding particular cases, he may cause the petitions he offers to embrace such various providential circumstances as are seldom far removed from the earnest feelings of some members of his flock. It is very certain that a living chord will thus be struck; and while the minister is prized and loved for his sympathy, his prayers will be backed by fervent Amens issuing from the inmost sanctuary of their hearts.

II. The next class of pastoral duties to which we shall advert

P

is that of meetings for prayer, reading the Scriptures, and collateral objects.

Ever since the evangelical revival of the last forty years, some such meetings have sprung up wherever there was any manifestation of religious earnestness. It must be owned, however, that in many cases they have not assumed a very definite shape, and that where the first fresh feeling out of which they sprung has subsided, the effort to keep them up has often been a laborious one.

In many cases the true conception of a " prayer-meeting " has not yet been realised. The meeting so termed is generally little else than a diluted edition of a pulpit service. It may be doubted whether this meeting, as it is often conducted, has in it the elements of permanent vigour. It is a kind of cross between the cottage lecture, the prayer-meeting proper, and the pulpit service—without what is most valuable in any. It is better, if possible, to keep these separate, and let each possess its characteristic features.

The cottage lecture derives its special charm from its domestic character, being a meeting of a few neighbouring families to hear the Word and join in praise and prayer. It is family worship on a larger scale. It has a kind of hallowing effect on the house and on the neighbourhood ; the simplicity, ease, and affectionateness of the service have a great charm, especially for the rural mind, and it tends, perhaps, to gender more of a kindly, neighbourly, Christian spirit than even the Lord's Day service, where many of the people are unacquainted, and a distant feeling towards one another must to some degree prevail.

Of the prayer-meeting proper we have had more characteristic samples among us of late years in connection with the revival of religion. Such meetings are really for prayer ; many Christian friends take part, and the prayers are like arrows from the bow of the mighty, jets of petition darting up to heaven. Intercession is a prominent and very blessed feature of such meetings, as it ought to be of all prayer-meetings. Intercession warms and expands the heart, and tends to deepen the spirit out of which it springs. It is a favoured congregation that can keep up such a meeting, leaving to the minister the duty of simply guiding the proceedings and drawing out the gifts and graces of his people.

A week-day congregational lecture entails a very great additional labour on a minister, and, where all the other pastoral duties are laboriously performed, is too exhausting to be looked for. Men with great facility of preaching may be able to overtake it, and to produce a discourse equal to those of the Lord's Day; but the temptation to slipshod preparation and crude performance is too great in ordinary cases. There seems to be no reason, however, why in towns a number of ministers should not combine, and taking a weekly lecture in turn, bestow their best strength upon it. The reason why such services have often died out is, that those who have taken part in them have not given their best strength to them, and instead of producing what was better, have been content with a weaker service than usual.

It may happen that for a time the minister finds it impossible to get members of the congregation of lively and earnest spirit to aid him in conducting a real prayer-meeting. The training of the younger men is a work of time, and meanwhile, in any meeting for prayer, the duty falls chiefly on himself. When it must be so, he ought still to study, as far as possible, to make the meeting answer to its name. His prayers ought not to be mere general devotions, but pleadings for the various classes of his flock, and for the various objects in which the congregation has an interest. His address ought to be directed, more than on ordinary occasions, to promote the spirit of devotion. The people ought to be able to feel, as they leave, that business has been done at the throne of grace, and to expect that in answer to such pleadings blessings will descend from above. It will be found, too, that when prayer assumes such a form at the prayer-meetings, it will by-and-by acquire more of it in the church. Every thoughtful minister will readily understand how important all this is. The Christian people of Scotland have got the character of being intensely fond of preaching, but not of praying. And undoubtedly there is a measure of truth in the charge.

A prayer-meeting for missionary objects is highly desirable and important, probably once a month. To give it variety and special interest, tidings from the mission-field should be given in some shape. But nothing can be more dry or cheerless than the mere reading of long letters from a Missionary Record. Pains must be taken to excite an interest in what is read. Explanations must be given, if necessary, about the place, the missionary, and the people. The narrative must be skilfully linked on to something that is stirring in the people's minds. In some cases there are narratives so absorbing that they require no comment; such, however, are exceptional. Such a service might at times take the place of an ordinary sermon; and generally, in the ordinary services of the sanctuary, a much higher place than has been common ought to be given to the great missionary enterprise. The hearts of the whole people ought to be directed habitually, and not by mere spasmodic efforts, to the missionary business of the Christian Church, so as to be expanded by the survey of the vast field of heathenism, and roused to pity, to effort, and to prayer, as St. Paul's was at Athens by the sight of the city given wholly to idolatry.

III. Is it ever desirable and proper to have special meetings with a view to deepen and concentrate religious feeling, and to bring about a revival? For such meetings some persons have a great horror, while to others they are the objects of the utmost delight. Not a few worthy persons, of the more orderly and correct stamp, regard them as mere emanations of fanaticism, and think that if encouragement is to be given to the illiterate and impetuous men that often come to the front on such occasions, Divine service will degenerate into mere sensuous excitement, and conscience and reason will be driven off the field by the surging force of spiritual passion. This, of course, is an extreme and therefore unsatisfactory view; the subject demands to be examined with more care and candour.

It is to be remarked, then, that even where the Word of God is fully and faithfully preached, there is a tendency in congregations to remain at rest. A preacher who has preached from week to week for many years to the same people, and who has the prospect of doing the same to the end of his life, can hardly fail to fall into a less urgent tone than one who is among them for one brief day or one brief week. The people, too, meeting quietly from week to week, without much outward difference between one week and another, do not ordinarily feel any necessity for immediate action in matters of religion. Accordingly, want of decision characterizes many persons who are not destitute of religious impressions, and who are not far from the kingdom of God. Something is needed to break in on the ordinary monotony and rouse an intenser feeling. In former days, in Scotland, communion occasions were often turned to account in this way; they were great preaching festivals, and such communion services as those of the Erskines were often times of awakening and refreshing. In the Highlands, too, the same state of things prevailed. But in most parts of the country the extra services on sacramental occasions have lost their former power, and the manifest tendency is to fewer extra services and to more frequent and simple arrangements for the communion. Those who desire to see the prevalent languor of our congregations broken in upon by special efforts to produce a livelier state of feeling resort to a succession of meetings, night after night, for prayer and evangelistic addresses. But the minister ought not to leave such meetings to be organized by others. He ought himself to be at the head of them, backed by the elders and the more godly and earnest members of the flock. All the earnest men and women of the flock should enter into a solemn league and covenant, looking for a blessing in the full assurance of hope, and wrestling, like Jacob, till the blessing come.

Meetings designed for the purpose of promoting a revival of spiritual life require to be organized with more skill and care than are often brought to bear on them. In the first place, the very word "revival" indicates that the first object is to resuscitate spiritual earnestness in those who have already been born of God. It is to rouse them to more vivid impressions of Divine truth, more solemn views of sin and guilt, more soul-stirring thoughts of the love of God and the grace of Christ, more grief and more love for a world lying in wickedness, and more intense prayer for the outpouring of the Holy Spirit. And any minister of the Gospel may be well assured that unless his own heart be stirred in this way, he cannot expect that he will be made the instrument of stirring up the hearts of others. If, however, by God's grace, there should come to the more godly part of his flock a spirit of special sensibility, prayerfulness, and expectation, he is entitled to regard the time as suitable for an effort on behalf of those who are outside the kingdom, or hovering about the door.

It is recommended by some who have made a study of such movements, that a gradation of subjects be followed in meetings designed to awaken the careless, and bring them safe within the kingdom of Christ. For the purpose of awakening, such topics as "the worth of the soul, the immediate and urgent claims of religion, the danger of delay, the death-bed of the sinner, the scenes of the last judgment, the final separation, the glories of heaven, and the retributions of eternity,"* are

* Pond's "Pastoral Theology," p. 162 (Boston, 1867). Dr. Pond has given special attention to this branch of pastoral work.

thought to be the most suitable. Next, it ought to be the aim
to produce true convictions of sin. The false standards which
men are wont to regard must be set aside, and the rule brought
forward, however strict and condemning, by which God will
judge us at the last day. The spirituality and searching
character of the law should be opened up, and at the same
time its excellence, fitness, and reasonableness. The aggrava-
tion of sin in neglecting the Son of God, notwithstanding his
coming from Heaven to Calvary for men's salvation, must be
specially urged. Mere agitation, or even distress of mind, is
not always a token of genuine conviction; nor can the conviction be sufficient either in quality or amount, until it prostrates
men in the dust as lost sinners before God, who have no plea
of their own to urge on their behalf, and must therefore lie
wholly at his mercy.

At this stage, it is of great importance to urge the freeness of
the gospel offer ; the completeness of the work of Christ ; the
call of God to the sinner to believe and live ; not to work or
wait indefinitely for some expected improvement on himself,
but to come *as he is*, accepting of Christ as all his salvation and
all his desire.

" Among the dangers incident to the management of a revival
movement, one is extreme caution, or fear of overdoing ; the
other is that of pushing the movement too fast, thereby injuring
its character and bringing it to a speedy close. . . . The pastor
rejoices in the work of begun revival ; he feels his own responsibility in regard to it ; his soul is excited and quickened
under its influence ; and he rushes into it under the impression
that he cannot labour too fast, or do too much in a given time
for the promotion of so good a cause. The consequence is
that he goes beyond his strength, is soon prostrated and unable
to do anything. Or in his heated, excited state of mind, he is
chargeable with indiscretions, which impair his influence and
hinder the progress of the work. He changes, it may be, the
whole character of the revival, and turns it into a scene of
excitement and extravagance." *

An acquaintance with the best narratives of awakenings, conversation with those who have had much to do with them, and
experience of the work itself, are far better fitted to guide one
in the management of them than any general instructions. The
"Narrative of Surprising Conversions" in New England by Pre-

* Pond, p. 172.

sident Edwards is one of the most interesting, impressive, and instructive memoirs ever published. It is eminently worthy of the study of every minister, for it combines the view of the philosopher and the saint, calm wisdom and deep spirituality, a burning desire for the welfare of souls, and a dread of the tares which the enemy is so ready to sow among the wheat. No single work is so well fitted to give one an intelligent view of the whole subject of a revival—its rise and progress, its crisis, and its decay; its risks and benefits, its good and evil. The life of Asahel Nettleton, the greatest of American revivalists, is also full of information and instruction, viewing the subject, as Nettleton did, from the strictly Calvinistic point, as Finney viewed it from the Arminian. Some of the writings of the late Isaac Taylor may be noted likewise as bearing on this subject, full of Christian wisdom and the results of careful and candid thought. The "Natural History of Enthusiasm" is in the main an apology for evangelical earnestness, with a careful exposition of the evils that come of it when allowed to run to seed. His "Fanaticism" indicates an advanced stage of religious degeneracy, when zeal for the Christian cause has become mixed with malignant feeling, and resorts to all manner of un-Christian devices to defeat its foes.

We have assumed throughout that any religious movement of the nature of a revival must be presided over by the minister himself. Sometimes he may be warranted in handing over the management to men of much experience, and much honoured by God in the work; but let these be regarded as exceptional cases. Even where the pastor is most deeply interested in the movement, it will sometimes be difficult to guide. Congregations have sometimes been brought to the verge of extinction through the injudicious management of revivals. In other cases they have been singularly built up by a wiser course. In an instance of the latter sort, where the congregation was doubled in numbers, and more than doubled in fervour and fruitfulness, the minister has told us that he kept his eye open to two opposite dangers—that of discouraging the development of life, on the one hand, and that of fostering the extravagances often adhering, but not necessarily cohering, to it, on the other. He found great benefit in a recipe which he called the three S's—Substitute, Suggest, Supplement. If any one wished a hymn of a somewhat ranting kind to be sung, he would invite the people to unite in singing, quietly substituting a more unexceptionable hymn; if they proposed an additional meeting at a late hour of the night, he would suggest that a meeting should be held next evening ; if any one gave a one-sided address, he would supplement it himself by presenting the other side of the question.   Thus, avoiding collision with the rushing stream, he contrived to guide it in a useful direction, and when the waters subsided a valuable deposit was left, and ever after richer clusters hung on the branches of his vines.*

* See Appendix A, Section IV.

CHAPTER XVIII.

ORGANIZATION OF WORK.

IF the question be asked, To whom does it belong to take an active part in the maintenance of Christian ordinances and the advancement of the kingdom of Christ ? the answers to the question may embrace two extremes. One extreme is, that all such work belongs to the ordained minister ; that he only has authority from his Master in the kingdom of Christ ; and that any one else who meddles with sacred things intrudes without warrant into the sacred enclosure. The other extreme is, that all who have themselves been taught of God are equally entitled, nay, bound and obliged, to minister in his kingdom ; and that for any one in that kingdom to assume and exercise authority over others, in virtue of his having been ordained by men, is to subvert the Master's order, and to hinder the full edification of the community. The one system, while it no doubt secures order and r.·gularity, tends to restrict the service of Christ to certain formal acts, and excludes Christians not ordained from all service in the house of God, except what is menial and mechanical ; the other, while affording ample scope for the exercise of gifts, makes no provision for order and authority, and tends to ecclesiastical anarchy. The best system must be one which combines both objects—secures order and authority, through office-bearers placed over the congregation, and yet affords free scope for the exercise of all their gifts and graces by those who are moved from above to help the cause of Christ.

The Presbyterian system, which just means the government of the Church by presbyters, when duly ordered and developed, tends to secure this double object. It is based on the principle of "many members in one body, and all members not having the same office." It does not hold that the gifts bestowed by the Head of the Church for the spiritual welfare of the body are all concentrated in one individual ; but, on the contrary, that they are distributed more or less throughout the members, and that scope for their orderly exercise ought to be freely afforded. It maintains, indeed, that over every congregation there ought to be one man who has been specially trained for the work of the ministry, and separated from secular pursuits in order that he may give his whole time and strength to the duties of his office. The right and warrant for this is partly that there were such men in the Church of the New Testament, and partly that experience is ever teaching that they are indispensable for the permanent order and edification of the Church. But however competent by natural gifts and spiritual grace any man may be to occupy the chief seat in a Christian synagogue, it is out of the question to suppose that he possesses all the gifts, and that no other member possesses any. In the flock of that very minister there may be some men who excel as judges of character, able to detect false pretence, and to form a just estimate of true worth ; some may have an unusual gift in prayer ; some, of very sympathetic heart, may be specially fitted for ministering to the sick and afflicted ; others have the faculty of winning the confidence of strangers, or of persons not connected with the flock ; others have a happy knack of instructing the young ; some have a great turn for evangelistic efforts ; others are interested in the improvement of the psalmody ; and some, endowed with rare persevering energy, will go on with the most trying work after others have abandoned it in despair. According to the constitution of the Presbyterian Church, certain qualified men, engaged in secular pursuits, ought to be selected and ordained to office in the congregation ; while others, though not ordained, ought to be recognised, directed, and superintended in their efforts to do good.

Two classes, elders and deacons, are specially recognised in the New Testament as ordained. In every congregation there was a *body* of elders, to whom the spiritual oversight of the congregation was committed. They are always spoken of in the plural number. The minister, indeed, is but an elder (1 Pet. v. 1), specially trained, however, and specially set apart for the service of the Church, and therefore entitled to preside, especially at the dispensation of word and sacraments, but differing from the other elders, not in the nature of his office, but in the extent of his qualifications. The spiritual authority of the Church is shared by the minister and the elders. While, therefore, the lay elders of a congregation (that is, those not separated from secular callings) are to concede to the

minister those duties for which his training and standing especially qualify him, they are to do what they can through their
own gifts for the spiritual welfare of the congregation over
which they bear rule equally with him. In like manner, though
in another sphere, deacons were ordained, in the time of the
apostles (Acts vi. 6), for the administration of the temporal
affairs of the Church. In the Presbyterian Church, however,
where the office of the deacon is regarded as instituted for the
management of secular interests, it has not been held imperative
to ordain deacons under all circumstances. On this point the
practice varies. What we are concerned to remark is, that every
duly-equipped congregation possesses a body of ordained office-
bearers, by whom, with the fullest regard to order and authority,
provision is made for the exercise of gifts and graces that tend
to edification.

But it is evident from the New Testament that elders and
deacons, though the only persons who are said to have been
formally ordained, were not the only persons who were allowed
to labour in the Church. The 16th chapter of Romans
contains the Apostle's greeting to many men and women who
were labouring in the Church at Rome. There is no reason to
suppose that all these were expressly ordained. At the top of
the list is Phebe—a servant or deaconess of the Church at
Cenchrea, but of whom we have no reason to believe that she
was ordained. Priscilla and Aquila, a married couple, come
next, the wife's name preceding the husband's. It is extremely
improbable that the long list of active men and women that
follows were persons who had all been ordained to office. But
all of them were actively using their abilities for the advancement of the kingdom, and in so doing they were not only
recognised but commended by the Apostle. It follows that in
every well-equipped congregation, in addition to those expressly
ordained, but under their sanction and superintendence, there
ought to be a body of active workers, engaged in the various
operations of Christian love and zeal which the circumstances
call for. In many such congregations we find a body of
Sunday-school teachers, or of helpers in a children's church ; a
body of district visitors ; a young men's association, a missionary
association, a psalmody association, a school committee, and a
mothers' meeting. It is right that all these should be both
recognised and superintended by the office-bearers. Their
work ought to be embraced in the prayers of the congregation,
and it ought to be made plain that they are not mere free

lances, but that they labour under the warm wing and paternal guidance of the Church.

It is not very easy to draw a line in theory between the services which are peculiar to the minister and those which may lawfully be performed by other members of a congregation. And as the line cannot easily be drawn in theory, it is not desirable to make it hard and fast in practice. It is evident that the apostles did not confine the deacons to serving tables, but allowed them, when qualified, to preach the word. Nor does it seem at all wise to try to shut the mouths of zealous men who on the streets, or at mission-meetings, try to address their fellow-sinners on the things of salvation. So long as no real interference with the stated functions of the ministry takes place, and so long as the proceedings are practically though it may be indirectly under the influence of the Church, it seems undesirable to interfere with the efforts of zealous men. Christian zeal at a white heat is so rare a quality, that even if it should be somewhat eccentric, it is well, if possible, to give it line. The real danger is connected with a class of men who are not under the superintendence of any Church, who do not believe in the Divine appointment of a regular ministry, and who are more given to deny its authority and undermine its influence than to accept its superintendence. But if more scope were afforded *within* for the labours of ardent and zealous men, there would be less opportunity for their subverting church order by operations *without*.

But there are other grounds on which this plan of co-operation in Christian work by all who have any fitness for it is to be encouraged in congregations. It is worthy of being earnestly fostered on the ground of its extraordinary benefit to the workers themselves. It is, indeed, a very important and valuable means of grace. To be doing good to others is one of the best means of getting good to one's self. "He that watereth shall be watered also himself" (Prov. xi. 29). There is an analogy here between the natural and the spiritual life. It is not merely by a process of direct nursing that the natural life becomes vigorous and robust. The man that confines himself to the house, that feeds on the tenderest dainties, that strives by every art to keep himself from draughts and damp, and on days entirely favourable takes a cautious airing at midday, is never strong. Bone and muscle are not developed by such treatment. If he would become strong, the coddling system must be abandoned, and his energies thrown into some pursuit *external to himself*, in following which his fibre may become firm and his organs vigorous. The analogy is but an imperfect one, but it may serve to set Christian men and women on their guard against the idea that a process of direct nursing, without the addition of some Christian occupation external to themselves, is the true way to preserve and develop their spiritual life. The most vigorous Christian men have found some such work not only beneficial but necessary. Dr. Chalmers had always a list of a few poor people among whom he visited, and Dr. Arnold of Rugby used to say that the two best safeguards against spiritual declension were prayer and visiting among the poor. Is there not something similar at the bottom of St. James's celebrated definition, " Pure religion and undefiled before God and the Father is this, to visit the fatherless and the widows in their affliction, and to keep himself unspotted from the world " (James i. 27).

Constituted as men are, they seem to require something over and above the direct instigation of duty, or the direct action of the highest spiritual motives, to carry them along the way of holiness, and stimulate them to the exercise of the highest graces. In ordinary life it helps a man to be moral and self-controlled, that he has others to care for who are physically weaker than himself; and in this arrangement we see a wise provision of the God of Providence. In the spiritual life it helps a Christian to be self-denied, that he has others to watch over who are spiritually weaker than himself; and in this arrangement we see a wise provision of the God of grace. Let us illustrate our position, first, by reference to one of the more mechanical of the Christian graces (although it is also, in its true exercise, much more than mechanical)—the giving of money to Christian objects. It is seldom that a mere *sense of duty* leads a rich Christian to be very liberal. But give him an interest in some definite Christian enterprise—attach him to some special mission or charity, where he sees or knows what is doing, and what needs to be done—his heart will be enlarged, and his hand will open with his heart, till he becomes a proverb for generosity. It is the same with the grace of prayer. Can any one fancy that the Apostle Paul would have prayed as he did if he had prayed only for himself? The fact of his having so many more to pray for drew out his desires, and kept him for ever repairing to the throne of grace—a duty which in other circumstances he might have sometimes neglected.

The same thing holds true of other graces, and of the

Christian life generally. The bare sense of duty, or the direct view of the unseen, has not a sufficient impulsive force on the souls of most men. It is a great advantage to be associated with religious work. It is useful to have their interests and sympathies drawn to some definite enterprise. At the same time, there is a risk in this direction as well as a benefit. The risk is, the substitution of a kind of *ecclesiastical activity* for personal and earnest godliness. A certain fussiness about church business may come practically to be regarded as a certificate of saintship. Intense sectarianism may be substituted for self-denying Christianity. Such a course is not less disastrous to ourselves than misleading to the world. It is a miserable thing to lead the men of the world to suppose, when we invite them to join us, that we just invite them to take a prominent place in certain church organizations, instead of inviting them to unite with us in trying to love and follow Jesus in every holy grace and beautiful habit of his spotless life. Connection with the Church, whether in the fellowship of worship or in the fellowship of work, is but a means to an end; and that end is, "the perfecting of the saints, till we all come in the unity of the faith, and of the knowledge of the Son of God, unto a perfect man, unto the measure of the stature of the fulness of Christ" (Eph. iv. 12, 13).

These views as to Christian usefulness are not of secondary but of primary importance for a living and thriving Church; and in order that they may be duly impressed on the people they ought to have no insignificant place among the lessons of the pulpit. They constitute a topic that should be frequently handled; indeed, it is not too much to say, that it ought to be one of the *marked* topics of the pulpit, one of the subjects on which the preacher may say, "To write" (or to speak) "the same things unto you, to me indeed is not grievous, but for you it is safe" (Phil. iii. 1). It should be the aim of the preacher to *indoctrinate* his people with this view of Christian duty and privilege, and to get them to regard it as one of the arrangements most necessary for the welfare of the Church, and for making her the blessing which she might be, and ought to be, to the world. Without going out of his way, the earnest minister will find many such opportunities. The parable of the talents; the parable of the labourers standing idle in the market-place; the mission of the seventy disciples by our Lord, apart from the twelve apostles; the commendations bestowed in the Epistles on the many men and women who served the

Church ; the counsels given us to exhort one another, to edify one another, to bear one another's burdens, to look not every man on his own things, but every man also on the things of others ; the example of Christ who came not to be ministered unto but to minister, and to give his life a ransom for many ; the genius of the Christian religion, where he who is the servant of all is the greatest of all ; the analogy of an army where not the commanding officer alone, but each soldier, is expected to fight ; the necessities of the world ; the necessities of the Church ; the danger to Christians themselves of a state of stagnation, and the numberless blessings of a state of activity ;— with related topics so pointed and so numerous as these, the minister will find no want of opportunity to press this theme. It is quite true that with a class of his people he will find it anything but popular. Reuben will prefer to abide in the sheepcotes, Gilead beyond Jordan, Asher on the seashore, and Dan in ships (Judges v. 16, 17). The selfish and the worldly will resent the summons to bestir themselves and come to the help of the Lord. But let not the minister be disheartened by a growl or a grumble. Deeper down, in the conscience of the objector, is a voice of approval, and there are times when even such persons feel a sort of pride in the zeal of their minister and the activity of his people. Only pride is not the feeling to be encouraged or tolerated. Let the spirit of self-satisfaction and pride get a footing in a vigorous congregation, alas for all that is lovely and of good report ! The best wine, according to the proverb, turns to the sourest vinegar ; and the best graces, whether in an individual or in a congregation, when thus perverted, become the most odious vices.

But it is time to address ourselves to the more practical aspect of the subject. How is the minister to go about this work of organization—how are the several agents to be selected and trained for this work, and how is the whole system to be maintained in vigour and efficiency ? But I must honestly confess that I shrink considerably from approaching this view of the subject, because, in truth, it is too much to expect that the minister shall carefully and zealously perform the laborious duties of his pulpit and his pastorate, and at the same time be the originator and the mainspring of a great system of evangelistic operations. Congregations must speedily contemplate arrangements that will give their minister some relief in pulpit and pastoral labour, if it is expected of him to superintend the varied machinery now so frequently at work in connection with congregational and territorial purposes. In the Church of England no minister in a charge of any magnitude bears the whole burden both of congregational and parochial work.

But suppose this difficulty to be got over—suppose the minister full of the desire to have an active congregation, and anxious to begin the varied operations—how is he to set about the work? In the first place, let him *pray* about it, and about every part of it, and about every agent that may be asked to take part in it, and about everything that may be undertaken by each. Let him seek to have the feeling deeply impressed on himself and all his coadjutors that this is not a warfare which he has begun on his own charges—that it is the Master's work, on which they may expect the Master's countenance if only it be directed to the advancement of his glory. Further, let him be careful to consult the office-bearers of the congregation. It may be that the elders will have little to say about it; they may have no help and no counsel to offer, and asking their advice and countenance may be a mere form, without practical result. But, on the other hand, there may be both counsel and help, and in any case there is such a tendency in men to complain if they are not sufficiently recognised in any undertaking, that it is always well to cut off all occasion for such complaint.

Suppose, then, that the elders devolve the active promotion of the work on the minister, the first thing he may have to settle is—the operations to be undertaken. This, of course, will depend on the nature of the case, the character of the population, and the composition of the flock. In general it is desirable to proceed cautiously, letting one branch of operations be pretty well established and consolidated before other branches are begun. Whether the work be a work of teaching, or of visiting, or of taking a part in meetings, the minister must not expect to find a sufficient staff of agents duly qualified at once. It will be well for him if he can find one or more capable of entering into the work intelligently, of giving it a tone, and of setting an example to the rest. But with regard to many he must lay his account with the need of a tolerably long process of education. Moreover, the minister must not expect that his people are to enter heartily at once into all that interests him, or are to rush to offer their services the moment he announces that he has need of them. He must take special means for awakening their interest.

And here it may be useful for us to consider what it is that gives to some ministers the remarkable power they possess of securing the services of others. We say of some men that they have a remarkable power of organization. They succeed wonderfully in getting others to work with them. What is the secret of this success? Not mere zeal, not mere activity (though these are included), but a combination of qualities deserving of careful study. Of these the following may be noted: 1. A clear aim and a firm will; the minister having a definite object which he can easily state and get others to understand, and holding firmly to it till it be attained. 2. Great readiness for personal labour; for a leader must not spare himself, but be forward in personal service. 3. Judgment and tact in finding out what other people are most fit for, and attaching them accordingly. 4. Elasticity and fertility of resource, capacity of adapting himself to circumstances. 5. Friendly interest in those whom he associates with him, a capacity to make common work a stepping-stone to mutual friendship, confidence, and affection. In a word, personal attractiveness and power to interest.

Further, the minister is not to deem it enough merely to announce from the pulpit the project he has on hand and his reasons for taking it up. He must first of all try to talk freely on the subject in his ordinary and pastoral intercourse with his people, taking them as it were into his confidence, making them the partners of his aims and of his plans, and asking them to become his fellow-workers in carrying them into effect. And when the work is going on he must try to make it the occasion of developing a social feeling among the workers, of associating with it a sense of social enjoyment, and likewise a sense of spiritual benefit to themselves. It is not easy to exaggerate the benefit of such frankness in dealing with one's associates.

With every class of agents in congregational or parochial work, it is most important to have regular meetings for prayer, conference, and quickening of interest. It is not desirable that these should be very frequent, but it is quite essential that they should be regular. At such meetings the minister may tell of what has been done, or of what is doing elsewhere in similar enterprises. Many is the wonderful narrative whose quickening effect time and space alike fail to impair. Works like "Praying and Working," by Mr. Fleming Stevenson; "Six Months among the Charities of Europe," by Mr. de Liefde; "The Book and its Mission," by Mrs. Ranyard; "English Hearts and English Hands," by Miss Marsh; "Haste to the Rescue," and "Arrest the Destroyer's March," by Mrs. Wight-

man ; and " Ragged Homes and how to Mend them," by Mrs.
Bayly, are adapted for being most useful both to the minister
and his people. It is, moreover, desirable to have occasional
or, perhaps, periodical meetings *of the various classes of workers*
in a congregation for social intercourse, and for addresses connected with the work. This tends to knit them together in
brotherly bonds, to develop a spirit of interest and mutual
affection, as well as to gather recruits from among the more
willing and interested members of the congregation, who may
be specially asked to be present on such occasions.*

The remarks now made are applicable chiefly to congregations in large towns and in the more populous districts elsewhere. To small flocks in the country they are applicable only
in a very limited degree. It is one of the difficulties connected
with small flocks how work is to be found for exercising and
developing the gifts and graces of the members. Some such
work, however, there obviously is, and probably by conferring
with friends and brethren interested in the subject, the young
minister will soon be able to settle what line it will be best for
him to follow. It has sometimes been said sarcastically that
Christianity has been a failure. The sunken masses are pointed
to in proof. If the Christian leaven were the right kind of
leaven, it is said that it would leaven the whole lump. But
the fault lies not with Christianity, but with Christians.
There is need of a more active, diffusive, affectionate Christian
spirit, not on the part of ministers only, but on the part of the
whole body of the Christian people. At the present day the
Holy Spirit seems to be pressing this truth home, and calling
on Christian men and women to act on it. It remains to be
seen whether the Christian people are willing to be led forth to
the enterprise ; or whether, preferring carnal ease and indulgence, they will fall under the curse of Meroz, " who came not
to the help of the Lord, to the help of the Lord against the
mighty " (Judges v. 23).

* See Appendix A, Section V.

CHAPTER XIX.

HITHERTO we have considered the minister almost exclusively in his relation to his own flock—first as a preacher,
and then as a pastor. But there is hardly any sphere, however
remote or humble, in which the minister does not sustain some
relation to a wider community. No small share of his influence, both with his flock and with the outer world, depends on
the manner in which he acquits himself in this wider relation;
and now that we have glanced at the leading topics that
concern the inner pastoral circle, it may be well to advert to
some of those that lie in the wider or more catholic sphere.
We are now to consider the minister as a public man—a
leading member of the general community—bound to take
an interest in public institutions, and to endeavour to give
a Christian tone and direction both to local and national procedure.

Two extremes present themselves here, between which, as in
most similar cases, the true path will be found.

One extreme is, when the minister is merely the pastor of
his own flock, and takes no concern in anything beyond; the
other, when he gets so overwhelmed with public engagements
that he is unable to discharge efficiently the duties of his own
charge. In the one case he has too little public spirit, in the
other too much. It is true, indeed, that the character of a
man's gifts goes far to determine whether or not he ought to
take much share in public business. Some men may be so cut
out for the quiet pastoral walk, and so awkward and miserable
on the platform or in the committee-room, that no reasonable
doubt can exist as to which is their proper sphere; while some,
on the other hand, may have such shining gifts for public life as
to make it a duty to take a large share of its burden, especially
in difficult times, even though certain parts of pastoral work

should suffer. But in truth every minister ought to concern himself in some way with the cause of Christianity at large. It was not the high priest only that had cause to tremble for the ark of God when it was carried into battle with the Philistines, but every Levite, nay, every Israelite, throughout the country. For a minister to shut himself up within the limits of his congregation, and leave all the more general interests of Christianity to their fate, is to forget that he is not merely the minister of that congregation, but that he is also the servant of Him who declares that the field is the world. In ordinary service nothing is worse than for a servant having a special charge in one department to take no interest in anything that concerns his master beyond it, and to neglect numberless opportunities of serving him because they lie in spheres that have not been especially committed to him. There are important matters connected with the cause of Christ that from their nature cannot be especially committed to individuals; it therefore becomes every minister to consider whether he be not called to give his help in some of them.

Undoubtedly, when one is first planted in his charge, his first and main duty is to work actively there. It would be unreasonable to deny him the opportunity of forming his plans and consolidating his arrangements there before he should be called actively to other work. The most essential reputation for any minister to earn is that of a faithful and laborious workman at home. The public will not be much disposed in his favour if he come to the platform or the committee board apparently because he has a craving for work more exciting and more public than his own. The Apostle's counsel to deacons is applicable, *mutatis mutandis*, to young ministers : " They that have used the office of a deacon well purchase to themselves a good degree [a good standing] and great boldness in the faith which is in Christ Jesus " (1 Tim. iii. 13). It were a great mistake to suppose that a man's antecedents in his pastoral sphere have no bearing upon his success on the platform or at the committee meeting. There is a secret disposition in his favour when he has acquired the character of a faithful and laborious minister, that gives weight to his counsels and force to his words. Public life is far more exposed than private to the influence of jealousies and cross currents of various kinds; but nothing is more fitted to smooth such jealousies, and conciliate favour for one who ventures on the public arena, than the fact of his having already proved himself a laborious worker, as well as a pure-hearted, humble Christian, in his own proper sphere.

Of the more public relations which ministers have to sustain, we may notice, as the most important—1. Relation to other denominations of Christians, and particularly to their ministers. 2. Relation to their own brethren, especially in church courts. 3. Relation to public institutions and movements of various kinds, local and general, charitable, social, educational, or political. 4. Relation to public controversies which may be agitating the community, or to matters of public morality. 5. Relation to literature and science, especially when these are much used in the interests of error, cr in opposition to Christian truth.

1. *Relation to other Denominations.*—Between two different if not opposite impulses, the conscientious minister may sometimes find himself in a difficulty. The instinct of neighbourliness will make him desire to be as friendly and as cordial as possible with ministers of other denominations ; whlle the impulse of faithfulness may somewhat restrain him, under the feeling that he is appointed to witness for truths which his brethren are neglecting or are even, perhaps, violating, and that his testimony for these truths requires him to maintain in public an attitude of isolation from them. But it is not correct to affirm that he is appointed merely to witness for these truths. A barren testimony is like faith without works, a shrivelled, useless thing. He is not less appointed to *commend* his principles, to endeavour to win the assent of others to them, so far as this can be done without concealment or compromise of their real nature. The question arises, Does a Christian man, and especially a Christian minister, best commend the truths which may be said to be committed to him by maintaining an attitude of separation, or by showing a kindly and brotherly spirit towards ministers of other denominations and co-operating with them so far as he freely can ?

Whatever, theoretically, may be said in answer to this question, and whatever may be the state of feeling in places overrun with prejudice, there can be little doubt that the Christian public and the public at large think better not only of the *man*, but of the *principles* of the man, who meets frankly with his brethren, where common action may be held, than of the man who stiffly retreats to a position of separation. Where there is frank and outspoken sincerity, and where a minister bears the character of a thorough and honest man, who holds no

opinion without cause, and who is both able and ready to give
an answer to every man that asks him concerning it, not only
is nothing lost by cordiality and affection, but much is gained.
The public, and notably the Christian public, have no favour
for quarrels or coldness among ministers. The points on which
they differ usually appear less important to the general community than to those who differ over them. By a sort of
instinct, bitterness of spirit and speech is judged by the world
to be unbecoming in Christian ministers. A minister whose
life and character attest his earnestness, whose active interest
in all that concerns the welfare of his own denomination attests
his loyalty, and who scruples not to speak out boldly and
strongly, but without bitterness, on suitable occasions, in
support of the distinctive principles of his Church, is much more
likely to commend his Church to the community than one who,
to show how much regard he has for denominational principles,
is distant and, perhaps, bitter to his brethren.

Affectionate cordiality, moreover, supported by consistent
action, has a wonderfully conciliating effect. It has been
observed, times without number, that men who keep aloof
have a tendency to imagine terrible evil of each other ; but
that commonly, when brought into friendly contact, they are
surprised to find how often their prejudices were unfounded,
and how much they have in common. It is seldom that men
think alike till they have learned to *feel* alike. Unions are
commonly effected in the heart before they are affirmed by the
head. Undoubtedly it is one of the most important yet difficult
aims a minister can have, to keep his heart warm and flowing,
when many things may be happening that are fitted to chill
it. But little though it is often heeded, the 13th chapter of
1 Corinthians is pre-eminently a minister's chapter ; and the
charity that is there enthroned still reigns, queen of all the
graces, and worthy to be coveted as the best of gifts.

2. *Relations to brother Ministers.*—The nature of a minister's
relations to the brethren of his own Church must depend considerably on the nature of the district in which he is situated.
If it be a thin rural district, the case will be widely different
from that of a city locality. In general, however, it will be
found, that while he sustains an obvious relation to all the
brethren in his neighbourhood, he gets into closer and more
social fellowship with a smaller number nearer him, perhaps, in
locality, or in age, or more congenial in tastes and habits. In
country districts especially ministers are pretty much thrown

upon each other for society—a circumstance that has both advantages and drawbacks. An unsocial and inhospitable minister, who shuns the society of his brethren, and indeed of his kind, is a misfortune, and gives too ready occasion to those who seek occasion against the servants of the gospel. Where ministers are inclined to social fellowship with one another, the disadvantage lies in their being so much alike that they learn little of the actual world, with its tastes and tendencies, and are sometimes confirmed in prejudices and narrow views.

The more formal gatherings of ministers ought to conduce to the increase both of personal devotedness and of professional activity. Some plan should be fallen upon whereby iron may sharpen iron, and the servant of the Lord may leave the society of his brethren not only with a heart refreshed by pleasant intercourse, but with all his activities quickened—with a more earnest desire to labour heartily in his work, and with a m₁re clear perception of the way in which he should do so. In country districts, which from their very nature are more inclined to stagnation, where the work of the minister is more uniform, and therefore more likely to become monotonous, the value of such meetings of brethren can hardly be over-estimated. At such meetings the opportunity presents itself to take stock, as it were, of the wants of the whole district ; to consider the prevailing tendencies, not only as to belief, but as to practice too ; and to concert measures in common by which its spiritual health may be improved and its moral temperature elevated. It must be borne in mind that our church system, rightly or wrongly, makes no provision for the episcopal superintendence of a district, otherwise than by the action of the united presbyters themselves. That which is everybody's business, we all know, is apt to be nobody's ; and though it might not be becoming in a young minister to put himself prominently forward in the way of calling his brethren to new duties or to unwonted enterprises, he cannot too soon begin to take a comprehensive view of the state of the whole district in which his lot is cast, or to consider the best means of providing for its necessities.

In regard to what is more properly the business of church courts—Presbyteries, Synods, and General Assemblies—it is obvious that the young minister must feel his way. It may be that he has no inclination for such work. The temptation then is to abstain from attending the meetings, and undoubtedly the temptation is considerable when one has other work in hand in

which one feels that one may be of some use, while one has no
such hope in attending meetings of church courts. Such a
practice—the practice of staying away—may arise from one or
other of two causes : either from the feeling that the business
is in the hands of better qualified men, and will be better conducted by them ; or from the feeling that the meetings are not
conducted as they ought to be, and that absence is the most
convenient way of testifying against them. But if the former
be the view, some consideration ought to be had for the depressing effect on those who do grapple with the business,
which the habitual or frequent absence of respected brethren
must have ; and if the latter be the view, it should be remembered that absence from meetings where one is understood to
be present, and for whose procedure one is officially responsible, is a mode of dissent only to be justified when the
circumstances are very extreme.

In connection with our church courts there are certain duties
which involve considerable labour, and there are other duties
with which there is connected a certain amount of honour.   It
would be unbecoming in younger members to aspire to the
latter without having been willing to take a fair share of the
former.   " *Juniores ad labores* " is a maxim from which there is
no appeal ; and not only is it in itself proper that work involving considerable physical exertion and mechanical labour should
be cheerfully done by the younger members, but it will be found
that this is the real road to honour—the true way not only to
influence, but to influence cordially acknowledged and readily
sustained by others.   In point of fact, there is no royal road to
influence in church courts.   The men who usually attain such
influence are men who have taken endless trouble—men who
have come at the beginning of the meetings, and waited to the
end—men who have plodded through weary details, and borne
the heat and burden of many a laborious day.   Even shining
gifts for public speaking do not command this place of influence
unless they are associated with willingness to take trouble.   It
may be said that, if such be the case, there is little chance for
any one gaining a conspicuous place, unless he have a physical
constitution capable of enduring the longest and most wearisome
meetings, and of returning early in the morning, after only half
a night's rest, as fresh and vigorous as ever.   And possibly this
is not very far from the truth.   But without entailing on men
of ordinary or of hardly ordinary strength, a duty which would
amount pretty nearly to martyrdom, it may be undoubtedly

affirmed that no man will readily command the confidence of an
assembly, in urging any course of procedure, who has not taken
a fair share of the more ordinary work—the drudgery, as it may
be called by some, of ecclesiastical business. This is especially
the case when a man stands up to object to some important
course which his more active brethren have proposed. The
objector may possibly begin by saying that he has not been a
prominent member—in other words, that he has been a most
irregular attender. The remark is a perilous one, for it is as
likely to operate against him as for him. And in every instance
care should be taken not to assume an attitude of mere resist-
ance. The lowest class of minds are capable of resisting, just
as the most mischievous of men can place a log across the rails
and upset a railway train. An attitude of mere opposition is
essentially weak. Those who offer opposition to the plans of
others are bound to produce better plans of their own, and
to give some practical security that they shall be efficiently
worked.

" Si quid novisti rectius istis,
Candidus imperti ; si non, his utere mecum."

3. *Relation to Public Institutions and Movements.*—In this
department, as in the preceding, much will depend on the
nature of the locality. Our institutions may be said, in theory
at least, to be the results of applied Christianity—our civilisation is a Christian civilisation ; and there cannot but be much
in the nature of these institutions, as well as in the way in
which it may be proposed to carry them out, that is interesting
and important in the eyes of the Christian minister. It is to be
remarked, too, that public opinion has very explicitly connected
the clergy with certain of our institutions, while with other
things it is much more chary of letting them meddle, and from
some it excludes them altogether. Education, the care of the
poor, and the management of public charities, have hitherto
been deemed appropriate to the clergy ; social and political
movements are in a somewhat doubtful category ; while from
financial, municipal, and parliamentary business they are wholly
excluded. This decision of the public voice is one with which
the clergy themselves have little cause to quarrel. The fact is,
that in our larger communities the conducting of public institutions and movements is not only work that may be done by our
Christian laymen, but it is the very work for which many of
them are peculiarly adapted. To drag the clergy from the

proper duties of a calling so laborious and extensive as theirs, to do work which our laymen are equally able to do, and which forms a wholesome occupation for their leisure hours, would be a singularly misdirected policy.

To such work, therefore, the clergy ought not ordinarily to consider themselves called, unless, perhaps, under two conditions. First, when in this way they get a door opened to extensive pastoral usefulness—let us say, among the inmates of a hospital, or the children of a school; and second, when there is a peculiar call to set things as it were in the right Christian groove—when Christianity, instead of being exemplified, is outraged by some institution, or when social or political arrangements are adjusted not to the benefit, but to the destruction, of the best interests of men.* We grant that whatever is fitted to promote human welfare has a certain character of sacredness, and may on that ground be counted not inappropriate in a minister; but regard must be had to its tendency to draw away his mind from the spiritual objects of the ministry, and tempt him, as a plain man once said, to make a by-job of his people's souls. Work which is merely useful, or merely benevolent, but not distinctively Christian, is not necessarily suitable employment for a minister.

On the other hand, it is suitable employment for a minister, from the pulpit, from the platform, or from the press, to show how Christianity has to do with all sorts of institutions, and to urge his people to carry it into effect in every relation of life. And here he must not be too timid. He must not avoid the

---

* No one, surely, would say that Dr. Andrew Thomson of St. George's did wrong in leaving the beaten tracks of the ministry to denounce the iniquity of West Indian slavery; or that Dr. Chalmers did wrong in contending for a more Christian mode of providing for the poor than that of the poor-law system; or that Dr. Duncan of Ruthwell did wrong in establishing savings-banks as a great encouragement to the habits of forethought and economy; or that Dr. Adam Thomson of Coldstream did wrong so far as he applied his energies to the abolition of the monopoly for printing the Bible; or that Dr. Guthrie did wrong in throwing his heart into the cause of ragged schools; or that those did wrong who strove to secure better houses and better days for working men. On the other hand, we question if Dr. Cartwright did right in turning his energies to machinery, although he became the inventor of the power-loom; or Dr. Forsyth, though he invented the percussion cap; or Dr. Bell, though he invented the reaping-machine. The difference between the two classes of cases is obvious. The one involve the application of some great law of Christianity for curing evils destructive of moral and religious habits; the other involve merely the application of a mechanical principle fitted to promote a temporal interest.

very forms of unchristian activity that exist around him. He must call on masters and employers to be considerate of their servants, and servants to be conscientiously careful of the interests of their masters. He must be fearless in rebuking sin wherever it is in mischievous activity, and in trying to promote a holier state of society, a more truly Christian civilisation. He will have to lay his account with considerable ill-will and opposition ; let him, on that account, make the more sure of his ground, and study the more carefully that wonderfully useful rule of the kingdom, "Be ye therefore wise as serpents, and harmless as doves."

4. *Relation to Public Controversies and Questions.*—Perhaps there is no department of his duty that demands more care and pains than this. Controversy, and emphatically religious controversy, invaluable though it is for quickening the faculties and intensifying enthusiasm in favour of truth, seems to have a marvellous power to elicit the qualities of the old man. Even good men are singularly apt to be thrown off their guard, and to forget the necessity of guarding tongue and temper, heart and head, in the excitement of controversial warfare. The Psalmist's resolution to put a bridle on his lips while the wicked was before him needs to be remembered, but is too often forgot. Of all kinds of writing, the controversial affords the least satisfaction to the author in the retrospect, and probably the largest number of passages which, dying, he would wish to blot. The great temptation in controversy is to deal hard hits to opponents. Whether in our present fallen condition men will ever be able to discuss great religious questions in a thoroughly Christian spirit—whether they will ever attain the needful excitement of their controversial faculties, without a corresponding excitement of their keener passions—whether they will ever come to a pure and simple love of truth without love of victory, and a pure and simple hatred of error without hatred of opponents— are questions on which theory might lead us to one conclusion, while experience, perhaps, would force us to another. But surely there is room for a much more careful self-control than is commonly practised, and a much more earnest endeavour to do Christ's controversial work in Christ's own spirit. For Christ *has* controversial work for his servants to do. And it is remarkable how much, amid the excitement and directly hostile influence of controversy, both personal and public religion have been advanced. So, also, when a minister deems it his duty to attack some prevalent or popular vice. He may encounter no

little opposition ; but most likely, through God's blessing, he will be the means of so stirring the consciences of some of his hearers, even of those who are most angry at the time, that a great change for the better shall be the ultimate result.

5. *Relation to Science and Literature.*—It is not reasonable to expect that all ministers shall be *savants*, or that every preacher shall be a *littérateur*. Much must be left to taste and natural ability, in the way of determining who shall specially devote themselves to these methods of serving the cause of Christ. The fact is that it is hardly possible for any man adequately to discharge the duties of an active ministry, and to be at the same time a man of science or of letters.

It was long ago seen clearly by Chalmers and others, that the perils arising to the interests of religion from literature and science could not be efficiently met except by the creation of situations in which Christian men would have leisure for such employment. The influence of science and literature at the present day on religious opinion and practice—the adverse influence, we may say, in many important quarters—is such that the Christian Church might well afford to encourage the efforts of any of her sons who were in any way competent to wield these weapons on the side of truth. Literature nowadays is not the starving profession it was last century, when, even under favourable circumstances, authors could aspire little higher than to a garret in Grub Street. Men of letters, nowadays are not the threadbare adventurers that could only hope to make way in the world by attaching themselves, in dedications of the most obsequious flattery, to the chariot-wheels of some noble lord. The products of our intellectual chiefs are not now given to the world in quarto or folio volumes, in which streams of large print flow luxuriously through ample "meadows of margin." Quick and hot as sparks from the anvil, many of our ablest writers coin their thoughts into words, and the periodical press carries them, day by day, in tens of thousands of copies, to every important centre and to every remote corner of the land.

No minister of the gospel, interested in the cause of truth, and aware how subtle many of the influences are that obstruct it, can view this state of things with indifference. There is great need at the present day of Christian writers of high ability, capable of commanding the ear of all classes and circles ; and our people should be reminded that, in their prayers to the Lord of the Harvest, they ought to keep in view this department of the Master's service; all the more that there is no regular provision for training such men, and that, even if there were, they are raised up rather than trained up, and come to the Christian community as special gifts from God.

What is the best thing to be done for Christianizing our literature and science at the present day, is undoubtedly a difficult problem. Those who make them mere matters of by-play, filling the *horæ subsecivæ* of an otherwise laborious life, can hardly expect to be of great service. Literature and science have now so many sons who give their whole energies to them, that mere *dilettanti* contributors must hold a very secondary place. And it is well worth noticing that there is a great jealousy of such outsiders among the regular members of the profession. A man must have done some good honest work in literature or science before his name will have weight or his writings influence in these circles. When theologians, for example, who are not known to have done scientific work come forward to criticise and blame the views of those who have, they are commonly dismissed rather contemptuously with the *ne sutor ultra crepidam* argument. There is no circle of *savants* where such a man as Livingstone would not have been listened to with profound respect, just because he was such a fearless, self-denying worker. If much is to be done in the way of Christianizing literature and science, it must be by a class of Christian men who shall make the one or the other their proper vocation.

The first duty of the clergy to literature is to cultivate that of their own profession. If they do so effectually they do a great service; a service, too, that may react on the general literature of the country, and secure for Christianity more respectful treatment there. It is also, doubtless, the duty of a minister to be in some degree familiar with the current literature and science of the day. If his sermons and conversation show utter ignorance of these things, it is little wonder if he excites the prejudices of those who are devoted to them. Such men feel that he takes no interest in what is interesting to them, and a great gulf immediately separates them. But in fact no man who is ignorant of literature and science can know what is stirring in educated men's minds, or be able to adapt his message to them. It is a common belief among some that in general the clergy know nothing of, and care nothing for, anything save what belongs to their own profession. They are counted guilty of ignorance and want of sympathy; and in many instances the charge may be just. But in those who have had a university training and the advantages of close contact with the best culture of their country, such ignorance and apathy are quite inexcusable.

Many examples show that ministers of active mind and habits may sometimes aid the cause of literature or of science without neglecting the proper duties of their sphere.   Such men as the late Dr. James Hamilton or Dr. Tristram have done yeoman's service in this way.   In the lighter departments of religious literature there is a wide field for able writers, provided they rise above that mediocrity which it is hard to condemn, yet impossible to encourage.   The position of a successful author is much to be desired, enabling one to command an audience in all parts of the country, and to exercise an influence that ramifies in every direction.   The toils of authorship, in such a profession as that of the ministry, are manifold and exhausting, but it is one of the great pleasures as well as surprises of life for a Christian author to learn that he has been useful to persons he never saw, and thrown brightness into abodes of whose very existence he had never heard.

CHAPTER XX.

BEFORE concluding our view of the work of the ministry, and the qualifications for performing it, one great subject yet remains—the influence of personal character.

Character, as it is one of the most impalpable, so it is one of the most powerful moral forces in a well-conditioned society. Built up imperceptibly by slow degrees, as the coral reef is built up from the minute secretions of the coral insect, and ripening as quietly and steadily as the apple which day by day receives its fresh touch from the sunbeam, the character of a good man becomes a force as sure, and in a sense as irresistible, as that of gravitation. It is a force not to be attained by direct aim or effort, but as the indirect result of a course of life consistently followed from youth to old age. Every Church and almost every district presents samples of such men, but probably it is in times of persecution that they become most conspicuous. Polycarp, in his extreme old age, going forth meekly to seal with his blood the testimony that he had borne so consistently to Christ, is the type of a noble army, of whom, as of Daniel, even their enemies have had to confess, that no fault could be found against them, unless it were in the matter of their God. Chaucer, referring, as is commonly believed, to the reformer Wycliffe, drew a picture which Dryden amplified in another connection :—

> " By preaching much, by practice more, he wrote
> A living sermon of the truths he taught."

Bunyan has drawn a similar portrait, with his usual skill: " The picture of a very grave person hung up against the wall; and this was the fashion of it. It had eyes lifted up to heaven; the best of books in his hand; the law of truth was written on his lips; the world was behind his back. It stood as if it pleaded with men, and a crown of glory was over its head."

But though it is persecution chiefly that drags such men into fame, they are often to be found in ordinary times in the quiet retreats of country places, or in the less conspicuous congregations in towns. They are pillars of the Christian edifice, epistles of Christ, known and read of all men. It is not in the ministry alone that men of this type are to be found; old " David Deans " is the representative of the class in the ranks of the laity. People feel that the very presence of such men has all the effect of a sermon; and infidelity has sometimes to confess, that though it can find an answer to every other argument in favour of the Bible, it can find none to that which is derived from the lives of the men who have imbibed its spirit and consistently followed its guidance.

It is a happy circumstance that this element of power does not depend on brilliant talents, lofty position, or even great professional skill. It is the crown which in the later years of his life the Church assigns to the faithful minister, whose powers of oratory may not have been great, but who has quietly and consistently done his duty, and shown unswerving allegiance to the principles which he has professed.

Consistency, indeed, reveals in one word the secret of weight of character. Conformity to the will of God, unselfish and unworldly devotion to the great objects of the ministry, singleness of heart in serving the Master and seeking the good of the flock, are the great qualities which secure this distinction in the end. An elastic conscience, a left-handed devotion to the interests of the world, the manœuvres of Mr. Facing-Bothways, and the dodges of Mr. By-ends, are utterly fatal to it. A man of poor ability and almost childish simplicity is far more likely to secure it than the cleverest orator and most skilful diplomatist who cannot forget himself.

" A clergyman," says Bishop Burnet, " by his character and design of life, ought to be a man separated from the cares and concerns of this world, and dedicated to the study and meditation of Divine matters, whose conversation ought to be a pattern for others; a constant preacher to his people, who ought to offer up the prayers of the people in their name and as their mouth to God; who ought to be praying and interceding for them in secret as well as officiating among them in public; who ought to be distributing among them the bread of life, the Word of God; and to be dispensing among them the sacred rites which are the badges, the union, and the support of Christians. . . . That he may perform all these duties with more advantage and better effect, he ought to behave himself so well that his own conversation may not only be without offence, but so exemplary that his people may have reason to conclude that he himself does firmly believe all those things which he proposes to them, that he thinks himself bound to follow all those rules that he sets them, and that they may see such a serious spirit of devotion in him that from thence they may be induced to believe that his chief design among them is to do them good and to save their souls ; which may prepare them so to esteem and love him that they may not be prejudiced against anything that he says or does in public by anything that they observe in himself in secret."*

It may be useful to notice in detail some of the elements on which weight of character depends.

1. In the apostolical enumeration of qualities necessary for a bishop, we find it laid down that he must be *grave.* The fitness of gravity in a minister will be evident to all who consider the special object of his office. That office, if we speak of it in general terms, is for urging on men a regard to the more serious and solemn aspects of life ; and the man who has chosen this for his life-work ought surely himself habitually to exemplify the seriousness which he seeks to impress on others. If we describe the office more exactly, in its Christian aspect, it is for promoting peace between God and man through the sacrifice of the cross ; and he who deals in so solemn a business ought to show himself habitually in sympathy with it. Unquestionably, therefore, gravity or seriousness should lie at the foundation, as it were, of the character of a Christian minister. But it does not need to be unmitigated gravity. For when parties stand to one another in the close personal relation of a minister to his people, unmitigated gravity is rather a hindrance than a help. It has a kind of repulsive effect, especially upon the young. A little playfulness of manner in private has a wonderful opening effect ; it softens the unapproachable solemnity with which the pulpit surrounds the preacher, and establishes a more frank and cordial relation between him and his youthful hearers. The play of a harmless humour sometimes proves to be that "touch of nature which makes the whole world kin." There is a medium path here between two extremes. At one extreme is an excess of frivolity. There are ministers who seem to think

* Burnet's " Pastoral Care," p. 2.

R

that as they are compelled to be grave in the pulpit, they may make up for that by unbounded levity in private. A professional propriety requires them to be serious in public, but, to show that they are not tied up by professional propriety, they take pleasure in throwing off all restraint and showing themselves elsewhere the most jovial of men. But there is a contradiction here which forfeits the esteem even of the worldly-minded. Such a course indicates a want of belief in those solemn truths which make the pulpit a place of such gravity. If the truths are real of which the Christian minister has charge, they not only demand of him a serious tone in the pulpit, but they demand a measure of habitual seriousness on all occasions and in all companies. It can never be right or becoming in one specially charged with the custody of these solemn truths to abandon himself to a frivolity which makes him the congenial companion of the most careless. Even worldly men cannot in their hearts esteem the man who can lay aside his cloth, as the world's phrase is, as occasion may tempt him, and be as completely one of themselves as if there were no truth in his sermons, no reality in God's wrath against sin and in the awful doom of the sinner.

For a similar reason, the minister who makes it his study to preserve a grim reserve and sombre demeanour on all occasions fails likewise to secure the respect he might have. With such a man the gravity of the clerical character is considered to be an assumed, not a real manner, a homage to the proprieties, instead of the product of a genuine feeling. It is not the artificial gravity into which a reverend pedant schools himself that is a real force in the world, but the gravity that results from *the true impression on himself* of those great truths with which it is his office to deal. And the minister whose habitual gravity is the result of real feeling is much less likely than the other to carry his gravity to a morbid pitch. He is much more likely to know the proper occasions for the play of lighter and more humorous feelings, and to give effect to his nature accordingly. He is more likely to know "the time to laugh," since he knows "the time to weep." A real man, obeying real forces, and not merely artificial regulations, his very instincts will show him that man's nature was not designed to be constantly occupied with the most solemn and awful relations of things, and that there are occasions in Providence, as well as moods of nature, that seem to invite us to a rejoicing and jubilant, and even a merry outpouring of the soul.

" The parson," says George Herbert, " sometimes refresheth himself, as knowing that nature will not bear everlasting droopings, and that pleasantness of disposition is a great key to do good, not only because all men shun the company of perpetual severity, but also for that, when they are in company, instructions seasoned with pleasantness both enter sooner and root deeper. Wherefore he condescends to human frailties both in himself and in others, and intermingles some mirth in his discourses occasionally, according to the pulse of the hearer." *

The remark has often been made, that a vein of genuine humour is closely allied to true pathos. The orators that have most power to make men weep are often those who have also most power to make them laugh. The fountain of tears and the fountain of laughter lie close to each other. Men of such temperament have a great faculty of rapid transition from one mood to another. Almost at a bound they can pass from the lightest humour to the deepest pathos. So abrupt sometimes are these transitions, that to men of ordinary temperament they appear irreverent. In many cases such a view of their character would be unjust. Men of extraordinary mental elasticity are not to be judged by the standard of the slowest and stiffest natures. At the same time, even a vein of natural humour needs, in a minister of the gospel especially, to be kept under control. The time is short, the solemn aspects of life are the decisive aspects; " it remaineth that they that weep be as though they wept not, and they that rejoice as though they rejoiced not, . . . fort he fashion of this world passeth away" (1 Cor. vii. 30, 31).

There are other aspects of ministerial deportment that this word " gravity " brings up. It suggests the question, Ought a minister to be affable or reserved? Ought he to take elaborate care of his dignity, or leave his dignity to take care of itself? Ought he to mingle with society, or to hold himself aloof? Ought he to countenance recreations, and, if so, what? Ought he to allow amusements to be carried on in his house, for the sake of his family and their friends, or ought his dwelling to exhibit a stern protest against all manner of worldly vanity, in literature, in dress, in amusements—in everything, in short, of a lighter kind, that is sought after by the age?

Into these questions we cannot enter elaborately or exhaus-

* Herbert's " Priest to the Temple," chap. xxvii.

tively. They are, many of them, so much questions of detail, that specific rules cannot be laid down regarding them, and ministers must try to shape their course in each case according to the best judgment they can form of the particular circumstances. For the most part affability, or at least accessibility, is a desirable quality, for frankness encourages frankness; and the man who locks up all his own thoughts and feelings from the gaze of others as carefully and as rigidly as a jailer locks up his prisoners, is not very likely to get his people to throw open their hearts to him. Yet, on the other hand, it is not to be desired that a minister should throw everything open. It is not for edification that he should quite readily place himself on a footing of equality with all. People respect a minister all the more when he keeps his own place, and does not allow persons who are not his equals to assume a tone of equality. This can be done, and by genuine and real men it is done without an artificial effort to maintain their dignity. The artificial effort to maintain dignity is commonly made by persons who lose the respect of the community by weak or foolish conduct, and try to save themselves from the effects of such conduct by falling back, on occasions, on what is due to the character of their office. But there is great force in the pithy observation, that if a minister cannot command respect he need not demand it. Respect is an unconscious homage; like the sensitive plant, it shuts itself up when force is applied.

As to the question of mingling in general society, if it be a matter which the minister has it in his own power to determine, and not a question providentially foreclosed, we should say that the degree to which society should be frequented must depend on the answers to such questions as these: What amount of time have I to give to it? What effect does it produce on my spiritual and ministerial character— does it quicken me or hinder me? And further, am I able to *hold my own* in society, or am I swept down by the current? Am I able to vindicate my views, to tell men their duty, to speak a word in season as an ambassador of Christ, or is the worldly stream that flows on such occasions too strong for me, too strong for my powers of conversation, and too strong for my courage and my faith? Duties of a determinate character are not to be shirked through a sense of weakness, but are to be courageously undertaken in reliance on the strength that is made perfect in weakness; but duties of an indeterminate character are not to be placed in the same category, and a minister of the gospel who feels that he cannot hold his ground in general society, and that he is under no obligation to frequent it, will do well to appear but seldom there.

In regard to *recreations*, the rule to be followed will probably depend on the question whether or not the prevalent feeling in regard to them is wholesome or morbid *in its degree*. In our own day, the feeling in favour of certain amusements has become so strong, that many ministers who have no ascetical tendencies are feeling it their duty to try to modify it. Intense devotion to such things seems to them to interfere with those habits of self-control and devotion to duty which are essential for the Christian life, and to which it is eminently salutary to train the young. And in regard to the families of ministers, while care should be taken not to bind by rules so strict as to produce reaction, it is reasonable that in some degree they should visibly share in that separation from the world to which the head of the house, by his very office, has devoted himself. If the members of the family do not heartily sympathize in this with its head, it is difficult, or rather impossible, to get the spirit of the household such as is desirable. But it is a blessed household in which all are of one heart and soul in their attachment to the Lord and to his work, and when the tone of holy cheerfulness by which all are pervaded proclaims to the world, that where Christian love has its reign, and where there is pleasure in serving God and in doing good to man, life does not need all kinds of artificial excitements, and that the sweetest enjoyment is inseparably connected with the highest duty. "Thou lovest righteousness, and hatest wickedness : *therefore* God, thy God, hath anointed thee with the oil of gladness above thy fellows " (Psalm xlv. 7).

2. Another most important element in weight of character is *openness and straightforwardness.* Nothing can be more hurtful to the growth of character than the practice of any kind of duplicity or fraud. Men in any rank of life who try to compass their ends by duplicity or diplomacy may be very able men, and may be highly successful in their immediate objects ; but such a course is never compatible with the attainment of great weight of character. In the life of a minister it is preeminently true that honesty is the best policy. The duty of aiming at honesty and straightforwardness is the more to be kept in view by men of facile nature or of obliging spirit, who often yield to temptation in order to avoid contradicting or hurting the feelings of those with whom they come into contact.

They may be brought into fellowship with men of various and
even of opposite opinions, but in consequence of this easiness of
mind they leave the impression that they do not differ very
much from any of them, to the great damage of their own
character for straightforwardness and honesty.

It follows that to enable the minister to be straightforward, it
is of vast importance that he be decided. It may be hard to
press this counsel on men of naturally vacillating temperament.
But it is precisely men of such temperament that have need to
lay it to heart. In any position, a vacillating man is feeble and
unsatisfactory. But a vacillating leader is a positive calamity.
The minister of the gospel is the leader of his congregation,
and for him to vacillate in any great question is practically to
bring the army to a stand-still, almost to proclaim the reign of
anarchy. On great questions, it is his duty to have his mind
made up. And on all questions which concern him and his
flock, it is his duty to have distinct opinions, opinions based on
the great leading convictions which he has been led to hold.
Thus he shall be able at once to state his opinion and to give his
reason for holding it. The reason thus given being manifestly
in accord with the great guiding principles of his life, will
command respect, if not concurrence. Strength and decision
of opinion, too, facilitate frankness of expression, whereas
feebleness of impression makes one utter one's self as if one
were ashamed of one's views.

Nor does this decisiveness of opinion and character necessarily
imply bigotry. Bigots there no doubt are among those who
are most decided and outspoken ; but there is nothing in such
decision and frankness to prevent one from feeling kindly and
from judging charitably in the case of persons on the other
side.

But while we thus speak of the advantage of frankness in
uttering one's views, as well as of having clear and decided
views to utter, let us remember that the basis of all that is truly
valuable in this habit is a moral basis. It is that attribute
which God especially demands—"truth in the inward parts"
(Psalm li. 6). It is only when there is inward sincerity that
there can be any reality in a seemingly transparent manner.
And that inward sincerity must ever be implored as the gift of
God, and habitually nursed and cherished, with the profoundest
sense of its value. For guile in the heart, as it is the ugliest
blot, and the most destructive cancer in any man's character,
so it is peculiarly offensive and peculiarly ruinous in the

character of a minister of Christ. Of all functionaries, an ambassador should be open and honest. Of all ambassadors, the ambassador of Christ should be true and real. The whole Bible, but especially the New Testament, makes war on guile. " Laying aside all malice, and all guile, and hypocrisies . . . as new-born babes, desire the sincere milk of the Word " (1 Peter ii. 1, 2). " Christ also suffered for us, leaving us an example . . . who did no sin, neither was guile found in his mouth " (1 Peter ii. 21, 22). One of the first of those whom Christ called to follow him was Nathanael, " an Israelite indeed, in whom was no guile " (John i. 47). Guilelessness is the characteristic of childhood, but not to be put away when you put away childish things. It is one of the noblest attributes of manhood. Never does man appear so great as when a great intellect and a large heart are allied to the transparent and guileless nature of a little child. And never does the Christian minister come so near to the ideal of his Master as when his whole life and his whole teaching are a faithful transcript of his own soul.

3. A third element of weight of character is a *patient, calm, reasonable temper.* It is an unhappy thing when a minister is prone to take offence, or when his temper is easily excited by any cause. It is, indeed, quite unworthy of a Christian minister to take offence at all, or even to appear to notice little things that in the world are counted offensive—little breaches of etiquette, want of proper consideration for him or his, or inattention to the formalities of society. There is no attitude in which a respectable man appears so little as when he is trying to prove that he has not been treated with due consideration. Our Lord struck at this foolish foible in instructing his disciples, when they were bidden to a feast, not to mind though they should occcupy the lowest place. And whatever may be the effect for the moment, a Christian minister who gives no heed to such matters will be sure ultimately to stand higher than one who fights for his place as for life itself. Even where wrong has manifestly been done to him, the minister should far rather forgive and forget, than cherish a grudge or manifest coldness. On him especially lies the force of the exhortation, " As much as lieth in you, live peaceably with all men." On him pre-eminently it is incumbent to show that Christianity supplies for the tear and wear of daily life a nobler fund of forbearance than does the natural heart. Let him be patient, too, and reasonable, when called to deal with the delinquencies of

his people.   I can never forget the words of an employer in the
West of Scotland, when explaining the principles on which he
dealt with his men, and through which he had been enabled in
a large degree to secure their regard and affection : "I make
it a point," he said, "when anything has been done wrong, not
to scold the workman until he has had an opportunity of giving
an explanation, for I find that after such explanation any
remonstrance falls with much more weight, especially when it
is conveyed in a mild and reasonable manner." Here surely is
a lesson for all sorts of persons in authority, and especially for
the Christian minister.   The minister of the gospel must ever
aim at being a peacemaker, a healer of strife, a sweetener of
the breath of society, a zealous promoter of glory to God in the
highest, on earth peace, good-will toward men.   Against one
very common form of mischief-making he will set himself with
the most rigid determination—against the habit of retailing
gossip, or opening one's ears to scandal.   There is no habit
that, especially in small communities, is so hurtful to the
Christian spirit.   There is nothing more likely to do harm than
for a minister to listen to the retailers of scandal, either
personally or by the instrumentality of those who have an
inclination towards it.   If he needs to learn the character of
his people, let it be from those who have no pleasure in bringing
down the character of their neighbours.

4. We add a single sentence on the great importance of habits
of *punctuality, accuracy, and exactness.*

A minister needs to be exact in his *statements.*   For it is both
awkward and injurious to his character, when, by any exaggeration or colouring, he affords a handle for a charge of untruth-
fulness.

Further, he needs to be very mindful of his *promises*—very
careful not to promise unless he distinctly sees his way to
perform ; remembering that though, through the very multiplicity of his engagements, he may forget to pay a visit or
to write a letter he has promised, the person to whom the
promise was made is sure to remember it, and very likely to
take a serious view of the omission.

A minister needs to be exact in *money matters.*   In the great
majority of cases he is subject to considerable financial pressure,
and the effort to keep all straight—the effort to maintain a
position for which the means are barely adequate—involves a
self-denial spread over the greater part of his life, that forms an
important discipline, and that often amounts to heroism.   With-

out such vigilance and care, the battle becomes too trying, and once the financial balance is lost it is almost hopeless to recover it. The cases are very numerous of embarrassment contracted at the commencement of public life, when there is necessarily considerable outlay, and when the young minister is probably ignorant at once of the expenses of his establishment and the practical limits of his income—embarrassment that has pressed like a millstone during all the rest of his career. The matter is all the more trying that in many districts the minister's lot is cast among those who, not comprehending his difficulty, are little likely to help him either with sympathy or material aid.

In all matters, great and small, a habit of business-like punctuality is invaluable to a minister. Let him make a point of being in time for every engagement. Let him never leave the answering of a letter which ought to be acknowledged at once to a more convenient opportunity, even though it should be a mere invitation, or allow minutes of meetings or records of accounts, if he has to do with such, to fall into neglect or arrear. Such matters, little though they seem to many, have an important bearing on character, and may be placed in the category of the minor morals. Exactness in them, if not made matter for a fussy and pedantic display, raises a minister in public estimation, and adds weight to his counsels when he urges his people, like the Apostle, "to exercise themselves to have always a conscience void of offence toward God and toward man" (Acts xxiv. 16).

Let it be observed, too, that perfect punctuality is a duty which is almost always attainable where it is sought. There are services and duties without number where we cannot be perfect; where in many cases we are woefully imperfect; depending on states of mind and heart which we cannot reach, or which we fail to reach, and in reference to all of which we have constant need to make the confession that we are unprofitable servants. But punctuality is not one of these. There, if we take pains, we may ordinarily do all that has to be done. And let us not despise the virtue because it is little: for he that is faithful in that which is least is faithful also in much; and he that is unjust in the least is unjust also in much.

5. Perhaps we ought to add a remark on the importance of a certain *refinement of manner*—meaning by this a result of refinement of mind. For though manner in itself may be but of lesser importance, and though manner, as manner, and fine manners, as fine manners, are very contemptible, yet a certain

culture of the outer man is unquestionably a fitting result of
that long process of culture, both intellectual and spiritual,
through which the ministers of our Church have to pass. Undoubtedly this is necessary to enable a minister of the gospel to
attain the full measure of efficiency in contact with the more
cultivated sections of the community.   It is a pity that he
should be exposed to disparaging remarks on that score, when
the cause for such disparagement might be so easily removed.
A great force of spirituality will indeed overbear everything,
and undoubtedly it is this which is most desirable.   The true
gentleman is not the disciple of Lord Chesterfield, devoted to
artificial rules and fashion ; he is the man of refined sympathies,
whose soul inspires him with a true refinement, and makes him
alert to avoid those little roughnesses of speech or manner, or
those little negligences in dress or appearance, which create a
prejudice against him and his message.   If cultivated society is
worth anything, it is as pointing out to us the conditions which
make social intercourse most agreeable and social influence
most impressive.

" The parson's yea is yea," says George Herbert, " and nay,
nay ; and his apparel plain, but reverend and clean, without
spots, or dust, or smell; the purity of the mind breaking out,
and dilating itself even to his body, clothes, and habitation."*

6. But matters such as have now been referred to are small
indeed compared to the importance of maintaining, earnestly
and diligently, the *habits of the inner life*.   The watching of the
state of his own soul, the guarding against declension and
decay, the keeping of a keen edge on the conscience, and the
maintaining of a close and real fellowship with God ; the
trimming of the lamp of faith, the strengthening of the things
that are ready to perish, the quickening of zeal, the stimulation
of all the Christian graces—if such things are not duly minded,
alas for the spiritual efficiency of the ministry !   For public
bustle and ecclesiastical activity will never make up for the
want of personal fellowship with God and personal appropria-
tion of the blessings of heaven.   No minister can be right who
does not look on the time spent in personal devotion as the
most important part of the day, giving a complexion to all the
rest, and determining whether or not any saving good may be
expected to result from his various employments.   The Bible
read with a direct and deliberate application to himself; the
mind solemnly exercised in meditation on his state, and in

* Herbert's " Priest to the Temple," chap. iii.

prayer to God for the corresponding blessings ; the whole work of each day spread out before God, and his guidance and blessing earnestly sought upon it—without such exercises, the ministry can be little else than a solemn form. In addition to the daily reading of the Scriptures, many earnest ministers find it of great benefit to read a portion of some spiritual book, one of the fragrant old authors, perhaps, and to add to this the perusal of some good biography and, perhaps, a hymn-book. Nor ought the practice which was so strongly recommended by Dr. Chalmers, and from which he himself derived so much benefit, to be forgot. Once a month, while engaged in the active duties of the ministry, he set apart a portion of a day for a more deliberate and full exercise of devotion. He began by asking a blessing on the exercise. He read a suitable portion or portions of Scripture.

" *June 1st.*—Rose at eight ; spent the forenoon in devotion, of which the following is the record : Invocation for God's blessing and direction on the exercise. . . . Read the promises to prayer, and prayed for acceptance through Jesus Christ, and general sanctification. . . . Prayed for knowledge, for the understanding and impression and remembrance of God's Word, for growth in grace, for personal holiness, for that sanctification which the redeemed undergo. Thought of the sins that most easily beset me ; confessed them, and prayed for correction and deliverance. They are—anxiety about worldly matters, when any suspicion or uncertainty attaches to them ; a disposition to brood over provocations ; impatience at the irksome peculiarities of others ; an industriousness from a mere principle of animal activity, without the glory of God and the service of mankind lying at the bottom of it ; and, above all, a taste and an appetite for human applause. My conscience smote me on the subject of pulpit exhibitions. I pray that God may make usefulness the grand principle of my appearances there. Read the promises annexed to faithful ministers, and prayed for zeal, diligence, and ability in the discharge of my ministerial office. Prayed for the people, individually for some, and generally for all descriptions of them. Prayed for friends individually, and relations. Read the promises relative to the progress of the gospel and conversion of the Jews. Prayed for those objects."*

It is difficult to say which part of the process is more to be admired—the humble earnestness with which he sought for himself to be made a vessel meet for the Master's use. or the

* " Memoirs of Dr. Chalmers," vol. i. p. 288.

affectionate concern which he felt for those for whom individually he pleaded before the throne. While every earnest minister will constantly pray for his flock as a whole and for the classes of which it is composed, it is in pleading for individuals that he will become most intense and get nearest to God. Nothing helps us or our people more than to make them individually the objects of supplication. From one to four or five, taken daily, will enable the minister in the course of a year to overtake his whole flock, whether it be larger or smaller. What a vast element of power will thus be added to his ministry !

It was not the splendour of his talents alone that made Chalmers the man of power that he was. A great part of his marvellous strength was got by the common process. Like Jacob, he wrestled with God, and he became a prince. The humblest student, if he will but trace his footsteps to the throne of grace, may obtain a measure of his blessing and of his power. There is a sense in which, in the kingdom of God, to be weak is to be strong ; to be empty is to be full ; to be poor is to be rich ; to have nothing is to possess all things.

APPENDIX A.

SUPPLEMENTARY HINTS.

I.—On Style.

In the body of this work some things have been laid down as *desirable* in style ; in this place we add a few hints, for the sake of younger students, as to how the *desirable* may be turned into the *actual*.

I. For attaining *Clearness* of style (1) the first necessity, as already indicated, is clear *thinking*. Through mental indolence, or other loose mental habits, we are exceedingly prone to vague thinking. There is no remedy for this but vigorous grappling with our thoughts, frequent asking of ourselves, what is the precise idea which we desire to convey ? In order that another may understand me, I must thoroughly understand myself ; and the more luminous the thing is to me, the more impressive will it be to him. The attainment is worth much. A luminous thinker is a public blessing. It is often by making our own thoughts and feelings clear that we help other people to understand theirs. And one of the best services we can render to others is to define to them their own thoughts and feelings. When we succeed here, we get a wonderful grip of their minds, and can wield them almost at will.

(2.) Hence it becomes an aid to clearness of style to think of our audience as we write. If we should suppose an average hearer sitting opposite to us, and if we should construct our discourse so that all its contents might be transferred to his mind and heart, we should be more likely to write clearly. It is one of the advantages of extemporaneous speaking (when one *can* speak extempore and does not merely pour out froth), that the audience insensibly shapes the style of the speaker, and compels him to adapt himself to it. The best written sermons are those which are composed as in the pulpit—as in the presence of a listening congregation.

(3.) Another help to clearness is familiarity with writers who excel in this quality. Unfortunately, these are not always models in other qualities. Paley is cold in tone and very deficient in evangelical aroma, but he is admirably clear as well as thoroughly idiomatic. John Henry Newman, another of our most luminous writers, is out of sympathy with us in very vital matters, having long been a member of the Church of Rome. Addison has always been esteemed a model writer, for clearness, purity, ease, and grace, but he was not a writer of sermons. John Bunyan is, perhaps, as good as any for clearness and idiomatic precision ; with this he combines scriptural depth and fervour, and a wonderful homiletical faculty. It is easy to conceive of Bunyan writing his works as with a hearer on the opposite side of the table.

(4.) In revision, clearness should be studied before any other quality. Beauty, rhythm, and all other secondary qualities must be sacrificed to clearness, without the least scruple. This must be matter of conscience, and to this rule there should be no exception.

To these hints let us add, that the training which students receive in languages ought to have a marked effect in promoting clearness both of thought and expression. The study of languages at once demands and promotes precision. The study of the English language, in its component parts, its grammar and its idiom, and especially the study of words and phrases apparently synonymous, will contribute in no slight degree to clearness of style.

II. *Force.*—Whatever makes style clear contributes *pro tanto* to make it forcible. If we inquire for other elements of force, we shall find them either in the substance or in the form of a discourse.

If we consider the *substance* of a discourse, its force will depend partly on the class of truths with which it deals. Of the forcible class, are truths bearing on the real, the certain, the positive ; truths relating to objects that are vast and grand, and that imply a great Power; truths that have great and solemn bearings, or that are connected with deep and earnest feelings that agitate the soul to its depths.

Now, no business in the world has so close dealings as the preacher's with such truths. A feeble style in handling the great themes of the pulpit is inexcusable. The preacher ought to begin early to handle some of the great truths. Death, judgment, and eternity furnish at once the most natural and the most suitable subjects for forcible words.

In regard to the *form* of words—force depends on (*a*) the selection of the best words, those of which the meaning is most plain and best understood. (*b*) On arranging them in the best order—usually the order of thought, but sometimes different; *e.g.* for *emphatic* words, the proper place is generally at the beginning, but occasionally at the end, of a clause—(" *Silver and gold* have I none ; " " *Unto us* a child is born ; " " *Great* is the mystery of godliness ; " " The Son of Man is come to seek and to save *that which is lost.*") (*c*) Making due use of *contrast* and other forms of antithesis ("It is sown in corruption, it is raised in incorruption ; it is sown in dishonour, it is raised in glory ; it is sown a natural body, it is raised a spiritual body.") (*d*) The occasional use of proverbial or other pithy expressions. (*e*) A happy selection of tropes, or figures (not necessarily flowers) of speech.

This last particular demands special attention. The element of force which figures of speech contribute is that of *vivacity*— the opposite of dulness. Vivacity is one of the most important features of popular and effective discourse. An excess of vivacity in the pulpit is much more rare than an excess of dulness, and much more readily pardoned.

In Dr. Campbell's " Philosophy of Rhetoric," the chief grounds on which figures of speech become subservient to vivacity are well explained. Generally, they present to the mind some image which, from the original principles of our nature, attaches the fancy more strongly than could have been done by the proper words whose place they occupy. They produce this effect in these four cases :—

(1.) When they represent a species by an individual, or a genus by a species—the more general by the less general. A Dorcas, a Judas, a Nathaniel, a Magdalene, a Demas, convey more lively impressions than a description of their respective qualities. " Consider the lilies," " consider the ravens," is far more forcible than, " Look to the vegetable and the animal kingdoms," or, as some would put it more grandly, " Study the flora and the fauna of Nature."

(2.) When they fix attention on the most interesting feature, or that with which the subject is most interestingly connected. " What, know ye not that your bodies are the *temples* of the living God, and that the Spirit of God dwelleth in you ? Defile not ye the temple of God ; for the temple of God is holy, which temple ye are." " Ye are the salt of the earth. Ye are the light of the world. A city that is set on an hill cannot be hid." " If they do these things in a green tree, what shall be done in the dry ? "

(3.) When they exhibit things spiritual by things sensible. " A man shall be as an hiding place from the wind and a covert from the storm : as rivers of water in a dry place, and as the shadow of a great rock in a weary land." " Fight the good fight of faith." " Run with patience the race set before us." " He that despised Moses' law died without mercy under two or three witnesses : of how much sorer punishment shall he be thought worthy who hath *trodden under foot the Son of God*, and counted the blood of the Covenant wherewith he was sanctified an unholy thing, and hath done despite unto the Spirit of grace ? " It is by this figure we are taught to ascribe such efficacy to the blood of Christ. The blood is the material emblem of spiritual things of transcendant value and mystery ; of loving self-surrender ; of endurance to the end ; of life substituted for life ; of a sacrificial offering, in which divinity and humanity met, and death was borne in such a way as to exalt infinitely the majesty of the Divine law.

(4.) When lifeless things are suggested by things animate. Thus Death, the very opposite of Life, is often represented as a living being, so often indeed that the figure has almost ceased to be a figure. In the Bible the sea (or the flood) lifts up its hands and roars ; the hills tremble ; the forest rejoices before the Lord ; the sun is like a bridegroom going out of his chamber; the wind bloweth where it listeth ; the wilderness and the solitary place rejoice, and the desert blossoms as the rose ; a river makes glad the city of God ; death is swallowed up of victory.

It is impossible to tell how much the vividness of Scripture is due to the use of such figures.

III. *Fulness.*—Of the many ways of giving the proper fulness or amplitude to a discourse, let us note the following :—

(1.) Repetition with variety. " If thy right eye offend thee, pluck it out and cast it from thee. . . . If thy right hand offend thee, cut it off and cast it from thee."

(2.) Resolving a general truth into its constituent elements, untwisting a cord, as it were, and exhibiting by itself each filament that composes it. This is especially true of descriptive discourse. " Charity suffereth long and is kind ; charity vaunteth not, is not puffed up, doth not behave itself unseemly, seeketh not her own, is not easily provoked, rejoiceth not in iniquity but rejoiceth in the truth, heareth all things, believeth all things, hopeth all things, endureth all things." " I was an hungered, and ye gave me meat ; I was thirsty, and ye gave me drink ; I was naked and ye clothed me ; sick and in prison, and ye visited me."

(3.) Accumulating contrasts and resemblances. " There is one glory of the sun and another glory of the moon, and another glory of the stars, even as one star differeth from another star in glory." " The Lord is my rock, and my fortress, and my deliverer ; my God, my strength in whom I trust ; my buckler, and the horn of my salvation, and my high tower."

(4.) Reference to examples. Thus, in Jude, the danger of self-security in religion is exemplified by (*a*) the case of the Israelites who were rescued from Egypt, but destroyed in the wilderness ; (*b*) the case of the angels who kept not their first estate ; (*c*) the case of Sodom and Gomorrah, and the cities about them.

(5.) Appeals to various faculties. A truth may in succession be (*a*) enforced by Divine authority, (*b*) commended to the reason, (*c*) urged on the conscience, (*d*) illustrated by the imagination, (*e*) carried home to the feelings, and by all these channels pressed on the will. The monotonous speaker appeals to but one faculty, generally the reason. This is the favourite door of the intellectual student, who, holding that there is nothing like thought, is ever addressing the intellect. But in uncultivated men, pure intellect is not very active ; it is easily tired, and when it gets tired it shuts its door, and leaves the intellectual orator to beat at it unheeded. The speaker skilled in expansion will divide his efforts between all the available faculties of the soul.

IV. *Beauty*, to a large degree, is the fruit or outcome of all the previous qualities of style. Clearness, neatness, simplicity, idiomatic purity, good arrangement and happy illustration, all conduce to beauty, and there can be little or no beauty without them. As there is beauty, great beauty, in a clear-flowing rivulet, so there is beauty in a clear-flowing discourse. Men of taste and culture hate tawdry metaphors and stilted periods, as they hate Brummagem trinkets and cheeks brilliant with rouge. Probably the highest beauty in a discourse, like the highest beauty in a woman, is that which is quite natural, and, as we may say, unconscious ; each is beautiful, not from aiming to be so, but from intrinsic qualities.

s

But in style, beauty, like force, is more especially connected, first with the substance of certain truths, and second with certain forms or modes of expression.

(1.) As to substance. It is evident that the quality of beauty attaches itself especially to *certain kinds* of truths. There are things eminently beautiful in themselves, both in the world of nature and in the world of spirit. The blue sky, the sunbeam, the rose, the lily, and innumerable other natural objects are beautiful, and any true description of them, or interesting discourse about them, is beautiful. Love, mercy, grace, self-sacrifice, and spiritual things of the like sort, are also beautiful, and cannot be suitably spoken of without beauty. It is usual for poets to choose for their themes subjects of this sort, and hence much of the beauty of poetry. Bolder and more original poets may choose subjects not having this quality in themselves, but, by connecting them through subtle links with what is beautiful, they may produce the same impression, or a stronger impression, in the end. In preaching, subjects that in themselves are beautiful, admit most readily of a beautiful style. But preachers of bold and original spirit are able so to handle even the less attractive subjects of the pulpit, are able so to connect them with what is beautiful, that in their hands the most prosaic subjects appear bright with the hues of the rainbow.

(2.) In turning to the *forms or modes of expression* that tend to beautify style, we are inevitably attracted by figurative language. Figures of speech constitute the ornaments of style. But, as we have remarked in this book, figures of speech cannot be truly ornamental unless they are at the same time useful. If they do not illustrate truth, they are worse than useless. Sometimes a figure, though not derived from a beautiful source, may, from its remarkable fitness, produce the effect of beauty. But generally the figures that produce the impression of beauty are derived from confessedly beautiful objects. The skill of the speaker lies in finding some resemblance between the non-beautiful and the beautiful, whereby the one is made to throw its brightness on the other. Skill of this kind in the use of figurative language is wonderfully fitted to beautify a discourse.

It results from these views that there is no necessary feebleness, as some seem to think, in the element of beauty, when applied legitimately to a religious discourse. On the contrary, whenever it is genuine, it is rather an element of strength. To despise beauty as a poor and unworthy adjunct of religious teaching is to show great want of sympathy with the writers of Scripture, guided as they were by the Holy Ghost. It is to neglect an element of power which tells on all kinds of people, but especially on the young and on cultivated minds. Beauty has a singularly refreshing effect on the mind, and there is an especial craving for it in dull and weary moods. It is like David's harp to Saul. In an age of great tension and pressure like the present, and especially in populous communities where this pressure is most felt, the element of refreshment which beauty is fitted to minister is not to be despised in the services of the sanctuary. In our pastoral work we have to minister to the whole nature of man, and to do this effectually we cannot safely neglect any mode or form of useful influence that God has made.

II.—ON VISITING THE SICK.

Any one desirous, as a matter of curiosity, to see a complete rubric on the visitation of the sick, should get hold of Dr. Stearne's "Tractatus de Visitatione Infirmorum," as contained in the "Clergyman's Instructor." There he will find instructions, cut and dried, for all sorts of cases, including that of criminals sentenced to be hanged. In the coldest and driest manner, he will find topics suggested as appropriate for conversation and prayer in such circumstances, as if the whole of a clergyman's duty were exhausted in saying the proper thing, and no consideration had to be given to the tone and spirit in which it was said.

The visitation of the sick is of all duties that for which the spirit of formality is most unsuitable, and where the speaking must be most thoroughly from the heart to the heart. Yet a rubric like that to which we have referred might not be without its use in the way of suggestion—it might show the minister how great a variety of cases he is called to deal with, and of what value it is for him to be provided with manifold Scripture texts and references, sayings and anecdotes of suffering Christians, counsels and encouragements of well-tried value, in order that to every sick and sorrowing person he may be able to give his portion of meat in due season.

I. *Manner of Visiting the Sick.*—" Long experience has convinced me that much more depends on the manner of entering a sick-room than young pastors are generally aware of. Always tread lightly on the stairs that lead to the chamber. . . . Approach the bed with a cheerful countenance. As the sick man extends his hand to welcome you, let him see and feel at once that he grasps the hand of a friend. Speak to him in a low and soothing voice. Let every word fall as gently and kindly on his ear as the dew of Hermon. The sick often need encouragement, as well as direction and prayer. In such cases, it has a bad effect for a minister to come in with the solemnity of death upon his countenance. . . . Were I satisfied that he would not live an hour, and ever so much afraid that he was unprepared to die, I would not virtually cut off that last hour of probation by the abrupt and distracting announcement. Nor, on the other hand, would I conceal from him his imminent danger. I would talk to him as one on the edge of eternity, and urge him to lay hold on the hope set before him without a moment's delay. If, when you come to the dying sinner's bedside, you find him stupid, you must if possible sound a note of alarm deep enough to rouse his slumbering conscience. If he listens, and the Spirit of God sets his transgressions before him, beware that you do not encourage him to hope that his sins are pardoned before he has cast himself on the mercy of God through a crucified Redeemer."—HUMPHREY's *Letters to a Son in the Ministry.*

II. *Time.*—"Make it a general rule to visit the sick in the early part of the day. They are then better able to see you and to enjoy your visit than in the afternoon or evening. Indeed, you should rarely call in the evening, and never at a late hour, unless you are sent for."—*Ibid.*

III. *Length of Visit.*—"In the early stages of disease, and while the mind of the invalid is clear and active, you may labour with him on any point that seems to require it at considerable length, always taking care, however, not to prolong the conversation beyond his ability to listen to advantage. As he grows weaker, your visits should be shortened, or you should select those topics which are most essential to immediate preparation for death, and which are most easily comprehended. When the patient is very low, when disease has apparently nearly done its work, and the mind sympathizes with the body in its extreme weakness, let your prayers be short and simple, and your words be few and directly to the purpose. It is cruel, under such circumstances, to give set dissertations, and to open long prayers in the sick-room, and it does no good, but hurt. It exhausts without benefiting the sufferer. It is common for the sick to lose the power of attention, and even of comprehending any but the simplest truths."—*Ibid.*

" What we *say* to the sick should be brief, and when we *pray* with the sick we should be short in our prayers."—DR. ANDREW BONAR.

IV. *Use of Scripture.*—" I am persuaded that those that visit the sick would do well to confine themselves to the simplest view of Scripture truth ; and it may be well also that these views should be embodied in some select texts of Scripture. It was in this way that Dr. C. treated me, and I have admired his wisdom. He approached my bedside, and after hearing my fears, he repeated the text, ' This is the record that God has given us eternal life, and this life is in his Son.' He again repeated it until he saw that I held it in my mind."—*Thoughts in the Prospect of Death.*

" When Bengel was dying, a student of the institution over which he presided called to inquire for him. Bengel requested from him a word of comfort before he left. The young student, abashed and confused, said that he did not know how to speak to one so learned, but at last contrived to utter the text, ' The blood of Jesus Christ, his Son, cleanseth us from all sin.' ' That is the very word I want,' said Bengel ; ' it is quite enough. ' "—DR. ANDREW BONAR.

Dr. Bonar's little book, " The Visitors' Book of Texts ; or, the Word brought nigh to the Sick and Sorrowing," is simply an application of this principle to the various classes of persons and states of mind comprehended under the word " sick." Of this very excellent manual we shall speak presently in detail.

V. *Other Helps.*—It is well to be familiar with some of the best practical works that have been written to indicate and impress the true uses of sickness. Such are—

Cecil's " Visit to the House of Mourning."
Flavel's " Token for Mourners."
Boston's " Crook in the Lot."
Hill's " It is Well."
Willison's " Afflicted Man's Companion."
Sibbe's " Bruised Reed."
Swinnoch's " Christian Man's Calling."
Adams's " Private Thoughts."
Samuel Rutherford's Letters.
Bonar's " Night of Weeping."

Some tracts and hymns adapted for the sick should be familiar to the visitor ; " Hymns for the Sick-chamber " have been published in large type. But in his ordinary reading the minister should mark anything that might be appropriate for

the sick, among other classes of his people, and have it ready
for use accordingly.

VI. *References to the Case of Others.*—It is an excellent way of
getting access to the minds of the sick to speak of others who
are or who have been in the like circumstances, and of the way
in which Christian men and women have felt and acted under
them. Even a verse of Scripture or a verse of a hymn acquires
a new interest when it is shown to have been useful to some
one in the like case. A dying Christian feels encouraged to
lay hold on " As many as received him to them gave he power
to become the sons of God," when he knows that it was the
stay of the dying Melancthon. Severe pain becomes more
bearable under the knowledge of Payson's experience, " I have
suffered twenty times as much as I could in being burned at the
stake, while my joy in God so abounded as to render my sufferings not only tolerable but welcome." Confidence in the will of
God is fostered by the words of Fénelon over the grave of the
Dauphin of France, " There lies my dear master ; all my
earthly hopes lie buried with him ; but if the turning of a straw
could restore him to life, I would not, for ten thousand worlds,
be the turner of that straw, in opposition to the will of God."
Church history and Christian biography come again here to
our help. Lives of Christians of mark who have come out of
great tribulation usually furnish many useful lessons. Not
only texts of Scripture but verses of hymns acquire fresh
interest and power from the experience of others. Who does
not feel a fresh power in that verse of " Rock of Ages," which
begins—

" Nothing in my hands I bring,
Simply to thy cross I cling,"

when he learns how that great prodigy of learning and genius,
the late Dr. John Duncan, had it read to him again and again
and again, while Death held him by the hand ? That hymn
has had a wonderful history, and it is remarkable how well
adapted it has been found to all conditions of men. Prince
Albert resorted to it in his dying hour. We knew a party of
fishermen whose boat was upset in a stormy night ; all the
night three of them clung to the keel, and one who alone survived
told how, expecting every moment to be washed off, they sung
" Rock of Ages." Perhaps no hymn expresses more deeply and
tenderly the heart's sense of emptiness and dependence, and its
trust in Another. Hence its universal power.

VII. *Benefits to the Minister from Visitation of the Sick.*—There is no duty in which the watering of others may be more fully accompanied by the watering of one's self. It is to the minister one of the best means of grace. Intercourse with the sick and dying is fitted to give him very vivid views of eternity, of sin, grace, and redemption. It is fitted to make his own heart more tender and affectionate. It gives a new sense of the reality and blessedness of the gospel, and the necessity and happiness of personal dealings with the Saviour. It counteracts scepticism, driving all the sophistries of unbelief like chaff before the wind, causing the Cross and its glorious gospel to shine with all the radiance of heaven. It makes prayer a reality, for the need of God's Divine power to effect a speedy change is often felt with overwhelming force. Let the duty be gone about with great solemnity and earnestness, and let abundant preparation be made for it in the closet. It is a duty in the prospect of which we may well say, "If thy presence go not with us, carry us not up hence."

CLASSIFICATION OF THE SICK, &c.

The classification given in Dr. A. Bonar's "Visitor's Text Book" is full, and the texts given under each head, with brief notes appended, are very appropriate. In Part I. texts are quoted applicable to the chief varieties of spiritual character which the sick present—believers, unknown, ignorant, self-righteous, anxious, backsliders, sceptical, and indifferent. In Part II. the texts are for those who may be met with in the sick-chamber — persons recovering from sickness, aged persons, young persons, children, attendants and friends of the sick. And, in Part III., the case of the sorrowful is dealt with, under the various phases which sorrow wears, whether it be personal trial, bereavement, worldly care, the ill-treatment of others, or sorrow arising from other causes.

We subjoin a few samples of texts adapted to the sick, and the use that may be made of them, chiefly from Dr. Bonar's book.

A sleepless night. Esther vi. 1. "On that night the King could not sleep; and he commanded to bring the book of the Chronicles, and they were read before the King."

"That sleepless night was sent by God for the very end that the King's thoughts might be led, through the record, to Mordecai. What if there be some truth of God, or some view

of duty, to which you are to be led by your sleeplessness ? "—
A. BONAR.

Sins remembered in sickness. Lam. iii. 20. " My soul hath
them still in remembrance, and is humbled in me."

" When saints are under trials, and well humbled, little sins
raise great cries in the conscience ; and in prosperity, conscience
is a pope that gives dispensations to our heart."—SAMUEL
RUTHERFORD.

Excessive pain consistent with Divine love. John xix. 32.
" Then came the soldiers, and brake the legs of the first, and of
the other which was crucified with him."

" See ! the converted thief, that saved man on his way to
Paradise, and very near it now, see, nevertheless, how the Lord
allows his body to be humbled. Oh, what racking, distracting
pain to him ! And yet, see how the Lord loved him, ready
within an hour to bathe him in bliss."—A. BONAR.

Crushing afflictions. Heb. xii. 6. " Whom the Lord loveth
he chasteneth, and scourgeth every son whom he receiveth."

" Nothing can be more severe than scourging—drawing the
blood by stroke after stroke. Yet it is God's treatment of (1)
those whom he loves, (2) his sons, (3) those whom he receives."

To the sceptical. Psalm cxix. 103. " How sweet are thy
words unto my taste ; yea, sweeter than honey to my mouth."

" Use the argument of personal experience ; what *you* have
felt, tasted, enjoyed. *You* have tried a way of happiness which
the sceptical man has never tried. So that you bring your
actual experience to bear against his non-experience—like a
traveller telling what he has seen to shut the mouths of those
who must confess they have never been in that country, and so
are not able to deny facts thus attested."—A. BONAR.

Boldness to enter into the holiest. Heb. x. 19, 21. " Having
boldness to enter into the holiest of the blood ; Jesus . . . And
having an high priest over the house of God."

" Two things give a sinner boldness in going to the Holy One
in the full blaze of his holiness : (1) *The blood of Jesus ;* He poured
out his life, and so the Father, looking on that outpoured life,
can justly say to us who point to the same, ' Live ! ' (2) *Jesus
himself,* the living priest ; he leads us in by his Spirit, and presents himself for us, the One for all who come."—A. BONAR.

Looking unto Jesus. Heb. xii. 2. " Looking unto Jesus,
the author and finisher of our faith ; who for the joy that was
set before him endured the cross, despising the shame, and is set
down at the right hand of the throne of God."

"Here is (1) Christ's atoning work ; (2) Christ strengthened in the midst of his sharpest pain by the thought of the kingdom ; (3) Christ now at rest in glory ; (4) Christ an example to us in the manner of bearing suffering ; (5) Christ able to yield us sympathy under pain; (6) Christ pointing the sufferer to the crown of glory and the throne."—A. BONAR.

Improvement of affliction. Heb. xii. 11. " Now no suffering for the present seemeth to be joyous but grievous ; nevertheless afterward it worketh the peaceable fruit of righteousness in them which are exercised thereby."

" It is *afterwards* that the fruit is to be reaped. For like ground lying fallow, body and soul seem ofttimes left useless and neglected in sickness ; or, we may say, like winter wheat, the seed lies underground till the snow and the frost of your sickness pass over, and then it springs up."—A. BONAR.

For the young in affliction. 2 Cor. vi. 17, 18. " Wherefore come out from among them, and be separated, saith the Lord, and touch not the unclean thing; and I will receive you, and will be a Father unto you, and ye shall be my sons and daughters, saith the Lord Almighty."

(1) " Connect with this invitation the *Parable of the Prodigal Son* in Luke xv. Is it not as if the Father had sent out messengers to seek his son, and had sent them to the very swine-trough over which his poor son was wistfully bending, to bid him remember the provision of his father's house, assuring him at the same time of a most cordial welcome in spite of all the past follies of his youth? (2) By sickness, is not the Lord sending a mighty famine upon you, to drive you out of the world, and send you to his home ? "—A. BONAR.

Sick children. 2 Kings iv. 18—21. " And when the child was grown, it fell on a day, that he went out to his father to the reapers. And he said unto his father : My head ! my head ! And he said to a lad, Carry him to his mother. And when he had taken him, and brought him to his mother, he sat on her knees till noon, and then died. And she went up, and laid him on the bed of the man of God, and shut the door upon him, and went out." Then at v. 33, 34, " Elisha prayed unto the Lord and stretched himself upon the child," till, v. 35, " The child sneezed seven times, and the child opened his eyes."

(1) " Every little circumstance in this boy's sickness and death is carefully told, to show God's care over the young—his playing among the reapers, the pain in his head, the lad carry-

ing him, his sitting on his mother's knee, &c.   Then (2) the
Lord brought him back to life, as he did the son of the widow
of Sarepta (1 Kings xvii. 23), showing his power and his willingness to deliver from death, when it is for his glory.   (3) Would
not that boy feel himself entirely the Lord's, soul and body?
(4) How would *you* live if you had once been dead?   Perhaps
you think, Oh, I would surely live for the Lord then.   But Christ
says, that if with your Bible telling you all this, you do not
live for Him, neither would you be persuaded to do so then
(Luke xvi. 31).   (5) The Holy Spirit must bless to you what
you now know and see, if ever if you are to be saved."—
A. BONAR. |
    The texts of Scripture adapted for the sorrowful are even
more full and striking than those bearing upon sickness.   Our
limits prevent further quotation, we must content ourselves
with referring to Dr. Bonar's little book.

III.—ON CONDUCTING BIBLE-CLASSES.

    A minister, we shall suppose, eager to get hold of the young
men of his congregation, announces his intention of opening a
Bible-class.   The time has been when a simple announcement of
this kind would be sure to draw together the chief part of those
whose presence was desired.   But it is seldom nowadays that
the minister has enough either of public authority or of private
influence to make so rapid a conquest.   In general he has to
interest the young men, to attract them, to inspire them with
confidence in himself and interest in his class.   It will usually
be found that a kind note addressed to each young man,
inviting the attendance of himself and any friends he may bring
with him, will secure, at the start, double or treble the attendance of a bare announcement.   For continued success, not a
little will depend on the first meeting.   The *character* of the
class has to be made at once.   It must start with the character
of an interesting class, a class where much is to be got, and
where much is to be got that is not generally got from the
pulpit or elsewhere.   Its tone must be warm, frank, and friendly,
and its business earnest, yet varied and lively.   If the class
gains this character it will be largely attended, and will leave
its mark on the young men of the place.   If it be cold and
formal, and its instructions merely a diluted edition of what is got
in sermons, it may hang languidly together, but it cannot be a
success.   In cases where such classes are failures, the cause

must be either that nothing of special value was taught in them, or that they were conducted in an uninteresting way.

A well-conducted Bible-class must have the same great aim as the pulpit—bringing souls to Christ and building up in them the Christian character. But it follows this aim in a different manner. The instruction it gives is more systematic on the one hand, and more varied on the other; its spirit is more free and social; the conductor has more freedom in using the theological stores which as a student he has laid up, and also his literary stores derived from his ordinary reading, to which he will always be making additions; he has also the opportunity of introducing some of the more current topics of the day, and of giving a more Christian direction to the thoughts of his young men on these than is usually done in the secular newspapers. A well-conducted Bible-class, by a minister of high character and gifts, is often the means of opening stagnant minds, of arousing a thirst for knowledge, of creating an interest in the kingdom of God, of begetting decision for Christ, of training workers and office-bearers, and of elevating the intellectual and spiritual tone of a neighbourhood. Out of it a wise minister will get many an aide-de-camp, whose services in future days may be quite invaluable.

No Bible-class is worthy of the name of which the object is not to teach what is contained in the Bible, and unless it be conducted *as a class*, that is, by the members actively taking part in it. The members may take part in various ways—by answering questions, by putting questions, if need be, and by writing exercises or essays. Skill in conducting a Bible-class is shown in getting the members to speak. In a small class this is usually less difficult than in a large miscellaneous one, where the method of question and answer has sometimes to be abandoned as impracticable.

Let us suppose that the Shorter Catechism is to be the basis of instruction in the class. It might be well to spend a few introductory minutes in telling the story of its origin;* but since but little is known of this, it will soon be disposed of, and the minister will find himself face to face with that striking statement of the purpose of man's life—" Man's chief end is to glorify God, and to enjoy Him for ever."

The division is simple—(1) the subject considered, Man's chief end ; and (2), What is said concerning it—it is to

* See Hetherington's " History of the Westminster Assembly."

glorify God and enjoy Him for ever. Any of the class who know grammar will recall the common division—*subject* and *predicate*.

(1.) Here it will be asked, What is meant by *end*, and then by *chief* end ? There will be no difficulty in obtaining the answer, " the chief purpose for which man exists." This assumes that there is a purpose for which man has received his being, and it will be useful to fix attention on this. It is fitted to make a young man think, if you can bring home to him that there is a definite purpose for which he was brought into the world. You might lead him up to the point by analogy. If you see an instrument constructed with much care—*e.g.* a musical box or a microscope—what do you infer as to the intention of its maker ? Would it be reasonable to say that he had no purpose in making it, and no interest in its fulfilling that purpose ? Now, what structure is that, which of all bodies in the world, has been made with most care ? What did the Psalmist say of his body (Psalm cxxxix. 14) ? And what is that part of man's nature which is far more wonderful than his body ? Is it conceivable that this wonderful organization should have been made for no purpose ? For no great purpose ?

Here it might be shown how it has ever been the great problem of intelligent, inquiring minds to know somewhat definitely for what purpose they were made. Biography, both ancient and modern, supplies interesting cases. Such an instance is that supplied in the autobiography of a celebrated Scottish minister of the seventeenth century, Mr. Robert Blair, of St. Andrew's. When left alone in his father's house one Sunday, in his seventh year, looking out of the window, he saw two objects that arrested him—the sun shining and a cow feeding. He concluded that the sun was made to give light, and the cow to give milk. But for what was he made ? He could find no answer. He thought that, perhaps, in the big house, called the kirk, he might be told. To the church he accordingly went, and though he got no clear answer to his question, he got an inkling of it which ultimately served to direct him.

At this stage the opportunity is given for a stroke of application—an earnest charge to the person examined, and all the class, to endeavour, first, to ascertain the purpose of their creation ; and, second, to see that it be not defeated.

(2.) The answer to the question—the *predicate*—now falls to be considered : it is obviously twofold—man was made (1) to glorify God, and (2) to enjoy Him for ever.

1. It is not very easy to explain this term. Most explanations are vague, and you must seek for one that will come home and *grip*.

You ask, first, what is the literal meaning of *glorify?* You are answered, " To make glorious." You ask an instance of its use in this sense, and are, perhaps, referred to Isaiah : " I will glorify the house of my glory." What is meant by glorifying a house ? Making it brilliant, splendid, beautiful, as Solomon glorified the temple by covering it with gold and silver and all precious things ? Is it in any such way that *we* were made to glorify God ? No. Why not ? Because God in himself, and from all eternity, is infinitely glorious—nothing can be added to his glory. Then has the word " glorify " any other meaning than to *make* glorious ? Yes—to manifest, to exhibit, to show the inherent glory of any person or thing. What is it to glorify God in this sense ? It is to show that in himself, and in all his ways, He is glorious, excellent, perfect. How is this most effectually done ? By that bearing, on our part, which is due to so excellent a Being—by submission, trust, honour, obedience, delight in Him and in all his ways and laws. Is this natural to us ? Do we naturally perceive all the excellence of God ? What blinds our eyes to this ? When is it revealed to any ? (2 Cor. iv. 4—6). When God is revealed to us in his true glory, what effect has this on us ? (2 Cor. iii. 18).

Here it may be advantageous again to make use of the principle of analogy. When you discover a man of rare gifts and excellence—say an excellent *physician*—how do you act towards him ? We trust and follow his prescriptions. A sagacious *adviser?* We apply to him in perplexity and follow his advice. A kind, warm-hearted friend ? We carry our troubles to him, and are relieved by his sympathy. If, then, God is infinitely more glorious than any human being, what should be the degree of our admiration, trust, and obedience to Him ? Without bounds. Illustrate this by the example of some good men—*e,g.* by the example of Abraham in offering up Isaac ; by that of Jesus in the Garden of Gethsemane ; by that of Shadrach, Meshach, and Abednego on the plain of Dura. Or, to come to common things, How did Eliezer, Abraham's servant, glorify God on his master's errand ? He committed himself to his guidance, and sought to know and follow his will. What is the rule for Christians in regard even to eating and drinking? (1 Cor. x. 31). Is this rule followed by men in their natural state? What change is necessary to make it effectual?

2. The other part of the answer. Explain the meaning of enjoying God. To derive our happiness from Him. Is this natural to men now? What is said of the carnal mind? (Rom. viii. 7.) What did Adam do, after the fall, when he heard God's voice? If a change of heart is needed to enable us to glorify God, is it less necessary to enable us to enjoy Him? When the change does take place, in what ways is man enabled to enjoy God? In such as these: (*a*) Contemplation of his excellence and goodness. This is the joy of *beholding*. Give analogies. Joy of beholding a beautiful picture, flower, landscape—all which are only faint rays of God, in whom all is infinitely lovely. (*b*) Possession of his favour and blessing. What does the Psalmist say of God's favour (Ps. xxx. 5)? Show that Christians may possess God as a *father* (2 Cor. v. 18), *companion* (Gen. v. 24), and *portion* (Psalm cxix. 57). (*c*) Glimpses of privileges not to be even conceived.

All this being brought out, the subject might be viewed from a different point. Does not this view imply that men are to give themselves wholly up to a religious life? Would not this view degrade such employments as digging, baking, tailoring, banking, painting, and the like, as too low, as unworthy of those those who were made to glorify and enjoy God? In answering this, notice should be taken of the word *chief*—"man's chief end." It should be explained that there are subordinate ends. The conditions of life in this world render other things necessary. The world's ordinary work has to be done, and men must be the instruments of doing it. Each must contribute his part to carry on the ordinary work of the world. But the doing of our little bit of the world's work is not our *chief* end. Even in that we must look to glorifying and enjoying God.

Here it will be well to point out how even the commonest pursuits are fitted to discipline the soul for its chief end. Even the commonest drudgery may be pursued with a view to please God. If the work be drudgery, it will be done better by being done as to the Lord. All life becomes holy when God is thus honoured and served.

A useful practical conclusion will be found in showing the infinite importance of the subject. A blunder here is an irremediable blunder. One may make bad investments of money, and suffer for it ; but a bad investment of one's life is utterly fatal. Yet blunders are infinitely common. The class should be requested to state some of the wrong ends to which many men devote their lives. And it might be shown that, however apparently successful, they are commonly disappointed. The ambitious soldier, Alexander the Great, disappointed, no new world to conquer. Successful writers, like Sir Walter Scott, unhappy in reviewing life. Successful scholars, like Henry Martyn, first wrangler—" I only grasped a bubble." Millionaires, unable to enjoy anything. Men of fashion, like Lord Chesterfield, disgusted. Contrast with experience of Christians —they only SATISFIED.

Jesus the way to the Father—through Him we enter on this blessed life ; through Him we persevere to the end.

Such are some of the materials for a Bible exercise on the first question of the Catechism. The chief difficulty lies in disposing of it all at one meeting. Perhaps two would be needed. From the sketch given, we may see the solidity of which this method is capable, along with variety. We suppose a class of some intelligence, capable of entering readily into the views that have been indicated. To a younger class such minuteness would be unseasonable and wearisome. It might be enough for such to learn that to glorify God means to respect and fear Him, and to enjoy God to be happy with Him, to find delight in his grace and love ; and then to show the need of a great change in order that this mode of life might be realised. For a Bible-class such a subject as this is well adapted, as showing from what varied sources material may be drawn, and yet how all may be made subservient to the highest ends.

IV.—ON SPIRITUAL COUNSEL.

Every well-furnished minister must be prepared to give counsel to his people when they apply to him in spiritual difficulties, or whenever he finds that their minds are unsettled or their views unsatisfactory. In this place we can only indicate some leading considerations bearing on the classes of cases which are most liable to occur.

I. *Persons inclined to Scepticism.*—These cases are generally of one or other of two kinds: the case of those who make sceptical difficulties an excuse for neglect of religion ; and that of those who desire to be believers, but are seriously impeded by difficulties in the way of faith.

In regard to the first, when persons of this sort come into contact with a minister, they will probably set before him a strong array of difficulties and objections, and he may find himself in the unfavourable position of having to act on the defensive, and that, too, when the objections are highly plausible, and can be but partially removed.

In dealing with objections, it is most desirable to avoid mere logomachies and narrow issues, and get upon the broad grounds on which the claims of the Bible rest. In any case, the pastor should be familiar with all important facts ; for in argument facts are the great weapons of efficient warfare, and there is nothing to which sceptics are more inclined than to assume what is uncertain or even unfounded, and use it for their ends.

In popular argument the principle of analogy is usually very efficient. In common matters men do not reason as they are apt to do in religious matters. When they are sick or in trouble they do not argue against medicine or against offered help as they do against religion. Objections are got over in the one case, which are yet declared to be insuperable in the other.

But in dealing with this class of sceptics, it should be the strenuous endeavour of the Christian pastor not to allow his own position to be merely that of defence. The sooner he can turn the tables on his opponent the better. Let him find an opportunity to press the objections and difficulties of unbelief. It is easy to show that though there are some things in the Bible hard to explain on the theory that it is from God, there are far more vital things which it is impossible to explain on the theory that it is not from God. In using scepticism as a refuge from difficulties, we plunge into difficulties infinitely greater. As a believer, I may have to keep my mind in suspense in regard to many difficulties ; as an unbeliever I must commit myself to the untenable position that a system of fraud and superstition has been the great instrument of promoting whatever of a heavenly nature has its abode in this world.

It is also most important to bear in mind that scepticism is very rarely cured by mere argument. The Bible appeals to far more in man's nature than his logical faculty. It appeals to his intuitions, his conscience, his whole spiritual nature. The claim of the gospel rests in a large measure on its fitness to meet the case of the sinner, on the adaptation of its provisions to the wants of man. It claims to be a supreme exhibition of Divine love, of such love as proves itself to be Divine. Dealings with the sceptic should not end without a strong appeal to his deepest feelings—without an earnest endeavour to place him in personal contact with the Lord of the gospel, and to get him to deal directly with his appeals.

The other class of sceptical persons, who wish to believe, but are staggered by difficulties, require to be dealt with patiently. In the end they usually come right, but for a time their difficulties are often very serious. In their case, too, much use should be made of the overwhelming positive evidence for the truth of the gospel, and the enormous increase of difficulty that would arise from rejecting its claims. Much should be made of those features of the Bible which hardly admit of any difficulty or objection, such as the life and character of Jesus, as well as the blessed purpose of the glorious gospel. Texts and statements of Scripture which have a wonderful self-evidencing power should be kept in front—the texts that have proved means of blessing to multitudes that no man can number. Books may be referred to, like Christlieb's " Modern Doubt and Christian Faith," or Luthard's "Fundamental" and " Saving Truths," in which many current objections are dealt with, and shown to be utterly incapable, in any fair view of the case, to subvert the faith of Christians. And it may be urged that it is not reasonable to demand the removal of every difficulty, or to demand that our difficulties shall be met precisely in the manner that we should like ; that were to repeat the obstinate demand of Thomas, " Except I shall see in his hands the print of the nails, and put my finger into the print of the nails, and thrust my hand into his side, I will not believe ; " and it would be to disregard all the glorious array of evidence from countless other and higher sources, fitted to evoke the confession, " My Lord and my God."

II. *Persons in Anxiety about Salvation.*—We suppose such persons to accept the full authority of Scripture, and to be prepared to bow to its teaching. The first business of the pastor must be to see that they understand clearly what the Bible teaches on the way of salvation. Especially he must see that they understand the method of grace, and are not mixing up works of their own with the work of Christ as the meritorious ground of their salvation.

Now, the salvation of the gospel being a free salvation, offered without money and without price, one might suppose that whenever an anxious person really understood the nature

T

of the transaction, his anxieties would at once terminate in his reception of the gospel offer. In ; practice, however, this is often found not to happen. It is important for the pastor to probe the heart more, and ascertain how it happens that the convictions of the understanding, coupled with at least a measure of inclination in the heart, do not lead to the desired result. The following may be found to be some of the causes :—

(1.) *A lurking desire to find in one's self some ground to recommend one to God.* Along with belief that the meritorious work of the Saviour is the only real ground of acceptance, there may be a reluctance to present one's self to God resting on that work, in the state of inward disorder in which one is, and a desire to be, at least, a little better, before one makes the venture. In reply, it must be shown that this is wrong in principle and ruinous in policy ; that the invitation to the sinner is at once to commit himself to the Saviour ; that—

> " If I tarry till I'm better,
>   I will never come at all ;"

and that the true and only right course is that indicated thus :—

> " Just as I am, without one plea,
>   But that thy blood was shed for me,
>   And that thou bid'st me come to thee,
>   O Lamb of God, I come."

(2.) *A lurking distrust of the generosity of God in the free offer of salvation.* God's ways are so much higher than man's ways, that even when we think we believe in his Word there may be an unconscious back-drawing. The heart is naturally so suspicious of God, so unwilling to believe in his infinite love and goodness, that it is apt to lag behind the understanding, and prevent the soul from closing with the offer. A false humility will sometimes put away the gospel offer as too good for one —too good news to be true. Like a prisoner who has spent months in a dark dungeon, and cannot at once adapt his retina to the light of the sun, some men have been so long surrounded with the darkness of sin and unbelief, that they cannot open their hearts to the marvellous light of Divine grace. The remedy for this must be found in urging passages of Scripture in which the love of God to sinners is expressed very clearly, and his desire that they should at once accept his salvation in all its fulness of blessing. It should be urged that disbelief in his generosity is extremely dishonouring to God, that in this matter man's highest privilege and God's glory coincide, and that the point of coincidence is the sinner's acceptance of the glorious offer.

(3.) *Distrust of one's self in reference to the future.* It cannot be forgotten by the more thoughtful inquirers that to accept of Christ is to commit themselves to great obligations in their future life. Many shrink from taking the decisive step, through fear that they will not be able to lead the kind of life to be expected of Christ's followers. The Christian life is such a high life, and their abilities and inclinations are so low. In reply to this it is to be urged that to accept Christ is the true and only way to get the strength and inclination to serve Him. All strength and grace are in Him, and if we would bear fruit we must abide in the Vine. It is out of his fulness that we must receive, even grace for grace.

(4.) *Lurking attachment to sinful and worldly ways.* There may be some besetting sin or some cherished unlawful pleasure with which they have not made up their mind to break. On the whole, they love and desire salvation, but there is a law in their members warring against the law of their minds, and making them recoil from the sacrifice of some cherished idol or secret indulgence. If it be found that this is at work, it must be strongly urged that it is madness to give effect to any such feeling; a right hand or a right eye must be sacrificed, lest the whole body be cast into hell. But such stern surgery loses its repulsiveness when the soul is flooded with the love of Christ. Let the heart be thus filled, and all that is against the will of God is easily parted with. Christ and his love are felt to be such treasures that all else in comparison is as dross.

Yet even when these and all such obstacles have been carefully removed, an indescribable something may keep back the inquirer from the act of accepting Christ. The faithful pastor will see in this the proof that in every case a Divine power is needed to bring the soul into vital contact with the Saviour, and his recourse will be to Him who quickens the dead and makes his strength perfect in our weakness.

III. Spiritual counsel is often sought of the minister in reference to certain classes of amusements and other details of practical life.

On such subjects it is comparatively easy to lay down general principles. We can explain why it is that so little is said in the New Testament bearing directly on such things. We can show that, unlike formal and mechanical religions, Christianity is a religion of the spirit, that is not carried out by any number of rigid rules, but that in matters which are not determinate the true principle is, that the Spirit of Christ guides to actions conformable to the mind of our Master. We can show that " to the upright there ariseth light in the darkness ; " that if we live as in the company of Jesus, we shall be insensibly influenced in many things in accordance with his will, and shall instinctively reject all amusements and employments in which we feel that we cannot enjoy his countenance and approval.

This, however, will not satisfy some of our people. It is not so much for themselves that they are perplexed as for their families. For themselves, they could quite readily give up the things in question. But their children do not share their feelings. They see no harm in them ; they wish to enjoy them. What, in such circumstances, are the children to do ?

Easy-going pastors, like pleasant physicians, are tempted to give the advice that will be easiest and most acceptable to follow. It will require considerable grace and wisdom to be faithful on the one hand, yet not extreme and unreasonable on the other.

Where parents have formed decided convictions on such matters for themselves, it is undoubtedly to be expected that their view shall dominate their households. It would be very unsafe for a pastor to advise a Christian to allow in his household what he would deem wrong in himself. If he thinks that he inclines to too rigid a course, it would be far better to try to modify the views which have been taken up than to recommend a laxity which, if it be not of faith, is not without sin.

In reference to cases of casuistry, generally, it must be remembered that the *rôle* of the Protestant pastor is essentially different from that of the father-confessor. His office is not to prescribe, but only to guide. It is less in his way to solve particular cases than it is to take all available means for enabling his people to solve them for themselves. And of such means one of the most essential is the attainment of that state of heart and mind which leads to the sounder decisions. Our Lord's words here are golden: " If thine eye be single, thy whole body shall be full of light; but if thine eye be evil, thy whole body shall be full of darkness." Singleness of heart is the great key to practical difficulties in the Christian life. Freedom from prejudice, freedom from selfish aims, absence of any secret purpose to please some one who has an interest in the matter, whole-hearted surrender to the will of God—such a state of mind will generally be followed by a perception of what God's will is, for " the secret of the Lord is with them that fear him." Often the indirect use for which some problems are intended is to show us how little we know the mind of God, and how far therefore we are from the state of heart which is commonly associated with the knowledge of his will. If we walked nearer to God we should see light in his light; we should hear a word as from behind us saying, " This is the way, walk ye in it."

V.—On Home Mission Work.

Home mission work differs from congregational work in one very obvious respect—it is carried on among those who have either lost the church-going habit or who never had it. It is true that many who go to church may be farther from the kingdom of God than some who do not, and it may really be a much harder thing to bring them into it. Still mission work, on its very surface, is the more difficult, and, from its obvious nature, it lays an imperative obligation on all who engage in it to see that they do not undertake it alone, but in the strength and in the company of their Great Master. A godless missionary is as great an anomaly, we might say absurdity, as a godless prophet or a worldly-minded apostle.

I. It is important for every one who enters on this field to have a clear understanding of the *causes* to which home heathenism is due. No doubt the fundamental cause is the natural dislike of the human heart to God and his ways, its distrust of Him and opposition to his will, the distastefulness of his service—in a word, inborn dislike to religion.

But as this is a universal feature, it does not explain the specific feature of home heathenism—utter neglect of the forms, as well as the substance, of God's service. To what causes is this phase of irreligion specially due ? The following are probably the most common:—

(1.) Ignorance, want of Christian training in youth, want of Christian influence of any kind—of Christian books, Christian acquaintances, comrades, or neighbours. Some grow up in entire isolation from all the Christian forces of the country.

(2.) Constitutional feebleness — physical, intellectual, or

moral—looseness of texture, inability for effort, want of self-control, liability to temptation, indolence, stupidity.

(3.) Drinking and debauchery, fostered by low and loose company and prevalent facilities for sensual indulgence, and by places of amusement and a light literature that tend to relax the reins of conscience and give a stimulus to carnal inclination.

(4.) Struggle, poverty, disappointment, and social changes and influences which cause people to lose heart, as well as remove them from the neighbourhood of those whose influence would be beneficial.

(5.) Scepticism, often fostered by inconsistencies of professing Christians, usually allying itself with secularism and the pursuit of present advantage, as the only sure and certain method of securing anything in the shape of good.

According as heathenism flows from one or other of these causes, the proper treatment of it must vary, and also the degree of hopefulness with which it may be attacked. The first and fourth classes, for example, present more ground for sympathy, and are generally more hopeful than the rest. The second class, from their very inertness, are peculiarly difficult to move. They will take any amount of charity, but to no good effect. The third appear to be possessed by evil spirits, of the kind that goeth not forth but by prayer and fasting. The last dwell in strongholds constructed with more art and defended with more skill, and demanding special qualifications on the part of any one who shall deal effectually with them. The difficulty of dealing with the whole is often increased by unfavourable social influences; crowded dwellings and polluted air; public-houses on the right hand and on the left; repulsive features in church-going people; and want of sympathy between the various classes of society, and especially between rich and poor.

II. It is of great importance for the home missionary to keep in view the great *end* which is to be aimed at in connection with all this class of people. The true object of a mission is never gained in the case of any one until his heart is turned to God. The breach between God and man must be healed through the acceptance on the part of man of God's offered reconciliation and blessing in Christ. Nothing short of this comes up to the object of a Christian mission. And in any mission which has a staff of workers, the missionary, or head worker, must be held to be specially intrusted with this object. He must regard himself as commissioned by God to present to the people his offers of reconciliation, and to urge the acceptance of them. He is not merely the missionary of a church or of a congregation; he is the missionary of Christ. If he feels this as he should, it will give him at once a tone of authority and a spirit of humility. Consciousness of a near relation to God, while it brings power of the highest order, inspires a godly fear which keeps down all kinds of conceit.

By keeping this great object constantly before him, the home missionary will be kept from letting his work assume a false character in the estimation of the people. Generally, the class among whom he works have a low idea of his motives. They are always suspicious, and most unwilling to believe in disinterestedness. They think his object is to fill a church or meeting-room, and by this means contribute to the advancement of his personal interests. A missionary who goes about merely pressing people to attend his meeting, unintentionally fosters this impression. He makes the people think that in coming to his meeting they are doing him a favour. But he who lets it be felt that his grand purpose is to bring the people into a state of peace with God, through faith in Jesus Christ, and to make them heirs of the kingdom of heaven, does not expose himself to such an imputation. Undoubtedly, in going about among the people, the first thing for the missionary is to get close to their hearts and consciences, and press them with the great realities of the gospel. A promise to attend a meeting not proceeding from a quickened conscience is worth nothing, and it is foolish to spend labour in exacting promises in these circumstances. Far better to press on people the wretchedness of having the great God against them, the misery of a disorderly heart and a godless life, the certain and awful doom of sin ; and seeing that a blessed provision has been made for their peace with God, for their deliverance from sin, and for their inheriting all the glories of eternal life, urge them in earnest to accept of Christ.

III. *Visitation.*—The purpose of a mission being to *seek* as well as save that which is lost, much time must be spent in visitation. The gospel must be carried to the people, when the people will not come to the gospel. The worse the district, the more need of much visiting. Generally, perhaps, there is a tendency to overdo meetings and underdo visiting. But that the visiting may be effective, it must be carried on with great care. The visits must be attractive, with something bright and cheering about them, like the visits of men *bringing good tidings*, publishing peace. The missionary must be encircled with an atmo-sphere of love and sympathy. He must take pains beforehand, by prayer and meditation, to go in this spirit. His visits should be such that when he leaves a house he should be asked to call again soon. He should always enter with words of courtesy, and with regard to the convenience of the family, remember-ing that every man has a right to privacy in his own house. He should try to put the family at ease with him. Frank, manly simplicity is ever the best policy. He should consider from time to time how to give fresh interest to these visits. It is well to be furnished with appropriate tracts for both young and old. But in these days tracts are almost a drug, and they will not be much attended to, unless interest be excited before-hand in some striking fact or incident on which they turn. In regard to the offering of *prayer*, let the missionary by all means beware of fostering an impression which the people naturally have, when they " get a prayer," that an act of priestly media-tion is performed on their behalf. Much prayer should be offered *for* each house, but not necessarily *in* each house.

IV. *Addresses.*—Avoiding the dogmatic form, and dwelling as much as possible on *facts*, mission addresses should be at once direct, simple, and earnest. For the most part the people are very ignorant of Scripture, and therefore very unable to profit by discourses which imply acquaintance with it. There is a vast field for suitable, attractive, and impressive home mission addresses in the historical parts of the Old Testament, and an even richer field in the New. It is the great facts of gospel history that have proved the means of arresting the heathen in all ages. Explanations of the facts, involving doctrinal subtleties, are sought at a later stage. The facts relating to the person and life of Christ were the lever that moved the world in the days of the apostles, and it cannot be supposed that they have lost their efficacy now. Much mission effort is wasted in unsuitable addresses, and, perhaps, by a too uniform kind of address. The proclamation of God's mercy to sinners must ever be in the centre ; but the ways of setting it forth should have all the variety of Scripture itself.

V. *Work among the Young.*—Such work has always a promi-nent place in home missions, and it may be regarded as a proof that a man is no missionary if he have not some aptitude and inclination for it. But how to deal with the young is far too wide a subject to be taken up here. It is necessary, however, to enter a caution against concluding that if a great multitude of children are under the influence of a mission, the object of the mission is all but secured. It is one of the saddest facts of modern experience that many criminals of both sexes are found to have been Sunday school children. Infinitely more important than the bringing together of hundreds of children is drafting them as they grow up into the church. Ministers as well as missionaries have need to bend their utmost energies to the problem of transferring promising scholars into diligent students of the Scriptures and servants of the Kingdom of God. The best security for this is the turning of the young heart to God while, like Josiah's, it is yet tender. A taste for improving reading should be earnestly encouraged. The ample stores of literature for the young at the present day give a great advantage to those who have to labour among them. The prevalent taste for hymns should likewise be taken advantage of, and, generally, good music should be much more made use of than it is in mission work.

VI. *The Mission Staff.*—No mission is really worthy of the name in which the missionary or missionary minister is not aided by a copious staff of volunteers. The district should be of course broken up into small districts, and every little cluster of families should have a visitor, with whom the missionary should be in frequent communication. On the duties of this mission staff some remarks will be found in our chapter " On the Organization of Work." We would only enter a caution against the employment of languid agents, who have no soul for the real work of a mission, and no right sense of what is needed to carry it on successfully.

VII. *Subsidiary Objects.*—There are many ways of helping on the temporal welfare of the people, well worthy of being looked to as subordinate features of a Christian mission. Godliness is profitable unto all things, having promise of the life that now is and of that which is to come. Our Lord is an example to us of how to combine supreme regard for the soul with a due regard for the welfare of the body. Savings-banks, clothing societies, benefit societies, building clubs, libraries, and such like institutions, are well worthy of a helping hand from the home missionary. It may be enough for me to refer to my little book, " Better Days for Working People," of which seventy-four thousand copies were circulated some years ago. Although it is now somewhat out of date, and therefore hardly suitable for present use, the success which it had in its day may be taken as a proof that it indicated correctly the kind of temporal objects at which the Christian Church might properly aim, and the spirit in which such th:ngs should be handled.

VIII. *Temperance Reform.*—With hardly an exception, intemperance is found to be the greatest of all hindrances to the work of Christ in a mission district. The readiness with which the authorities usually plant drinking-houses in such districts is in every way most lamentable. It is quite necessary for the mission agent to assume a very decided attitude towards the drinking tendencies and habits of the time. In fact, earnest men almost invariably feel that if they would have any influence for good in this matter, they must be avowed and thorough-going abstainers. To counteract the public-house, it is most desirable to have an attractive temperance refreshment-room, but it requires much pains and skill to make it in every way successful.

IX. *Prayer-meetings.*—It is out of the question to carry on a congregational or other home mission without much earnest prayer. The work visibly and palpably defies mere human appliances, and demands a copious and constant exercise of Divine power. At every corner there are cases where the evil spirit goeth not forth but by prayer and fasting. But who ought to pray for this? Surely not the missionary alone. He ought to be sustained by the whole praying force of the congregation in connection with which the work goes on. But here there is commonly a lamentable want of a proper sense of responsibility. It is but a few individuals that feel any interest in the mission, or any obligation to charge themselves in earnest with helping it on. It is vain to expect that the true kind Jof prayer-meetings shall be made up, at least at first, of the people of the district. It is, perhaps, unwise in the missionary to give the title of prayer-meetings to gatherings which are not so much for prayer as for instruction. The congregation sustaining the mission should furnish materials for earnest prayer-meetings. The mission staff should form the nucleus for this purpose, but others should gather around them—Aarons and Hurs to hold up the hands of Moses, to sustain by prayer those who are called to bear the heat and burden of the day. But whatever be the fate of prayer-meetings, let each agent pray without ceasing for a blessing on his work. Let him make the case of each man, woman, and child a subject of prayer. Let him encourage all associated with him to do the same. Let all remember that it is God's enterprise, not theirs; and that if only appealed to duly, God is sure to aid a work in which his interest is so infinitely greater than can be that of any of his servants. Let them, in short, expect a blessing.

X. *Habits of Working.*—Regularity, punctuality, and unceasing diligence are indispensable in this work. They are necessary for the missionary himself, and they are most desirable in him as a means of training his whole staff to the same modes of work. It never does for him to let his hands hang down. An atmosphere of cheerfulness, buoyancy, and hopefulness will encompass every successful mission. When his nervous energy falls low, it is far more economical to take a brief rest than to work on with dull eye and languid heart. From every meeting over which he presides people should go away refreshed, quickened, and in better heart. No man needs more the motto, and no motto suits better for the man—" Therefore, my beloved brethren, be ye stedfast, unmoveable, always abounding in the work of the Lord, forasmuch as ye know that your labour is not in vain in the Lord."

VI.—On Evangelistic Movements.

When it is contemplated to make a special effort to promote earnestness and decision in religion, through special meetings for that purpose, the following points ought to be borne in mind from the beginning.

(1.) It is better to make no such movement at all than to do it languidly or formally. Sometimes an earnest man will say to his minister, " Ought *we* not to have a series of meetings, like those which have been so useful at M. or N. ? " Desirous of doing good, the minister may consent, and forthwith proceed to arrange for a week of meetings, in which Dr. A., Mr. B., and Lord C., are expected to take part. A measure of interest is excited, the meetings are fairly attended, but when inquiry is made as to results, there is little to point to, except some of those vague considerations which can always be made the groundwork of a hope that some good has been done. But it is not in this easy-going way that the tone of a neighbourhood is to be raised regarding spiritual and eternal things. The very nature of a religious awakening implies that by a spiritual force that cannot be resisted men's souls are filled with the very truths to which habitually they shut their eyes and their hearts. Is it to be supposed that such a result shall be accomplished by a mere succession of meetings, even though addressed by prac-

tised speakers ?   On the contrary, are not evangelistic meetings
of this kind, like feeble assaults on a strong fortress, productive
of more harm than good ?   Men become used to the views of
truths that are commonly urged at such meetings, and then
these truths lose their edge.   If such meetings are to be useful
they must be occasions for the delivery of a great, combined
attack on the kingdom of darkness.   Every effort must be
bent towards this.   We feel the need of much prayer and
effort when it is proposed to have a mission week in a vast town
like London ; but, in truth, prayer and effort are just as needful
in any village, hamlet, or highland glen.

(2.) Revival in the congregation precedes, and indeed promotes, awakening and conversion in the outer world.   The
spiritual temperature first rises in the Church, and through the
Church in the surrounding world.   It is unreasonable to find
fault with a religious movement which is directed, in the first
place, to warm the piety and brighten the zeal of existing
Christians.   The Church, when truly revived, will throw out
its energies on the outside community.   Round any real revival movement there will gather meetings like those of the
Glasgow Tent and the Edinburgh Drill Hall.   What is necessary
is, whenever symptoms of new life appear in a congregation, to
press the condition of the world that lieth in wickedness and
the obligations of the Lord's servants to be up and doing.

(3.) The most satisfactory and enduring revivals of religion are
those which begin with a revival of prayer.   The spirit of dependence, and the spirit of expectation, both of which are fostered
by prayer, are usually the forerunners of those other gifts and
graces that mark an awakening.   This was so remarkably the
case with the first great Christian awakening on the day of Pentecost, that it may well be relied on in all future time.   In some
churches, e.g. the Dutch, where the Christian festivals, Christmas,
Good Friday, Easter, Whit Sunday, and Pentecost, are observed,
the ten days between the last two are often devoted to united
prayer for the Holy Spirit.   Where prayer is offered in the
spirit of the early Church, a time of blessing is sure to follow.
When no spirit of earnest prayer exists among the godly
members of a congregation, the mere holding of evangelistic
meetings cannot be expected to be followed by great results.
When the men and women of prayer are especially roused to
ask and expect a blessing, it is a token that a shower of grace is
near at hand.

4. It ought to be felt deeply that any true revival movement

must begin from above. To lash men's minds into an excited condition by sensational means can produce no permanent good. Men never can be induced to lay hold of God unless God first lays hold of them. The great thing to be sought is the glorious presence of God and the working of his Holy Spirit. The cry of those who desire blessing should ever be for God to reveal himself—to shine forth, to discover to men his beauty, his grace, his holiness, and his love. It is this Divine manifestation that moves and melts men's souls and draws them Godwards. God must be the mighty worker, using men as his instruments, and bringing about those Divine results which constitute a revival worthy of the name.

These things being borne in mind, some hints may now be given as to steps to be taken to bring about a revival, to guide it while it is in progress, and to improve it when it is past.

(1.) The ordinary ministrations ought to be pointed towards it for some weeks previously. In many ways this may be done. The prevalent indifference and worldliness, the rareness of Christian decision, the activity of all the Christian's enemies, the wonderful promises of God, the glorious freeness and abundance of gospel blessings, the completeness of the work of Christ as our substitute, the blessed freeness of the offer which is nevertheless accepted by so few, the fact of such multitudes perishing for lack of knowledge, the nature and effects of the new birth, the doctrine of the Holy Spirit, the great love of God, are among the topics which would be easily brought forward in preparation for special revival movement. In the application of such topics there should be unusual earnestness, and very special pains to show the guilt, infatuation, and inexcusableness of all who neglect the great salvation.

(2.) Meetings for prayer should be specially encouraged, and the spirit of dependence and expectation abundantly fostered. At such meetings narratives of revivals may be of much service, especially in leading people to expect a Divine movement; and tidings of whatever of the like kind is going on in other places are often extremely useful. Let much stress be laid at such meetings on the glorious riches of God's grace, the pleasure which it must give Him to save sinners, the joy there is in heaven over one sinner that repenteth.

(3.) When meetings have been arranged for, full notice should be given of them, and efforts made to interest all the neighbourhood in them. A brief invitation explaining their object, and setting forth their unspeakable importance and value, has often proved of much use, especially in rousing attention, and exciting expectation and prayer.

(4.) At first the meetings should not extend beyond a week, and their prolongation should not be resolved on unless insuperable reasons emerge for this course. The aim will be to rouse the community during that week, and unless this object has been so far accomplished as to make it imperative to go on longer, the special movement should be limited to that time.

(5.) The services of one or more of those who have had most skill in evangelistic meetings, and been most blessed in them, should be secured. Other things being equal, it is desirable to have one leading speaker all or most of the time. The plan of a separate speaker, or of two speakers for each night, is apt to be distracting, even when the pastor is himself constantly present and taking part. It is desirable that any impression made at one meeting should be followed up at the next, and where one leading speaker is present most of the time, this object may be accomplished without much difficulty.

(6.) Speakers at such meetings must ever feel that the preparation of the heart is at least equally important with that of the head. Regarding themselves as mere instruments in the hand of God, they must seek that He would employ them, would give them their message, and bless it for the purpose for which it is sent. The soul should be exercised with these views until they fill it, until the speaker is able to go forth with the calm confidence of the shepherd-lad against the giant of the Philistines. To expect a blessing is the way to receive it. Nor should the speaker begin his work without thinking of his audience, and seeking to have his heart full of longing for their good. Let him think of their eternity, of woe unmitigated if they reject the gospel, of blessing unspeakable if they receive it; and let him try to have his own heart so thrilled and moved by this feeling that no fear of man, no conferring with flesh and blood, shall hinder him from coming close to every conscience, and dealing with people as directly and nearly, and with as tender and urgent pathos, as if he were urging them to leave a sinking ship or fly from a dwelling-house on fire.

(7.) In his address the speaker should be eminently biblical. It is the simple message of salvation he is to deliver, the message of God's love and of Christ's grace, as contrasted with man's sin, and the wages of sin which is death. It is a time to lead his hearers to the cross, and to set forth for their redemption Jesus Christ and Him crucified. Christ in us and Christ for us are, in some form, the great pillars of the structure he is to build; no address, however suitable and excellent for other purposes, can be suitable for the present purpose of which the tendency is not to set forth Jesus as the only Saviour, and constrain men to think of their personal relation to Him.

(8.) Impressions made at the public meetings should be followed up at once by personal dealings. Every facility should be given for this. If there be at first a shyness to remain to a second meeting, those who seem anxious should be approached, in order that they may be urged to come at once to a decision. Experience will soon make an earnest man familiar with the difficulties, the objections, the temptations to delay and indecision, that beset those in whose hearts the arrow of conviction has stuck fast. He will come to know the texts that are of most avail, the ways of putting the truth that usually remove obstructions to the gospel, and the lines along which the inquirer may most probably be guided to peace. Usually he will find that obstacles are removed by the clearer exhibition of the loving God, the grace of Christ who finished the work given him to do. No tendency is stronger than to look as a ground of peace to something in our own hearts, instead of looking outwards to Christ and his finished work; and no skill is of more value than that by which the inquirer is guided to make full use of a completed redemption, and throw himself just as he is on the all-sufficiency of Christ.

(9.) In arranging for after meetings, much care must be taken as to the views and character of those who are employed or allowed to speak to the anxious. It is true that in extensive revival movements, much less harm has arisen than might have been feared from persons being allowed to speak to the anxious, actuated on the one hand by sectarian motives, or, on the other, ignorant and incompetent; but it is of great importance that, if possible, no single case of this kind should occur, and much pains should be taken to secure in the inquiry-room the aid of none but competent Christians.

(10.) In urging on young Christians the duty of consecration to Christ, full regard should be had to the various ways in which this is to be carried out—in the heart, in the life, and by the tongue. In powerful revivals there is sometimes a one-sidedness here, bearing fatal results afterwards. Some young converts, reversing the law of reticence which so often and so painfully binds Christians, cannot restrain their speech, and act as if their whole duty to Christ was expressed in the text, " Come near and hear, all that fear God, and I will declare what he hath done for my soul." A prudent minister, when he sees a vehement tendency of this kind, will take care not to thwart it, but will set himself to guide and modify it. Converts with ready speech and unabashed in public are liable to be spoiled, and to degenerate into effusive, fussy, talking men and women, with little of the lowliness of Christ in their hearts or the blamelessness of Christ in their lives. It is very unwise to repress entirely the tendency to speak, but public occasions for it ought to be but sparingly given, and such persons should be taught most urgently that consecration to Christ includes the heart and the life quite as much as the tongue. It is remarkable how much a work of God is often spoiled by fussy, talkative, and by no means solid and trustworthy agents.

(11.) Young converts require much careful handling after a revival. Often they are very deficient in knowledge, and Bible-classes and Bible readings are necessary to supplement their defects. And it is not always that they have sense to know this, or patience to apply themselves quietly to supply their want. At first, all their craving is for the kind of meetings at which they received their first impressions. Despising the ordinary services of the Church as too slow and tame, some go off to Plymouthism and other sects. It is not difficult, however, to deal with these tendencies if the minister show some sympathy with the converts in their special circumstances. Where ardent converts are driven off, it is commonly because their minister showed himself out of all sympathy with them, perhaps even rebuked and scolded them. A minister in full sympathy with a revival movement may be able to show young converts that religious worship is not merely a festive luxury, that the head has to be instructed and the conscience regulated, as well as the feelings regaled. He may be able to convince them that the organization of a Church is necessary to keep things together, to prevent the members from flying off into so many chips and fragments. By opening up the Scriptures in his ordinary ministrations, and showing them the hidden treasures of wisdom, he will show them how much they have yet to learn, and how much, like the Ethiopian treasurer, they need some one to teach them.

(12.) Revival movements should be carefully directed towards giving fresh life and interest to the established means of grace. Sometimes there is a tendency to neglect these. Where there is real revival, those who have partaken of it will feel a strong drawing to one another, and meetings for fellowship on a common level will have great attraction for them. They will delight in singing the hymns that have come home to their hearts, and speaking of their experience both in their life and their work. To a certain extent this is right and natural, but the revival will not hold its ground unless it is made to quicken the usual Sunday services, to enliven the prayer-meeting, to give new life to the Sunday school, to make family worship more of a real, urgent, and very blessed service. Most earnestly should the new life of a revival be sought to be turned into these channels.

(13.) Revival movements should be directed very specially towards fostering a very high regard for the Word of God. Wherever they issue in a strong Bible-reading habit, in a profound belief that stores of spiritual wealth are treasured up in its pages and are to be found by the diligent seeker, there is a guarantee for the wholesome and abiding influence of the movement. Good habits are the best human security for abiding impressions. It is to be remembered that at a time of religious awakening, the hearts of those who are impressed are singularly open and susceptible, and that there is no time so favourable for the formation of sound Christian habits.

(14.) It is of great importance to find some suitable way of employing young converts in the service of Christ. True, they must be taught that doing their worldly work well is serving Christ, and they must be urged to all those ways and habits which will prove to the world that they have undergone a change for the better. But in young converts the evangelistic instinct is strong, and it ought to be turned to action. The Sunday school will afford a field to some, and their ordinary companions or associates in work to others. And the feeling should be encouraged that working for Christ is a life-long work. Often, an awakening supplies the Church with some of its most useful ministers. Ministers will be on the outlook for those adapted for this highest form of service, remembering, however, that a great number of separate qualifications are needed here. It will indeed be a blessed thing if the awakening serves at once to replenish all the ordinary forms of service in the congregation, and to send the best and choicest onward to the work of the ministry.

(15.) All care must be taken to foster humility, meekness, self-control, and charity among the fruits of a revival. Experience shows that the tendency to conceit, spiritual pride, censoriousness, and self-indulgence, in some subtle forms, often lamentably mars the whole movement. In the days of Jonathan Edwards the reaction in this form was terrible. His " Narrative of Surprising Conversions " will be found an excellent guide, both as to what is to be done and what is to be avoided in times of awakening. Among us intemperance is by far the greatest source of scandal and backsliding. Nettleton says that no class of persons are so apt to deceive themselves and deceive others at a revival time as drunkards, and that the only security for such is to abandon the use of drink entirely and for ever. It is remarkable how deeply it has been impressed on those who have had to do with recent revivals, that in the present frightful condition of things the practice of abstinence is the only effectual way of protesting against the ruinous drinking habits of the age.

(16.) It must not be supposed that revival times are the only harvest seasons in the Christian Church. Ministers should ever be looking for the Spirit to work in times of affliction, at communion occasions, and in all the ordinary services. It becomes unwholesome to be depending wholly on a revival for every saving result. Let ministers not despise the ordinary periods of careful instruction, and calm, earnest appeal. Let them go on building up the house, laying the train, boring the quarry, rejoicing in such cases of spiritual good as are accorded to them ; and when another time of special grace is given, the fruit of their labours will be found in solid additions to the living Church, lively stones which will form true contributions both to the strength and to the beauty of the temple.

APPENDIX B

HOMILETICAL AND PASTORAL LITERATURE

*A complete list of all works of this class would fill a volume ; what follows ιο
but a selection from the more notable.*

1.—PATRISTIC AND MEDIÆVAL WRITERS

1. CHRYSOSTOM. Περὶ Ἱερωσύνης. *Of the Priesthood.* [Deepl;
and intensely earnest, magnifying the office of the Ministry, but with
a strong leaning to Sacerdotalism.]

2. AUGUSTINE. *De Doctrina Christiana.* [Liber iv. treats of the
best way of conveying the truth to others. It describes, among other
things, the various kinds of style, and urges prayer and devout living
as most essential to a successful ministry.]
De Catechizandis Rudibus. [Counsels to Deogratias, a young and
somewhat timid deacon at Carthage, on instructing the ignorant.]

3. CYRIL OF JERUSALEM. *Eighteen Books of Catechetical Discourses.* [Little value in *doctrine* : earnestly practical and eloquent.]

4. GREGORY NAZIANZEN. Λόγος ἀπολογήτικος, τῆς φυγῆς ἕνεκεν.
Apologetic Oration for his flight. [Eloquent, and intensely impressed
with the solemnity of the priesthood.]

5. JEROME. *Epistle to Nepotian.* [Solemn counsels to the clergy.]

6. BERNARD OF CLAIRVAUX. *De Moribus et Officio Episcoporum.
Ad Clericos. De Conversione.* [These works consist largely of rebukes
and exhortations on the manner of conducting the duties of the
ministry.]

7. GILBERT OF NOVIGENTIUM. *Quo ordi. e sermo fieri debeat ?* [A
French abbot of the thirteenth century. This was a period of considerable Homiletic literature, the Church being desirous to train
preachers who would counteract the unlearned but popular preaching
of the Albigenses and Waldenses. See Neander's *Ch. Hist.* vol. viii.]

8. BONAVENTURA. *Ars Concionandi,* A.D. 1274. [A summary of
the Homiletical precepts of Augustine.]

9. THOMAS AQUINAS. *De Arte et vero modo Concionandi.* [Not
a formal treatise of Aquinas, but a subsequent compilation from his
writings. Van Oosterzee says that the sermons of Aquinas that have
come down to us are a pure type of the scholastic method, concise,
sharply formulated and divided, and addressed to the intellect.]

10. HUMBERT DE ROMANIS. *De Eruditione Predicatorum,* A.D.
1277. [General of the Dominican order ; deeply impressed with the
importance of preaching, and most eager to induce his monks to be
zealous, ardent, unwearied preachers.]

11. REUCHLIN. *Liber Congestorum de Arte Predicandi*, A.D. 1500.
12. BORROMEO, Cardinal. *De Instructione Predicatoris*, A.D. 1580.
13. ERASMUS. *Ecclesiastes, sive Concionator Evangelicus.*
[For a large number of writers, now little remembered, that wrote
on the subject about the time of the Reformation, see Bp. WILKINS,
Gift of Preaching; DRAUDIUS, *Bibliotheca Classica* (under " *Concion-
atorum Instructio* ") ; and KIDDER, *Homiletics*, p. 331. See also J.
M. NEALE, M.A., *Mediæval Preachers and Preaching* ; and J. M.
ASHLEY, *A Year with Great Preachers* ; also, *A Festival Year with
Great Preachers*, the preachers being chiefly distinguished Franciscans
and Dominicans.]

2.—FRENCH AND SWISS WRITERS.

1. FÉNELON, Archbishop. *Dialogues concerning Eloquence in
general, and particularly that kind which is fit for the Pulpit.* [Good
sense and ability ; but not much depth either of thought or feeling.]
2. MAURY, Cardinal. *Essay on the Eloquence of the Pulpit.*
3. CLAUDE, J. (Reformed Church.) *Essay on the Composition
of a Sermon.* [Re-edited by Rev. C. Simeon in connection with his
Horæ Homileticæ.]
4. E. GAUSSEN (of Saumur). *De ratione Concionandi*, A.D. 1678.
5. OSTERWALD (of Neuchâtel). *Exercice du Ministère Sacré*, 2
tomes, A.D. 1737.
6. LE MAITRE. *Réflexions sur la manière de prêcher*, A.D. 1745.
7. CHENEVRIÈRE. *Observations sur l'éloquence de la chaire.*
8. VINCENT. *Recherches Homilétiques*, A.D. 1858.
9. VINET (of Lausanne). 1. *Pastoral Theology: the Theory of a
Gospel Ministry.* 2. *Homiletics, or the Theory of Preaching.* [The
last, posthumous and fragmentary. Both devout, original, sparkling
with genius, and at same time Scriptural and earnest.] 3. *Histoire de
la Prédication parmi les Réformés de France au Dix-Septième Siècle.*
[Shows his fine critical faculty.]
10. COQUEREL, A. *Observations pratiques sur la prédication*, A.D.
1860.
11. MONOD, ADOLPHE. *Eloquence Sacrée.* (*Revue Théologique*,
A.D. 1841.)
12. BAUTAIN, M. *The art of Extempore Speaking : Hints for the
Senate, the Pulpit, and the Bar*, A.D. 1867. [An earnest plea by
a R.C. Professor of the Sorbonne in favour of extemporaneous
preaching.]
13. BUNGENER. *The Preacher and the King ; or, Bourdaloue in
the Court of Louis XIV.* [A vivid fancy-sketch of Bourdaloue supposed to be in communication with Claude.]
14. TURNBULL. *Pulpit Orators of France and Switzerland.*

3.—GERMAN WRITERS.

Probably the best introduction to the German bibliography of
Homiletic and Pastoral Theology is to be got from the several articles

on the subject in Herzog and Plitt's *Real-Encyclopädie der Pro-testantischen Theologie und Kirche*, by the late Professor Christlieb of Bonn, author of the well-known Apologetic work, *Modern Doubt and Christian Belief*. These articles embrace Homiletik, Predigt, Praktische Theologie, Katechetik, Goddes-dienst, Liturgie, Seelsorge, and Innere Mission. We shall give a short account of the first three.

I. HOMILETIK, from the German Point of View.—1. First, the meaning of the term is considered, and it is defined as the scientific treatment of preaching, viewed as a witnessing for Christ. Some Germans have restricted the term to " preaching to believers " (Schleier-macher, Schweizer, Palmer, Harnack, and others), but this is too limited. 2. *Homiletics and Rhetoric.*—Though at first rhetoric was disregarded and even disparaged, a change took place in the fourth century, when, many of the great preachers having been teachers of rhetoric, its aid was sought in preaching. Hence, by some preaching has been considered a branch of rhetoric or oratory (Erasmus, Melan-chthon, Herder, Theremin, Vinet). Others (Pietists, Spener, Stier) have demanded an absolute divorce from rhetoric. This, however, is not desirable ; rhetoric may lend power to preaching, yet the features in which rhetoric and Christian preaching agree are far fewer than those in which they differ. 3. *Theories of Preaching.*—The great object of preaching is to direct the world to the way of salvation by Christ, to call the unconverted to repentance and to confirm believers in their faith. 4. *History of Homiletics.*—(This branch is treated very fully under the article " Predigt," *q.v.*) After noticing the dry scholastic form which preaching had assumed in Germany, the author remarks : " With Schleiermacher and Claus Harms a new period begins, which is marked by the treatment of Homiletics as a branch of Practical Theo-logy. Marheineke's work on Homiletics contends for the introduction of the fundamental doctrines of Christianity into the pulpit, and, with Schleiermacher, insists on edification as the aim of preaching. Claus Harms followed with his essay on *Speaking with Tongues*, which fell like a bombshell under the lamps of those students who were seeking to copy strictly logical and rhetorical models. With great freshness and originality he declared war against the artificial pulpit productions of the schools." Stier in his *Kerytik* (A.D. 1830), and to some extent Sickel (*Halieutik*, A.D. 1829), insist on the Biblical character of preaching. The most important works since then are Palmer, *Homi-letik*, A.D. 1842 ; G. Baur, *Grundzüge d. Homiletik*, A.D. 1848 ; Gaup, *Hom.*, A.D. 1852 ; Harnack, *Prakt. Theol.*, A.D. 1878.

II. PREDIGT.—The desirableness of a fuller account of the History of Preaching seems to have been an afterthought of the conductors of the Encyclopædia, as it forms a very elaborate article of about two hundred closely printed pages in the Appendix to the second edition. See last volume, A.D. 1888.

In this paper Professor Christlieb surveys the Christian pulpit in all its varied phases, schools, and countries, from the days of the Apostles to the latter part of the nineteenth century. He shows throughout a warm appreciation of protestant evangelical preaching. In three great divisions he discusses the preaching of—1, the Early Church ; 2, the Middle Ages ; 3, Modern Times.

1. The first division embraces the Genesis of preaching, in the first and second centuries ; the Patristic Homilies of the third ; the period of brilliancy and bloom, from the fourth to the middle of the fifth ; and the period of decline, from the end of the fifth and throughout the sixth.

2. The period of the Middle Ages is divided into two—(*a*) From A.D. 600 to 1200, a period for the most part of neglect and decadence, though not without exceptions, particularly in the case of the mission preachers, who, from Iona and Lindisfarne, strove to spread the light of the truth on the Continent of Europe. (*b*) From A.D. 1200 to the Reformation. Preaching was of two forms—in Latin to monks and other educated persons ; in the vernacular to the people. The Scholastic preaching has special notice, and also the preaching of the mystics, on which the author dwells with affectionate appreciation. Then come notices of the mendicants, Dominican and Franciscan, till we reach the dawn of the Reformation, distinguished by such names as those of Wycliffe, Huss, and Savonarola.

3. The Modern Period is introduced by remarks on the revival, at the Reformation, of preaching on the basis of Holy Scripture. Then, as to Germany, we have notices of the preachers (*a*) of the Lutheran Church, and (*b*) of the Reformed. Passing to other countries, we are introduced to the preachers of Switzerland, the Netherlands, Italy, Spain, England, and Scotland. There are also notices of the Catholic preachers of the same period, but such as to show how extremely meagre the Catholic pulpit was both in numbers and in power. Proceeding to post-Reformation times, from A.D. 1580 to the time of Spener (A.D. 1700), we have a poor array for Germany ; but for France, the brilliant period of Louis XIV., both in the Protestant and Catholic pulpit ; and in England, the Puritan preachers, and the famous Church preachers of the seventeenth century. Proceeding to the eighteenth century and beginning of the nineteenth, our author dwells with great interest on the revival of the light and power of the Gospel under Spener and the Pietists, which, imperfect though it may have been, came as such a relief to the dry and formal sermons of incipient and advancing Rationalism. There were a few stars in Germany in the eighteenth century, but for the most part this was a very barren period. The nineteenth century witnessed the revival of faith, imperfectly in the school of Schleiermacher, more thoroughly under Tholuck, Krummacher, and others. Outside Germany there were a few men of mark, in the pulpits of Scandinavia, Holland, and France ; but by far the richest harvest during that period has been reaped in England, Wales, Ireland, Scotland, and America. Of our recent preachers in Britain, we have notices of J. H. Newman, Frederick Robertson, Liddon, and Spurgeon ; also of Chalmers, Guthrie, Candlish, and Caird.

This sketch of the history of the pulpit is accompanied with short notes on the characteristic features both of the different periods and of the men, and with an abundant bibliography on all departments of the subject. Perhaps it is this last department that contains most that is new to the present generation. Histories of the pulpit at different periods have been very numerous, far beyond the general supposition. The existence of so many gifted preachers in all ages and countries, and of so many works about them, is a striking testimony to the

vitality of the pulpit in the past, and to its prospects of endurance in the future. (See *ante*, Chapters I. II. and III.)
III. PRAKTISCHE THEOLOGIE.—1. The *idea* of practical theology. 2. The *History* [many casual notices occur earlier, but only in the nineteenth century is it a branch of scientific theology]. 3. *Method.* 4. *Literature* [very full, including books on the various departments of spiritual life and culture, *e.g.* for rich and poor, sick and dying, mourners, doubters and disbelievers ; mostly German, some English].

The author has received the following notes from his learned and accomplished friend, the Rev. Professor Salmond, D.D., of Aberdeen, a well-known proficient in German Theology.
Among the older books of real value :—
1. EHRENFEUCHTER. *Praktische Theologie.* Göttingen, 1859.
2. A. SCHWEITZER. *Pastoral-theologie.* Leipzig, 1875.
3. TH. HARNACK. [Father of Professor Adolf Harnack of Berlin.] *Praktische Theologie.* Erlangen, 1877.
4. G. VON ZEZSCHWITZ. *System der praktischen Theologie.* [Very good.] Leipzig, 1876-78.
5. W. OTTO. *Grundzüge der evangelischen praktischen Theologie.* Dillenburg, 1867.
6. W. OTTO. *Evangelische praktische Theologie.* Gotha, 1869-1870.
7. R. KÜBEL. *Umriss der Pastoraltheologie.* Stuttgart, 1874.
Books on Katechetik, Cultus, etc., *e.g.*—
8. G. VON ZEZSCHWITZ. *System der christlichkirchl. Katechetik.* Second Edition, Leipzig, 1872-74. (The largest and completest book I know on the subject.)
9. R. KÜBEL. *Katechetik.* Stuttgart, 1877.
10. K. R. HAGENBACH. *Grundlinien der Liturgik und Homiletik.* Leipzig, 1863.
11. E. L. TH. HENKE. *Vorlesungen über Liturgik und Homiletik.* Halle, 1876.
12. CH. PALMER. *Evangelische Homiletik.* Stuttgart, Fifth Edition, 1867. [Much recommended.]
13. A. F. C. VILMAR. *Lehrbuch der Pastoral-Theologie.* Gütersloh, 1872.
14. W. LÖHE. *Der evangelische Geistliche.* Stuttgart, Third Edition, 1876.
Among more recent books, these are best known to me :—
15. PROF. ALFRED KRAUSS. *Lehrbuch der praktischen Theologie.* 2 vols. Freiburg, J. C. B. Mohr, 1890-93.
16. PROF. E. CHR. ACHELIS. *Praktische Theologie* (in the *Sammlung theologischer Lehrbücher* series). Freiburg: J. C. B. Mohr, 2 vols., 1890-92.
17. CLAUS HARMS. *Pastoral-Theologie, in Reden an Theologie-studierende.* New Edition. Gotha : Perthes, 1891.
18. ZIMMER. *Handbibliothek der praktischen Theologie.* Gotha : Perthes, 1892.

19. Th. Christlieb. *Homiletik. Vorlesungen ; Losg. von Th. Haarbeck.* Basel : Jaeger und Korber, 1893.
20. E. Chr. Achelis. *Praktische Theologie* (in the *Grundriss der theologischen Wissenschaften* series ; a smaller form or condensed edition of the work appears in the *Sammlung theologischer Lehrbücher* series). Freiburg, J. C. B. Mohr.
21. *Sammlung von Lehrbüchern der praktischen Theologie in gedrängter Darstellung.* A series of small vols. of sixty or seventy pages each, edited by H. Hering in Verbindung mit J. Hesekiel, K. Köhler, G. Rietschel, E. Sachse, P. Wurster. Published by Reuther und Reichard, Berlin, 1894, etc.
22. F. Zimmer. *Die Grundlegung der praktischen Theologie.* Berlin : Reuther und Reichard, 1894.

To this list of Professor Salmond's, another friend adds—
23. Nitzsch. *Praktische Theologie,* especially vol. iii. :—*Die eigenthümliche Seelenpflege des Evangelischen Hirtenamtes, mit Rücksicht auf die innere Mission.*

4.—DUTCH WRITERS.

The fullest book in any language on Homiletical and Pastoral Theology is that of the late Professor J. J. Van Oosterzee, D.D., of which an English translation has been published, entitled *Practical Theology: a Manual for Theological Students,* translated by Maurice J. Evans, B.A. In this massive volume of more than 600 pages, we have ample treatises on Homiletics, Liturgics, Catechetics, and Poimenics, each branch being discussed with ample recognition of underlying principles and the authority of Scripture, large knowledge of Christian history and biography, and an almost inexhaustible acquaintance with the literature of the subject. The tone is sensible, earnest, devout ; and the only serious drawback to the book is that, being so long, it can hardly be mastered by the student, who would often prefer to get the gist of the subject in smaller compass.

5.—BRITISH WRITERS.

1. William Perkins. *The Art of Prophesying; or a Treatise, concerning the only true manner and method of preaching.* A.D. 1613. [Once very celebrated.]
2. Richard Baxter. *Gildas Salvianus, the Reformed Pastor: showing the Nature of the Pastoral Work, especially in Private Instruction and Catechizing.* A.D. 1656. [Founded on Acts xx. 28, chiefly on personal dealing with souls. Baxter's *Life and Times* contains full statements of his pastoral methods, especially his catechizing, at Kidderminster.]
3. George Herbert. *A Priest to the Temple: or, the Country Parson, his Character and Rule of Holy Life.* [Devout, simple, quaint, with High-church flavour.]
4. Gilbert Burnet, D.D., Bishop of Salisbury. *A Discourse of the Pastoral Care.* A.D. 1692. [Chiefly on Parochial duties.]

5. BISHOP WILKINS. *Ecclesiastes; or, a Discourse concerning the Gift of Preaching, as it falls under the Rules of Art.* [A work much esteemed in its day.]

6. GILBERT GERARD, D.D. *The Pastoral Care.*

7. GEORGE CAMPBELL, D.D. *Lectures on Pulpit Eloquence.*

8. PHILIP DODDRIDGE. *Lectures on Preaching and the Ministerial Office.*

9. GEORGE HILL, D.D. *Counsels concerning the duties of the Pastoral Office.*

10. STEVENSON MACGILL, D.D. *Considerations addressed to a Young Clergyman on some Trials of Principle and Character which may arise in the course of his Ministry.*

11. ADAM CLARKE, LL.D. *Letter to a Preacher on his Entrance into the Work of the Ministry.*

12. REV. ARCHIBALD BRUCE. *Introductory and Occasional Lectures, for forming the Minds of Young Men intending the Holy Ministry to Theological and Useful Learning, Religion, and Good Manners.* With Preface by Thomas M'Crie, D.D. [Mr. Bruce was Professor to the Secession Church; an able and remarkable man.]

13. HENRY FOSTER BURDER. *Mental Discipline; or, Hints on the Cultivation of Moral and Intellectual Habits.* Addressed to Students in Theology and Young Preachers.

14. W. GRESLEY. *Ecclesiastes Anglicanus: a Treatise on Preaching, as adapted to a Church of England Congregation.*

15. ROBERT VAUGHAN, D.D. *The Modern Pulpit viewed in Relation to the State of Society.*

16. REV. CHARLES SIMEON. *Horæ Homileticæ; or, Discourses digested into one continued Series, and forming a Commentary on every Book of the Old and New Testament.* 21 volumes.

17. REV. CHARLES BRIDGES. *The Christian Ministry, with an Inquiry into the Causes of its Inefficiency, and with a Special Reference to the Ministry of the Establishment.*

18. REV. J. J. BLUNT, B.D. *The Acquirements and Principal Duties of the Parish Priest.*

19. ARCHBISHOP WHATELY. *The Parish Pastor.* [Six Lectures: I. The Parochial System, embracing the chief pastoral duties of the ministry. II. Explanations of the Bible. III. Explanations of the Prayer Book. IV. On Baptism. V. On the Lord's Supper. VI. Christian Moral Instruction, showing the right place and great importance of ethical Christian teaching. Dr. Whately shows his characteristic dislike of everything priestly by using the terms Pastor and Minister, and avoiding the terms Clergyman and Clergy.]

20. REV. DANIEL MOORE. *Thoughts on Preaching, especially in Relation to the Requirements of the Age.*

21. REV. JOHN BROWN. *The Christian Pastor's Manual.* [A Selection of Tracts by Jennings, Booth, Erskine, Watts, Mason, Bostwich, Newton, Scott, and Cecil.]

22. REV. JOHN ANGELL JAMES. *An Earnest Ministry the Want of the Times. The Church in Earnest.*

23. Rev. William Arthur. *The Tongue of Fire.* [Admirably rousing and earnest.]

24. Charles J. Brown, D.D. *The Ministry, being Addresses to Students of Divinity.*

25. C. H. Spurgeon. *Lectures to my Students.* Three volumes. [Racy, practical, solemn, yet sometimes humorous ; often pointed and powerful, with constant application to highest ends of the ministry. The third series is on *The Art of Illustration.*]

26. Patrick Fairbairn, D.D. *Pastoral Theology.* [A posthumous volume, marked by combination of sobriety with evangelical earnestness, and showing results of much reading and thinking.]

27. Sturtevant., S. T. *The Preacher's Manual.*

28. Octavius Winslow, D.D. *Eminent Holiness Essential to an Efficient Ministry.*

29. Potter. *Sacred Eloquence and the Theory and Practice of Preaching.* [A Roman Catholic author, strongly against *reading* of sermons.]

30. Joseph Parker, D.D. *Ad Clerum: Advice to a Young Preacher.* [Characteristically unconventional and vigorous.]

31. James Begg, D.D. *The Art of Preaching.*

32. Canon Liddon, D.D. *Clerical Life and Work: A Collection of Sermons.*

33. *Papers on Preaching.* (By various—Balwin, Rainy, etc.) 1887.

34. Rev. William Ross, LL.D. *Glimpses of Pastoral Work in Covenanting Times. A Record of the Labours of Andrew Donaldson, A.M., Minister of Dalgety, Fifeshire,* 1644-1662.

35. G. W. Sprott, D.D. *The Worship and Offices of the Church of Scotland,* 1882.

36. Rev. H. W. Smith. *The Pastor as Preacher.* 1882.

37. *The Book of Common Order, or Knox's Liturgy.*

38. *Euchologion, or Book of Common Order.*

39. C. G. M'Crie, D.D. *Scotland's Presbyterian Worship Historically Treated* (Cunningham Lectures, 1892).

40. D. D. Bannerman, D.D. *Worship of the Presbyterian Church and Liturgies.* 1884.

41. W. Garden Blaikie, D.D., LL.D. I. *For the Work of the Ministry* [the present volume]. II. *The Public Ministry and Pastoral Methods of our Lord.* III. *The Preachers of Scotland from the Sixth to the Nineteenth Century* (Cunningham Lectures, 1888).

42. J. Stalker, D.D. *The Preacher and his Models* (Yale Lectures, 1891).

43. J. Ker, D.D. *Lectures on the History of Preaching.* [Chiefly of the early Church ; of modern preaching, only German.]

44. Rev. H. C. G. Moule. *To my Younger Brethren.* Chapters on Pastoral Life and Work. 1892.

45. *Echoes from the Welsh Hills: or, Reminiscences of the Preachers and People of Wales.*

6. AMERICAN WRITERS. '

1. COTTON MATHER. "*Manuductio ad Ministerium*"; *the Student and the Preacher.* [The first work written in America on the subject —about A.D. 1710.]
2. EBENEZER PORTER, D.D. *Lectures on Homiletics and Preaching, and on Public Prayer.*
3. DANIEL P. KIDDER, D.D. *Treatise on Homiletics; designed to Illustrate the True Theory and Practice of the Preaching of the Gospel.*
4. WILLIAM T. G. SHEDD, D.D. *Homiletics and Pastoral Theology.* [Remarkable as exemplifying the union of the philosophy and practice of homiletics.]
5. JAMES W. ALEXANDER, D.D. *Thoughts on Preaching, being Contributions to Homiletics.* [Fragmentary, but vivid, unconventional, full of historical, practical, and spiritual interest.]
6. SAMUEL MILLER, D.D. *Letters on Clerical Manners and Habits: addressed to a Student in the Theological Seminary at Princeton, N.J.* [This book is almost unique. It corresponds with its title, and bears mainly on clerical habits and manners. The author is especially desirous that ministers should be free from low, coarse, and vulgar manners. He goes down to the minutest details of personal cleanliness—the hands, the hair, and the nails. He touches the science of etiquette, loves good-breeding and pleasant manners, and would have no boors in the ministry.]
7. REV. H. HUMPHREY. *Thirty-four Letters to a Son in the Ministry.* [Embraces many details on minute questions connected with ministerial work, not often taken up.]
8. W. H. MURCH, D.D. *Essays on the Sacred Ministry*, selected from the *Bibliotheca Sacra* and other American periodicals.
9. J. A. BROADUS, D.D., LL.D. I. *On the Preparation and Delivery of Sermons.* II. *On the History of Preaching.*
10. JAMES MASON HOPPIN, D.D. I. *Office and Work of the Christian Ministry.* II. *Homiletics.* III. *Pastoral Theology* (being I. and II. combined).
11. REV. HENRY C. FISH. *History and Repository of Pulpit Eloquence.* 2 vols.
12. SPRAGUE. *Annals of the American Pulpit.* 5 vols.
13. J. S. SPENCER, D.D. *A Pastor's Sketches.*
14. *Yale Lectures on Preaching.* This is now a yearly series, to which useful contributions have been made by HENRY WARD BEECHER, JOHN HALL, D.D.; W. M. TAYLOR, D.D.; R. W. DALE, BISHOP SIMPSON, HOWARD CROSBY, D.D.; BISHOP PHILLIPS BROOKS, D.D.; J. STALKER, D.D., and others. The lectures of PHILLIPS BROOKS are eminently fresh and suggestive.
15. T. L. CUYLER, D.D. *How to be a Pastor.*
16. STORRS, R. S., D.D. *Preaching without Notes.*
17. TAYLOR, W. M., D.D. *The Ministry of the Word. Scottish Pulpit from the Reformation.*

INDEX.

Printed by T. and A. CONSTABLE, Printers to Her Majesty
at the Edinburgh University Press

Other Related Solid Ground Titles

In addition to *For the Work of the Ministry* which you hold in your hand we are delighted to offer the following titles for those committed to the faithful preaching of God's Word:

THE PREPARATION AND DELIVERY OF SERMONS
The Classic Dargan Edition by *John A. Broadus*

THEOLOGY ON FIRE: Sermons from the Heart of J.A. Alexander by *Joseph Addison Alexander*

A SHEPHERD'S HEART: Sermons from the Pastoral Ministry of J.W. Alexander by *James Waddel Alexander*

THE BUNYAN OF BROOKLYN: The Life and Practical Sermons of Ichabod Spencer, author of *A Pastor's Sketches*

EVANGELICAL TRUTH: Practical Sermons for the Christian Family by *Archibald Alexander*

THE SCOTTISH PULPIT: From the Reformation to the Present by *William M. Taylor*

THE NATIONAL PREACHER: Revival Sermons from the Second Great Awakening, Volumes One and Two (June 1826 - May 1828) *Edited by Austin Dickinson*

LECTURES ON THE HISTORY OF PREACHING by *John A. Broadus*

HOMILETICS & PASTORAL THEOLOGY by *William G.T. Shedd*

A HISTORY OF PREACHING: in Two Volumes by *Edwin Charles Dargan*

THE PREACHER AND HIS MODELS: Yale Lectures by *James Stalker*

Call us Toll Free at 1-877-666-9469
Send us an e-mail at sgcb@charter.net
Visit our web site at solid-ground-books.com

Printed in the United States
38533LVS00004B/37-42

9 781932 474824